WOMEN IN NAZI SOCIETY

WOMEN IN NAZI SOCIETY

JILL STEPHENSON

CROOM HELM LONDON

First published 1975
© 1975 by Jill Stephenson

Croom Helm Ltd
2-10 St John's Road, London SW11

ISBN   0–85664–225–X

Printed and bound in Great Britain by
REDWOOD BURN LIMITED
Trowbridge & Esher

CONTENTS

ACKNOWLEDGEMENTS

The idea of studying the position of women in Germany between the wars was suggested to me as a subject for a doctoral thesis by Mr Esmonde Robertson, formerly of Edinburgh University, now of the London School of Economics. For his advice and great kindness to me, especially in the early years of this work, I am deeply grateful. I am also indebted to Professor V. G. Kiernan, of Edinburgh University, who has generously given me much of his time and wise advice over many years. Dr J. S. Conway, of the University of British Columbia, Professor Arthur Marwick, formerly of Edinburgh University, now of the Open University, and Mr A. J. Nicholls, of St Antony's College, Oxford, gave valuable advice and encouragement at critical points, and Professor James Joll of the London School of Economics was kind enough to advise me about the publication of this work. I have received invaluable assistance from various libraries and archives, most particularly from the Bundesarchiv, Koblenz, the Berlin Document Center, the Institut für Zeitgeschichte, Munich, and, especially, the Wiener Library in London and, of course, Edinburgh University Library. I owe a particular debt to Mrs Sheila Somerville who has typed first my thesis and then this book with admirable efficiency. The encouragement and support of my parents and of my husband have provided the context in which it has been possible to complete this work. Its content, and consequently its shortcomings, are, of course, my responsibility alone.

To my parents, Andrew and Alice McIntyre

INTRODUCTION

The rising tide of feminism, or 'women's lib', in the 1960s and 1970s
has led to a dramatic growth in interest in the position of women in
society in both recent and ancient history. In the light of this, and given
the continuing fascination of inter-war Germany for the general reader
as well as the historian, it is perhaps remarkable that little of substance
has been written about the position of women in German society in the
1920s and 1930s, although piecemeal attempts have been made in
recent years to rectify this.[1] Before the Second World War, the Nazis,
particularly, produced myriad pamphlets which painted an idyllic picture of their ideology in practice, of their 'liberation' of women from
the degradation into which they had been plunged by the 'Weimar
system'. Communists, too, in Britain and elsewhere, wrote copiously
and extravagantly on the subject, claiming that the Nazis had enslaved
German women, distorting the picture to fit their own rigid ideology.
The net result is that relatively little is known about the actual position
of women in German society in the 1920s and 1930s, although a substantial corpus of mythology exists.

The aim here therefore is to describe and discuss some aspects of the
status of, and opportunities for, women in Germany in one inter-war
decade, the 1930s, and in so doing to explode some of the myths. The
years 1930-40 form a logical unit whose bounds are the impact of the
world economic crisis on Germany and the Nazi regime's attempt to
wage war with only a partial war economy, while the German army is
still victorious. To have tried to cover the years of the Second World
War would have introduced a disproportionate amount of material
referring to a highly abnormal situation, one which the Nazis saw as an
interruption of their domestic policy, but one which was necessary if
this were ever to be implemented. To have drawn to a close in 1939,
with the outbreak of war, would not, however, have been much more
satisfactory, since trends which were apparent then, and which had
manifested themselves even earlier, can be conveniently followed into
the first full year of the war, and largely left there because the failure to
defeat or make peace with Germany's only remaining foe, Britain,
meant that the *ad hoc* arrangements made in 1939-40 for war production, and the gearing of society to a war situation on a temporary basis,
would have to be transformed into a longer term system.

Within the decade 1930 to 1940, the significance of the year 1933 is
inescapable; the appointment of Adolf Hitler as German Chancellor on

1

30 January and the rapid progress towards the creation of a one party State, effected in July 1933, had far-reaching implications for all Germans. But to have begun this book in 1933 would have been to neglect — as others have done — the vital last years of the Weimar Republic, when trends were already apparent in many aspects of economic and social, as well as political, development which would be intensified, or, more often, distorted after the *Machtübernahme* (Nazi assumption of power). The year 1933 continues to hold a magnetic attraction for Germans and for historians of Germany; to this extent, Nazi propaganda has been highly successful, since it was the Nazis themselves who first depicted 1933 as a great turning point in German history, as the year of 'the national awakening'.

Indeed, the events of 1933 heralded changes in every aspect of German life; but these were conditioned by German traditions and experience as well as by Nazi ideology. It is not, in any case, easy to gauge the significance of Nazi policies without some knowledge of what they replaced. Study of developments in the last years before the Nazi takeover, particularly from 1930, reveals that there is a strong degree of continuity in German domestic policy in the years 1930 to 1935-6. It has long been realised that 'the descent into dictatorship' began even under the Brüning Government, with resort to the use of Article 48 of the Weimar Constitution resulting in the overriding of the parliamentary system by Presidential decree, but there has been little attempt to investigate whether this trend in the political sphere is paralleled in economic and social policy.[2] One of the major themes of this work is that there was continuity in domestic policy in the first half of the 1930s, in spite of the momentous events of 1933, simply because of the cataclysmic and all-pervading effect on Germany of the world economic crisis, which began in autumn 1929. The changes which took place in 1935-6 are indicative of two factors: by this time, the Nazis had made their medium term plans, and were beginning to implement them within the context of their long term aims; but at least as important is the end of the depression, and the consequent end to the emergency measures initiated to alleviate its effects, particularly the massive unemployment which was its chief characteristic.

To say this is not to deny that the position of women was affected by the coming to power of a Party which, indeed, had very fixed ideas about the role women should play in the life of the nation. But before the Nazis came to power the position of women in Germany had already been deeply affected by the economic crisis which had thrown millions of people in manual, clerical, managerial and professional positions out of work. It was the condition of the labour market which was undoubtedly the single most influential factor in the development of attitudes to and opportunities for women in wage and salary earning positions outside the home, throughout the 1930s. Its impact went far beyond the narrow employment situation, affecting also educational policy and official attitudes to women in the family context, and brought Nazi theory about women's role into sharp conflict with the needs of the German economy, in its widest sense, in the later 1930s, particularly once Germany was at war.

The broad sections into which this book falls therefore include the position of women in marriage and family life, employment outside the home, higher education, and the professions. The relative, or even complete, neglect of subjects which fall outside these confines is to be regretted, and is due more to lack of space than to the absence of material. It has seemed sensible, for example, to omit more than passing reference to the Nazis' attempt to organise women in the Third Reich, to the girls' section of the Hitler Youth, the *Bund deutscher Mädel*, and to the women's Labour Service, and to aim to give these absorbing topics the coverage they merit in another work. Only fleeting mention is made of social mores, although there is a fairly full discussion of the position of the unmarried mother; and nothing is said about the contribution of women – like Ricarda Huch and Käthe Kollwitz, for example – to the cultural life of the Weimar Republic. The daily life of the working-class woman is alluded to, but not described in any systematic way. Particularly in the chapters dealing with education and the professions, the emphasis is on an extremely small minority of German women. But it was in these two areas that questions of women's rights were most alive, in Germany as in other European countries and North America. If the women affected by reforms in these areas even now constitute only a larger minority, it is nevertheless true that achievements there have eventually opened up questions of equality for women generally, in legal, economic and social affairs.

In the international context, it appears that, on the whole, women in Germany in the late 1930s were neither better nor worse off than women in other countries in terms of status and opportunities, even in the Third Reich. In the Weimar years there was, admittedly, the impression, at least, that German women were in a particularly fortunate position: for one thing, Germany had a far higher proportion of women legislators than most other countries. In 1926, when there were three women in the United States' Congress and six women in the Austrian parliament, there were thirty-two female Reichstag deputies. Again, in 1929, women constituted 1.1 per cent of the membership of the House of Representatives, 2.1 per cent of the House of Commons, and 6.7 per cent of the Reichstag.[3] Still in early 1933, there were fifteen women Members of Parliament in Britain and thirty-five women deputies in the Reichstag.[4] But, as the feminists were well aware, membership of the legislative body did not guarantee progress towards equality for women.

Much is made of how women lost their representation in the Reichstag under the Nazis, once Germany became a one party State; but it ought also to be remembered that in two of Germany's neighbours, France and Switzerland, women did not even have the vote in the 1920s and 1930s.

Clearly, it is felt to be less reprehensible not to introduce a reform than to reverse one that has taken place. Much of the time the Nazis are − generally rightly − criticised for revoking progressive measures, whether they had been effective or not, and putting German women once again in a position similar to that obtaining in countries where reforms had not been effected. Perhaps the outstanding example of this is the law of 30 June 1933, which permitted the dismissal of married women from the civil service and departure from the principle of equal pay for men and women in civil service positions.[5] But in Britain, for example, women in the civil service had been, and were still being, discriminated against: British women had to wait until the mid-1950s before equal pay in the civil service was introduced,[6] while married women were − other than exceptionally − banned from the teaching profession until after the Butler Act of 1944.[7] The implication, then, is that Germany of the Weimar Republic was in the vanguard of those countries which accepted a more equitable position for women in public and professional life.

But the problem in Germany in the 1920s, as the feminists never tired of complaining, was that the Weimar Constitution, which affirmed equality of the sexes in education, in civil service appointments, and in terms of remuneration in the professions, was not the law of the land; it was possible at times to ignore its provisions, or at least to try to circumvent them, as some Land governments did in the 1920s. Where the intentions of the Constitution were observed, progress in winning a more equitable position for women was slow; but those who imagined that it could be otherwise were surely naive. In the Soviet Union, too, where the Constitutions of 1918 and 1936 declared equality of rights between the sexes, men continued to hold a near monopoly of the senior administrative positions, although women did increase their representation significantly in administrative and professional positions which carried less authority and responsibility.[8] Indeed, women quickly came to dominate − numerically, if not in terms of authority − the medical profession; but it is suggested that this was because doctors were poorly paid in the Soviet Union.[9]

Certainly, if there was no distinction between the sexes as regards professional opportunities in some other countries − for example, Czechoslovakia, Lithuania and Iceland, as well as the Soviet Union − in two of Germany's western neighbours, France and Belgium, the professions were not universally open to women; in addition, in other countries, including Italy, Bulgaria, Greece, Norway (until 1938) and the Netherlands, there remained restrictions on women's eligibility for professional positions throughout the inter-war years. In Austria, under the Dollfuss regime, an order was issued in 1933 which was very similar to the German law of 30 June 1933, restricting opportunities for married women in the civil service.[10] Germany was, in fact, in the majority camp in the 1930s, with the Nazis' more reactionary measures well according with the trend in the many other European countries which in the 1920s and 1930s were falling under right-wing dictatorships.

Reactionary measures included the attempt to eliminate abortion and contraception in the Third Reich, a policy that was being followed in other European countries, particularly the predominantly Roman Catholic ones. In France, for example, where there was, as in Germany, deep concern about the declining birth rate, abortion was illegal and harsh penalties were afforded in the Penal Code for offenders. In 1920 a law was passed which provided that those manufacturing, selling or advocating contraceptive devices could be punished by a fine or imprisonment; it was to this obstacle to effective contraception that a rate of abortion estimated at between 300,000 and 500,000 per year during the 1930s was largely attributed. The one concession made was that therapeutic abortion — where the life of the mother was endangered — was permitted in 1939; but it was in the same year that the *Code de la Famille* sanctioned the imposition of more severe penalties for those selling abortifacients and contraceptives. No doubt influenced by wartime German policy, the French government in 1942 made abortion a crime carrying very severe sanctions, including the possibility of the death penalty.[11]

Toleration of abortion and free access to contraceptive advice were generally associated with Communism and, above all, Soviet Russia. Certainly, the Draconian penalties for abortion in Tsarist Russia were revoked by decree immediately after the Bolshevik Revolution, and in November 1920 abortion was formally legalised.[12] Those who criticised this policy as 'licentious' failed to add that the Soviet authorities regarded abortion as an evil, but one which would remain until adequate contraceptive provision obviated the need for it. It was less because this *desideratum* had been achieved than because of the growing international tension of the 1930s that abortion was banned in the 1936 Constitution of the Soviet Union; the raising of the birth rate became in the USSR, as in Hitler's Germany, a major official preoccupation, and Stalin's government, again like Hitler's, offered at the same time a number of incentives for procreation. The carnage of the Second World War led to the provision of more, and more attractive, incentives in 1944 to encourage the citizens of the USSR to compensate for the immense losses, in the field and among civilians.[13]

To this extent, dictatorships of 'left' and 'right' followed similar, even identical, policies: Mussolini, too, imposed heavy penalties for abortion and the dissemination of contraceptive advice, and offered tax incentives and allowances to large families to encourage procreation. Again like Hitler and the Soviet regime, he provided improved welfare for mothers and infants, and attempted to remove the stigma from unmarried motherhood.[14] If their attitude towards abortion and contraception was repressive and harsh, the dictators gave the impression — for bellicose motives, no doubt — that they were more enlightened in matters of social welfare than most democratic governments, including the British ones in the inter-war years.

With regard specifically to the 1930s in Germany, it has been firmly asserted, and equally firmly believed, that the assumption of power by the Nazis meant a complete transformation in the position of women, and a transformation for the worse. Writing in January 1934, Alice Hamilton, an American doctor, asserted, on the basis of her own observations and information from inside Germany, that

> 'German women had a long and hard fight but they had won a fair measure of equality under the Republic. Now all seems to be lost and suddenly they are set back, perhaps as much as a hundred years.'[15]

This was the view that tended to be given by those who had emigrated from Germany in and after 1933 for political reasons.[16] But it is an accurate representation of neither the situation between the end of the Great War and 1933 nor that after 1933. The 'fair measure of equality' promised in the Weimar Constitution remained in many instances a dead letter because the Civil Code of the Empire, which became effective in 1900, and which had given men decisive superiority within the marriage relationship, remained the law of the land. While legislation was not forthcoming to implement the clauses of the Weimar Constitution which declared, for example, that both parents should have responsibility for the upbringing of their children, they remained purely pious affirmations of intent, without any legal effect. And while it was no doubt reasonable to assume from Nazi utterances before 1933 that in the Third Reich women would be sent back to the home *en masse*, the fact is that the Nazis, like any other party, found that proclaiming ideology in the safety of opposition was one thing, but that when they were put in the position of exercising power circumstances which were partly beyond their control, partly of their own making, obliged them to modify, and in some cases to abandon, previously formulated policy. Thus they found that during the Second World War they had to try to persuade married women and even mothers to go out to work, and not devote themselves entirely to home and family — the role

6

deemed most suitable for women in Nazi theory.

There is a risk in trying to revise earlier views of an historical phenomenon like National Socialism: one reviewer has expressed concern that revision may lead to a softening of attitudes towards this most evil of movements.[17] Thus, the difficulty in pointing out where critics of the Nazis have been in error, and especially where they have wrongly attributed bad or philistine policies to them, is that one may be suspected of consciously or unconsciously defending the Nazis. To try to avoid this, I must therefore now assert that I do not believe that it is possible to defend those who ruled Germany between 1933 and 1945. We all know that they committed the most heinous of crimes, of courting and causing a long and terrible war which brought death or immense suffering to millions of people throughout the world, and of treating with revolting and unspeakable brutality certain minorities, especially the Jews, for whom they nurtured an implacable and irrational hatred. Recognition of this makes it impossible for us to regard any aspect of Nazism dispassionately, and rightly so, I believe. But this should not place a taboo on analysing parts of the Nazi system in a methodical way; to explain it is not to justify it. I say this because at various places in this work I am obliged to state or to imply that 'this aspect of Nazi policy brought some benefit to women' or 'the Nazis did not initiate this policy which was disadvantageous to women'. To make such remarks, within highly restricted areas of discussion, is not to say that the net result of Nazi policies towards women was favourable, nor that the motives behind any apparently beneficial actions were benevolent.

Some understanding of basic Nazi beliefs and aims is essential to a discussion of their policies towards any group in society, in this case the female sex. From the hotchpotch that was Nazi ideology, the following assumptions consistently emerge. In the first place, the traditional divisions of class and creed were superseded by the fundamental division — in the Nazi view — of race. The Nazi leaders genuinely and fanatically believed that Jews, Slavs and the coloured peoples were inferior types of being; had they been less sincere in this belief, they might have been less dangerous. As it was, they claimed that the 'Aryan' race, to which those of German stock belonged, had, in order to protect and preserve itself, to use every means at its disposal to destroy these 'inferior peoples' before they destroyed the 'Aryan' race. The inherent malevolence of non-'Aryans' towards the 'Aryan' race was accepted as the logical corollary of their inferiority.

To further the survival of the race most fitted for leadership, physical exercise became a cult, while strength and 'Nordic' features became vital attributes. Quality, in this sense, was not, however, enough; in order to overcome the teeming hordes of these 'inferior peoples', the relatively small numbers of the 'Aryan' race would have to be increased, urgently and on a huge scale. It was this obsessive line of thought, absolutely basic to the Nazi *Weltanschauung* (philosophy of life), which conditioned the Party's attitude to the role of women, since women are the childbearers of a nation. Men, as the other half of the genetic equation, were by no means exempt from official concern in this context: they were exhorted to marry young, and even, if they were public employees, threatened with being passed over for promotion if they did not marry and start a family.[18] But woman's biological function made her much more the focus of Nazi leaders' concern in questions of population policy. This applied only, of course, to the 'Aryan' race; women of other races could be worked to death or tortured in concentration camps, while intricate legislation was prepared to protect the reproductive capacity of 'Aryan' women. It was, after all, not at all desirable, in the Nazi view, that non-'Aryans' should procreate, since this only increased in number the enemies of the 'Aryan' race. For this reason, it was pointed out in 1939 that the strict prohibition of abortion did not apply to Jews.[19]

Within the 'Aryan' race, the primary division was that of sex, providing two complementary, not antagonistic, elements which each played a predetermined part in the gigantic jigsaw which was the life of the *Volksgemeinschaft* (national community). As Frau Scholtz-Klink, leader of the Nazi women's organisation, said in 1936, 'the guiding principle of German women today is not to campaign against men but to campaign alongside men'.[20] While men very definitely played the leading role in the Nazi State, with women excluded from political life, the Nazis did not accept that they were subordinating women completely to men; rather, they claimed, they were drawing a distinction — the natural distinction — between the areas of activity of men and women, so that each sex might better perform its function for the good of the nation. This insistence on the separation of the sexes is a crucial feature of Nazi policy towards women, in all areas of life. The sexes, then, were to come together only for what was seen as the most important function of all, procreation. The Nazis turned to the ancient Teutonic relationship — or, at least, what they thought it had been — where man was the warrior and woman the homemaker. They claimed that civilisation, especially in industrial society, had undermined the relationship between the sexes by altering the 'natural' roles of man and woman, and held that the differences between the sexes should not be denied or ignored, but gladly accepted, and indeed emphasised.

In the Nazi view, the chief difference was that man was essentially productive, and woman fundamentally reproductive. By the same token, man was creative while woman was imitative.[21] Thus, woman's position in Nazi society was to be one which gave her the chance to

8

exhibit her 'natural' qualities, sympathy, self-sacrifice and comradeship, rather than demanding of her the 'unnatural' attributes of independence, intellectual ability or a competitive spirit. Following from this, then, the Nazis were at once ideologically opposed to the employment of women outside the home, to more than a very limited amount of academic education for girls, and, above all, to feminists and all proponents of equal rights for women who, they claimed, treated the sexes as identical when they were rather *'gleichwertig aber nicht gleichartig'* (equivalent but not the same).[22]

In matters relating to women in society, then, the Nazis were diametrically opposed to all that the liberals and socialists, both men and women, had campaigned for before 1918 and had continued to support in the 1920s. The franchise, too often regarded as itself constituting emancipation, was the symbol of the struggle to win equal rights for women, and so although the Nazis did not propose to deny women the right to vote, they claimed that they would bring an end to the — in their view — disgraceful situation where women were present at, and even participated in, the activities of the Reichstag.[23] The 'liberal-democratic-Marxists' and 'Jewish-intellectuals' who had brought this about had tried, said the Nazis, to disguise the differences between the sexes, and the result had been the aping of men by some women in a ridiculous caricature, in terms of character, aspirations and outward appearance.[24]

There were indeed grounds for these accusations, however masked they might seem to be by the Nazis' vicious hysteria. It was not only in the most noticeable aspects, such as the wearing of trousers, the copying of men's hair styles, the ostentatious smoking of cigarettes in public, that women had tried to imitate men, and thus prove their equality with them. The founding of the Open Door International for the Economic Emancipation of the Woman Worker in 1929 by radical feminists from several countries had led to the raising of demands in Germany that measures of labour protection — measures actually favourable to women in terms of their physical health — be revoked, since they prevented women from enjoying complete equality on the labour market.[25] The Communists could perhaps be accused of wanting the best of both worlds, but their demands for equal pay for equal work and, in addition, increased maternity benefit and labour protection for women, were more sensible than the Open Door's indiscriminate demands for equality at any price.[26]

The Open Door and its supporters were, however, in a tiny minority, and by characterising Weimar democrats as sharing their views the Nazis deliberately misrepresented the political and social climate of the Republic, for their own ends. The large body of conservative opinion, a majority of which was female, in the influential Roman Catholic Centre

Party and in the German Nationalist camp,[27] opposed the excesses of radical feminists, the more consistent but still extreme views of the Communists, and even the cautious and at times half-hearted egalitarianism of the Social Democrats, while liberals in the People's Party and even in the Democratic Party were coming to the conclusion by the late 1920s that in some cases freedom had been abused. Together the Nationalists, the Centre and the People's Party, with some support from the Democratic Party, planned to introduce a Bill to permit censorship as part of their campaign against 'filth in the theatre and in literature'.[28] The Churches were active in the front line of those fighting to uphold traditional moral values as they saw them,[29] and the moderate feminists were concerned only to consolidate the modest gains they had made since the turn of the century, not to promote an egalitarian revolution. Gertrud Bäumer, leader of this group, found it completely natural that even her most gifted pupils should want more than anything to marry and have a family, which would absorb all their interest and energy.[30] In domestic affairs, then, apart from minority fringe groups of extremists, the word most applicable to the political and social atmosphere in the Weimar Republic is possibly 'moderate', but much of the time more probably 'conservative'.

The governments of the Republic were bound to look conservative, with the Centre Party unique in participating in every one from 1919-32. The coalition nature of these governments tended to mean stalemate, particularly when the Social Democrats joined the Centre in government in the years 1919-23 and 1928-30. The Centre was pathologically terrified of any change which would undermine the position of the Roman Catholic Church or promote 'Bolshevism', and it therefore endeavoured to block any measure proposed by the nominally Marxist SPD, in spite of the latter's conservatism as demonstrated in the events of 1918-19. There was minimal room for manoeuvre in a situation where the secession of one of these parties from government would precipitate the government's fall, and necessitate once again a casting about for a viable partnership among the parties, or else a new general election. The disastrous outcome of Brüning's resort to the latter method in September 1930, when the Nazis increased their parliamentary representation from 12 to 107, might seem to justify the reluctance of earlier coalitions to use it, and their preference for compromise instead.

But compromise meant the abdicating of legislative initiative in any issue that was mildly contentious; the result was that the clauses of the Weimar Constitution which declared the equality of women in the family and in the opportunities available in education and the professions were not transformed into law. The agitation of the radical feminists throughout the Weimar years, and to some extent the increased activity of the Communist Party in the late 1920s and early 1930s, were a response to governmental inaction on this front. But it was not only political differences and political convenience that conditioned this situation. The chief preoccupation in Germany for most of the Weimar period was the financial and economic position of the country after the disasters of the Great War and the inflation of the early 1920s; there was only a brief period of apparent recovery before renewed disaster in 1929-30 again demanded the full attention of the government, and relegated serious discussion of equal rights for women to the realm of theory. Indeed, the economic crisis created a situation where not only was progress towards equality for women halted, but where voices were increasingly raised which demanded that men be given preference in job opportunities of every kind, with jobs in very short supply. The call for a restriction of women to their 'natural' occupations, in the home and with children, was raised by many who were not Nazis, and became increasingly popular as the depression grew deeper. Thus, the Nazis were able to win support not in spite of their view of women's role — which would no doubt have been far less popular in time of economic stability — but actually because of it.[31] The groundwork for measures they would introduce to reverse the progress made in opening up opportunities for women was laid before they came to power.

NOTES

1.   David Schoenbaum, *Hitler's Social Revolution*, London, 1967, ch. VI; Joachim Fest, *Das Gesicht des Dritten Reiches*, Munich, 1964, part 3; Richard Grunberger, *A Social History of the Third Reich*, London, 1971, ch. 17; Werner Thönnessen, *Frauenemanzipation*, Frankfurt am Main, 1969; Renate Bridenthal, 'Beyond *Kinder, Küche, Kirche*: Weimar Women at Work', *Central European History*, 1973. I am grateful to H. M. Scott for kindly sending me a copy of this article; Michael Kater, 'Krisis des Frauenstudiums in der Weimarer Republik', *Vierteljahrschrift für Sozial- und Wirtschaftsgeschichte*, 1972.
2.   An exception is Christoph Führ, 'Schulpolitik im Spannungsfeld zwischen Reich und Ländern', *Das Parlament*, 17 October 1970.
3.   Robert H. Lowie, *Towards Understanding Germany*, Illinois, 1954, p. 209.
4.   'Women MPs', *The Women's Who's Who*, 1933; report in *Die Bayerische Frau (BF)*, January 1933, p. 5.
5.   'Gesetz zur Änderung von Vorschriften auf dem gebiet des allgemeinen Beamten-, des Besoldungs- und des Versorgungsrechts', *Reichsgesetzblatt (RGB)*, 1933 I, 30 June 1933, pp. 434-5.
6.   *Keesing's Contemporary Archives*, vol. X, 1955-6, 'Equal Pay for Women in the Non-Industrial Civil Service and for Women Teachers', 25 January 1955, p. 14165.
7.   H. C. Dent, *The Education Act, 1944*, London, 1964, p. 35.
8.   M. Fainsod, *How Russia is Ruled*, London, 1963, p. 377.
9.   Maurice Larkin, *Gathering Pace*, London, 1969, p. 292.

11

10.   Vera Douie (ed.), *The Professional Position of Women: a World Survey immediately preceding World War II*, London, 1947, pp. 10-14, 20.

11.   C. Watson, 'Birth Control and Abortion in France since 1939', *Population Studies*, 1951-2, pp. 261-8.

12.   Fannina Halle, *Woman in Soviet Russia*, London, 1933, p. 39.

13.   Rudolf Schlesinger, *The Family in the USSR*, London, 1949, pp. 269-79, 371-2.

14.   S. W. Halperin, *Mussolini and Italian Fascism*, New York, 1964, pp. 63-4; *ILO Yearbook, 1937-38*, pp. 260-2.

15.   Alice Hamilton, 'Woman's Place in Germany', *Survey Graphic*, January 1934, p. 26.

16.   E.g., Judith Grunfeld, 'Women Workers in Nazi Germany', *Nation*, 12 March 1937. The author was an active member of the SPD in Germany up to 1933.

17.   Gordon Brook-Shepherd, 'More Noises from the Bunker', *Sunday Telegraph*, 15 July 1973, says 'How can you reassess Hitler except upwards?'

18.   'Der Beamte soll frühzeitig heiraten', *Westdeutscher Beobachter*, 3 August 1937.

19.   BA, NSD30/vorl. 1836, *Informationsdienst* . . . , March 1939, 'Anwendung nur auf das deutsche Volk'.

20.   'Die Aufgaben der deutschen Frau', *VB*, 27 May 1936.

21.   Elfriede Eggener, 'Die organische Eingliederung der Frau in den national-sozialistischen Staat', doctoral dissertation for Leipzig University, 1938, pp. 22-4.

22.   'Die Geschlechter im Dritten Reich', *Fränkische Tageszeitung*, 17 April 1934; 'Dies aber ist die "Lady" ', *Das Schwarze Korps*, 2 May 1940.

23.   Hitler expressed his view on this frequently, e.g. in *Hitler's Table-Talk*, London, 1953, pp. 251-2, 26 January 1942; BA, R45 II/64, DVP Reichsgeschäftsstelle, *Frauenrundschau*, 4 March 1932, 'Nationalsozialisten und Frau', p. 1141.

24.   Hitler's speech to the Nazi women's organisation at the 1934 Party rally, Max Domarus, *Hitler: Reden und Proklamationen*, Würzburg, 1962, p. 451; Rudolf Hess, 'Die Aufgaben der deutschen Frau', *VB*, 27 May 1936; G. Vogel, *Die Deutsche Frau: Im Weltkrieg und im Dritten Reich*, Breslau, 1936, vol. III, p. 5.

25.   Report in *Jahrbuch des Allgemeinen Deutschen Gewerkschaftsbundes, (JADG)*, 1930, pp. 191-2. For amplification, see Chapter 4, pp. 77-8.

26.   BA, R2/18554, proposal for a Bill put to the Reichstag by KPD members, 16 October 1931.

27.   Gabrielle Bremme, *Die politische Rolle der Frau in Deutschland*, Göttingen, 1956, p. 68.

28.   BA, *Kl. Erw.*, no. 267-(1) letter from R. Glöckler (DDP Ortsgruppe Hildesheim) to Gertrud Bäumer, 23 December 1928; Reinhard Opitz, *Der deutsche Sozialliberalismus 1917-1933*, Cologne, 1973, p. 197.

29.   *Verhandlungen des dritten Deutschen Evangelischen Kirchentages*, 1930, pp. 115-17, 247, 334; Flann Campbell, 'Birth Control and the Christian Churches', *Population Studies*, 1960, pp. 136-8.

30.   BA, *op. cit.*, no. 258-(1), letter from Gertrud Bäumer to Marianne Weber, 12 September 1931.

31.   Renate Bridenthal, *op. cit.*, p. 166, makes a similar point.

1 EMANCIPATION AND REACTION AFTER THE GREAT WAR

The granting of the national franchise to all German women over twenty in November 1918 was the symbol of the emancipation for which the feminist movement in its various branches had fought since the founding of the *Allgemeiner Deutscher Frauenverein* (General German Women's Association) by Luise Otto in 1865.[1] In some respects it was merely a symbol: the Imperial Civil Code, which had come into effect as recently as 1900, and which remained in force regardless of the change in 1918 from Empire to Republic, was permeated by a paternalistic assumption of women's dependence on man which had ceased to be valid before the Great War. Indeed single women were put on an equal footing with men so far as written law went; but the vast majority of women would marry at some time and thus accept the authority a husband might choose to exert in most aspects of family life. The husband, for example, had the right to choose the place of residence, the names and religion of the children of the marriage, and the character and duration of their education. The wife was 'entitled and obliged to conduct the family household', and she was also obliged to work in her husband's business, insofar as this was customary in their social position. The husband was entitled to prevent his wife from working for another person if it was clear that her employment was 'prejudicial to the interests of the marriage'; he also had direct control of any money his wife might have or acquire, as a dowry or legacy, for example.

There was one clause in the Civil Code which was of novel significance for the married woman: this was the provision that she might dispose freely of any money which she earned by her own effort from gainful employment outside the home.[2] The 1907 census showed that there were 8,243,498 women in full-time employment — constituting almost 34 per cent of all employed Germans — of whom 2.8 million were married. If 1.8 million of these probably did not, as 'assisting family members'[3] receive a formal wage, there nevertheless remained a million married women who were in a position to benefit from the independent earnings clause of the Civil Code, and the enhanced status in marriage which it implied. While this provision was realistic, the Civil Code did on the whole treat women in a backward looking way; but, as a British commentator observed, to adopt a more modern approach to the status of women would have raised irreconcilable opposition, and doubtless been an obstacle to the acceptance of the Code as a whole.[4]

If some of the new legal provisions did seem patriarchal in both tone and substance, they nevertheless lacked the complete subjugation implied in the codes of some other countries, including the two at the political extremes of pre-1914 Europe. In Republican France, the clause 'le mari conserve toujours sa prérogative de "puissance maritale" avec son droit à "l'obéissance" ' remained in force until 1938.[5] In Tsarist Russia, section 107 of the Imperial Code was even more dogmatic: a wife's duty was 'to obey her husband as the head of the family, to be loving and respectful, to be submissive in every respect, and show him every compliance and affection, he being the master of the house'.[6] This conception of marriage is highly reminiscent of the Pauline view, expressed in Ephesians V: 'Wives, submit yourselves unto your husbands as unto the Lord. For the husband is the head of the wife, even as Christ is head of the Church . . .' St Paul's teachings certainly influenced and informed the attitude of the Christian Churches towards marriage, after as well as before the Great War.

Although German women's legal position within marriage left much to be desired, the feminists had nevertheless made some gains in the years before the Great War, most notably in education. By 1914, women were admitted to full matriculation in the universities of every state of the Empire. The corollary of this, the provision of facilities for academic secondary schooling – as an alternative to the genteel, anti-intellectual *Höhere Töchterschule* – had also been realised. These achievements were largely the result of a sustained campaign begun by the middle-class women's movement in the 1860s and brought to success around the turn of the century under the leadership of Helene Lange.[7] Education was the feminists' first point of attack on a male dominated society because they realised that adequate educational opportunities were essential if women were ever to challenge men in the more specialised categories of employment, whether skilled manual, clerical or professional. In addition, it was clear that the undereducation of women was a continual, if spurious, justification for their relegation to political inactivity and gentle submission in the home.

The feminists' campaign here was directed only at those areas of education where women were at a noticeable disadvantage, senior schooling and higher education; the numbers involved were therefore extremely small, since for every girl who attended a senior school of any kind in 1911 there were twenty-five girls at elementary school, and, further, only 9 per cent of all senior school pupils attended the new *Lyzeen* or *Studienanstalten*, which alone provided an avenue to higher education.[8] But the pioneering work in the interests of a tiny minority was to prove of inestimable value to the somewhat larger numbers of girls who would enjoy the chance to exploit their academic abilities to the full in future decades, particularly once a wide range of professional opportunities — restricted to teaching, medicine and social work before 1918 — was accessible to women.

It was the Great War that gave women the chance to obtain positions which had previously been exclusively male preserves. This was particularly the case in industry, where women were increasingly brought into skilled and responsible positions as men were called up for active service. Women were not included in the Hindenburg Programme of 1916, which provided for the conscription into industry of all civilian men, but they were strongly encouraged to volunteer for work and working-class women, particularly, responded in large numbers.[9] Their reward was a moderate narrowing of wage differentials, so that by the end of the war they were, on average, being paid about half of men's wage rates.[10] Middle-class women, too, contributed to the war effort; Gertrud Bäumer, leader of the *Bund deutscher Frauenvereine* (League of German Women's Associations), founded the *Nationale Frauendienst* (National Women's Service) in 1914 to mobilise volunteers for welfare work and for the making of clothing for the armed forces. Large numbers of middle-class women also volunteered for the Red Cross.[11]

The wartime situation also provided greater opportunities in higher education for those middle-class girls who had been the first to benefit from the reforms in senior schooling immediately before the war. With potential male students at the front, girls were admitted to German universities in increasing numbers; whereas their immediately pre-war share in the student body had been 5 or 6 per cent, by 1916 it had risen to 9.5 per cent, a level that would be maintained until it rose again after 1923.[12] All these developments suggested that when the war ended women would be in a strong position to demand greater opportunities, even equality of opportunity, in employment of all kinds, including freer access to the professions; in addition, it was becoming increasingly less defensible to deny women a voice, through the suffrage, in the affairs of the nation.

The end of the Imperial regime, coming at the same time as the armistice in 1918, meant the removal of one of the major obstacles to women's advancement generally and to their enfranchisement in particular, the Kaiser. The caretaker Socialist Government was quick to extend the suffrage to women, and the election of forty-one women deputies as almost 10 per cent of the membership of the National Assembly in January 1919 seemed to bode well for rapid progress towards equality of opportunity between the sexes.[13] It was thus in a mood of optimism that Marie Juchacz of the SPD made the first speech to be delivered by a woman in a national representative capacity, in the National Assembly at Weimar on 11 February 1919:

'I should like to say now that the "woman question" in Germany no longer exists in the old sense of the term; it has been solved. It will no longer be necessary for us to campaign for our rights with meetings, resolutions and petitions. Political conflict, which will always exist, will from now on take place in another form. We women now have the opportunity to allow our influence to be exerted within the context of party groupings on the basis of ideology.'[14]

It needed only a decade to show that the claims made by Marie Juchacz had been premature, and the hope implicit in them illusory. By 1930 the radical feminists were convinced that progress towards equality for women had been frustrated throughout the 1920s because of the continuing majority of men in every parliamentary party. In fact, women's representation in the Reichstag actually dropped in the mid-1920s, to a share of around 6 per cent,[15] although after the election of November 1932 it again reached a figure of 9 per cent, when there were thirty-five women deputies.[16] The enfranchisement of women had meant only, said the radicals, that they were now represented; they remained powerless.[17] More moderate feminists echoed this view: for Katharina von Kardorff, one-time People's Party deputy in the Reichstag, the chief obstacle to progress was precisely the arrangement which Marie Juchacz had welcomed, namely the dispersal of the women representatives into a large number of political parties, with partisan allegiance given priority over the solidarity of the female sex. If women were ever to make progress towards equality, they would, she claimed, have to act together as a combined non-party pressure group, although she and her associates did have reservations about the creation of a Women's Party as such.[18]

In fact, given the sharp differences of opinion both between and among socialist and non-socialist feminists, the formation of a Women's Party by women of all shades of political opinion was not a practical proposition at any time during the Weimar years. A degree of cooperation was achieved briefly, in 1930, when women Reichstag deputies from all political parties — except the Economics Party and the NSDAP, neither of which had women representatives — came together in a study group to discuss matters of particular interest to women. But this arrangement lapsed after July 1932, as increasing political bitterness made collaboration impossible.[19]

The basic reason for the disappointment of the high hopes entertained by feminists immediately after the war was neatly pinpointed by Katharina von Kardorff: 'Our equality with men', she observed, 'is written into the Constitution but not into the Civil Code.'[20] Indeed Article 109 of the Weimar Constitution stated that 'All Germans are equal before the law. Men and women have fundamentally the same civil rights and obligations.' Then, Article 119 acknowledged that the Civil Code's view of the marriage relationship was out of date: 'Marriage is based on the equality of the sexes.' And Article 128 affirmed the right of women to equality of opportunity in public life and the public service with the words: 'All citizens without distinction are eligible for public office in accordance with the laws and according to their abilities and achievements. All discriminations against women in the civil service are abolished.' But these statements were not of themselves sufficient to transform the position of women in Germany: legislation alone could alter existing laws and, particularly, the Civil Code, and until it was forthcoming, they remained in force as before.

The continuing majority of men in all parties should not of itself have prevented the enactment of measures to promote equality for women, since several of the post-war political parties were pledged to support the implementation of the Constitution, including the clauses which would reform the Civil Code where it discriminated against women and which would provide equality of opportunity for women in employment and public life. Of the middle-class parties the Democratic Party (DDP) was the most unequivocally in favour of equality for women; indeed, the outstanding figure in the pre-war middle-class women's movement, Helene Lange, was one of the founders of the DDP,[21] and other prominent feminists, including Gertrud Bäumer and Marie-Elisabeth Lüders, joined it in 1918. Esteem for Helene Lange was such that she was created Honorary President of the DDP.[22] The People's Party (DVP) was almost as committed to the achievement of women's rights: its 1919 programme stated, in a paragraph entitled 'The Woman Question', that the party was in favour of the 'political, economic and legal equality of the sexes . . . and . . . the admission of women to all offices and positions on condition of having the requisite preparatory training . . .'[23]

During the 1920s both these parties developed a network of local groups of women party workers, coordinated in each case by a National Women's Committee which published a newsletter to circulate information about the party activity of women at the local level and to feature items of particular interest to women.[24] The aims of the DDP's National Women's Committee were to defend and propagate the idea of democracy, to promote the DDP, to educate German women to civic responsibility, and to achieve equality for women.[25] Doubtless in recognition of the active part played by women in the party, and in the hope of attracting more female support, the party — now the 'Staatspartei' — held discussions in summer 1932 about the possibility of giving second place on the national list of candidates for the next general election to a woman,[26] a practice adopted in some state elections,[27] but nothing came of them.[28] The DVP, however, did put forward their long serving deputy Dr Elsa Matz as the third candidate on their list for the election in March 1933.[29] Dr Matz was President of the DVP's Women's Committee and a member of the executive committee of the party.[30] The DVP's *Women's Review* paid tribute to the loyalty of the party's women members in March 1932, describing their 'tireless' activity in supporting the party throughout the country.[31] But by this time both the liberal parties were becoming very weak indeed, to the extent that the radical feminist Lida Gustava Heymann, referring to the DDP even in November 1930 had asked, in a parenthesis, 'Does it still exist?'[32]

The mass of women continued to be strongly influenced by the more conservative power groups, the Roman Catholic and Lutheran Churches and, to some extent, the Nationalist Party (DNVP). The latter had admitted women to political activity before the war more out of self-defence against the socialists and the liberals, who had gladly enlisted women's aid, than out of conviction; in fact, the DNVP's chief women's organisation, the *Deutscher Frauenbund 1909*, was specifically opposed to feminists of any political colour.[33] Nevertheless, the DNVP had its own National Women's Committee, which in 1933 claimed that it was obvious that the party was in favour of 'protecting equal rights for women'.[34] After all, the DNVP had consistently presented women candidates at general elections throughout the Weimar period, the most distinguished of whom was Paula Müller-Ottfried, President of the Evangelical Women's Association, who was a Reichstag deputy throughout the 1920s.[35]

It was abundantly clear, however, that the DNVP and the Evangelical Church, whose political views were very similar, aimed to mobilise women for the purpose of forming an opposition to progressive ideas which included pacifism, increased employment opportunities for women at all levels, and any kind of 'permissiveness' in social behaviour or sexual morality.[36] Certainly, it did seem that women preferred order to disorder; there was a higher proportion of women's votes among those for Hindenburg in the Presidential election of March 1932 than among those for any other candidate, and women were in a minority of voters for the extremist candidates, both Communist and Nazi.[37] The *raison d'être* of Evangelical women seemed to be to uphold the idea that women's role was, and should be, that of housewife and mother; the Evangelical Women's Association made its position clear in January 1932 with the pronouncement that 'German Evangelical women see in the child the God-given natural perfection of marriage'. In their view, only medical reasons could justify refusal by a married couple to have children.[38]

The views of the Roman Catholic Church were certainly as uncompromising as those of the Evangelical Church; but, even so, the Catholic Church realised that to give no ground at all on the 'woman question' would be only to its own disadvantage. Therefore the political wing of the Church, the Centre Party, reluctantly made some concessions to the feminists in its 1918 programme 'Centre Party and the New Political Order'. For the first time a Centre Party manifesto supported women's suffrage and made mention of 'the contribution of women in political life'. While regretting that circumstances necessitated the sanctioning of women's admission to the 'brawling and quarrelling' of politics, the Centre Party put a good face on it by asserting that 'we are convinced that we shall find in our women enthusiastic fellow-combatants and energetic helpers . . . The counsel of experienced women will be indispensable to us in creating a new state structure . . .'[39] But the continuing reactionary attitude of the Roman Catholic Church was epitomised in the Papal Encyclical 'Quadragesimo Anno' of 1931, which demanded an end to the employment of married women,[40] and which aroused the ire even of women who could in no way be termed radical or socialist.[41] On the other hand, a representative of the Centre claimed to have found considerable support, particularly among women, for the party's view that women could not fulfil the demands of two full-time jobs — one of these being that of housewife and mother — satisfactorily; he also maintained that the man 'is, and remains, the provider for and head of the family'.[42] This, then, was the attitude towards the position of women in society of the one political party which was in every German government from 1919 to 1932.

The ascendancy of the Centre was to some extent facilitated by the splitting of the SPD during the war, a circumstance which was particularly serious for the working women's movement.[43] Most of the leading women socialists of the pre-war period, notably Rosa Luxemburg and Clara Zetkin, belonged to the radical wing of the party, and therefore found themselves in opposition to the SPD's wartime policies, finally becoming leading members of the German Communist Party (KPD) on its founding at the end of 1918. These women had always disliked the at times latent, at times overt antifeminism of the rank and file of the SPD.[44] In the KPD, the radicals were determined to return to basic Marxist ideals, and so the liberation of women from all kinds of discrimination would follow naturally from the liberation of the working class from capitalism, since it was the capitalist system, with its bourgeois morality, which had brought about the subordination of women in society and in the economy.[45]

If the SPD had become bureaucratised before 1914, the process was only intensified by the secession of the radicals and its new-found respectability as a party of government. Docile moderates like Marie Juchacz and Gertrud Hanna became the chief spokeswomen of the party; these loyally upheld official party policy, and were at pains to

19

remind women members that they were first and foremost members of the SPD, and that their women's organisation was only one constituent of 'this great party'.[46] Gertrud Hanna firmly believed that in the socialist trade union movement, at any rate, positive harm would result from any attempt to isolate women in their own groups, and found herself having to remind male trade unionists at times that the interests of their movement would be better served by keeping women in it as full members, alongside the men.[47] More than one delegate to the SPD's 1927 congress voiced the opinion that not nearly enough was being done by the party to interest women in all aspects of party work and to mobilise their support for SPD policies generally, not just those of particular relevance to women; the middle-class women's movement and the liberal parties were felt to be much more active and successful in this.[48]

But although the SPD was nominally committed to the pursuit of equality between the sexes, it had been a party to the Demobilisation Orders of the post-war years which had the effect of dismissing women from jobs to make way for men returning from the forces. In addition, the onset of the depression in 1929-30 gave rise again to hostility among working men and within the socialist unions towards what they regarded as female competition for the ever-decreasing number of jobs.[49] The SPD could boast that women were better represented in its parliamentary party than in any other; but women never held positions of the first importance in the party.[50] During the Weimar period the SPD was incapable of shaking off prejudices which had a long tradition, while at the same time exhibiting complacence about the things it had achieved.

On the other side of the socialist camp there was no equivocation whatsoever. The breakaway KPD trade union organisation, the Revolutionary Trade Union Opposition (RGO), founded in 1929,[51] was fully explicit about its policy, which included the abolition of wage differentials between men and women, within the context of a campaign for a general rise in wages, as well as more thorough protection for women workers and longer paid leave for expectant and nursing mothers. The RGO also campaigned for equal salaries for men and women white collar workers, and for the repeal of provisions, reintroduced in 1932, permitting the dismissal of married women civil servants. In a clear reference to the contentious question about whether a woman should be dismissed from public employment if she had an illegitimate child, the RGO's manifesto asserted its opposition to 'any interference in the personal life of women civil servants'.[52]

The end of the 1920s saw the intensification of KPD activity in Germany, with the directive from Stalin that Social Democracy, above all, must be combated. Intensive propaganda campaigns were launched with the aim of encouraging women, especially, to join the proletarian

struggle for a 'Soviet Germany'.[53] The belief that capitalism in
Germany was reaching its crisis with the depression led to particularly
energetic recruiting drives in 1931 and 1932. These did bear fruit, but,
given that the situation was particularly favourable to Communist
agitation — with compulsory wage cuts and the shortage of jobs — the
results were disappointing, especially among women in the heavy industrial areas. Local women shop stewards were felt by the executive to
have neglected opportunities, and so greater central control was proposed and new targets for women's recruitment were set in March
1932.[54]

In addition to the split in the socialist camp, the middle-class
women's movement, in which there had already been sharp differences
of opinion before the war,[55] was now divided into two groups whose
attitudes had diverged considerably. Those who had been in the leadership of the *Bund deutscher Frauenvereine* (BDF)[56] before the war, and
who had organised the *Nationale Frauendienst* during it — the group led
by Gertrud Bäumer — largely associated themselves with the DDP in
local and national politics, but also continued to be active in their
separate women's organisations within the BDF. The other, smaller
group was more radical, not affiliated to any political party but wholeheartedly Republican; it was strongly feminist, pacifist, and thoroughly
disenchanted with the 'establishment' of the women's movement
which, felt the radicals, had been tamed and institutionalised by its
nationalist stance in the war, and bought off by a few concessions to
the feminist lobby after it.

The final split had come in 1915 when a small group of middle-class
feminists, led by Lida Gustava Heymann and Anita Augspurg, had condemned the BDF for volunteering to assist the war effort, and had preferred to join with women pacifists from other countries in founding
the Women's International League for Peace and Freedom at The Hague.
The WILPF pledged itself to work for peace and disarmament and to
lobby governments in all countries to try to achieve this.[57] As the
organisation developed, in time of peace, its demands became more far-
reaching with as decisive an application to domestic as to international
affairs. In the election campaign of 1930 the German branch of the
WILPF urged its members to canvass and vote for candidates from
any party which supported its twelve demands, which included the
abolition of the death penalty, the implementing of the Constitution's
provisions which promoted equality for women and for the illegitimate
child, the repeal of the severe abortion law, paragraph 218 of the
Criminal Code, and a ban on the production of and trade in wea-
pons.[58] Campaigning for total disarmament, the WILPF preached the
pointlessness of trying to create protective devices against the use of
poison gas and air attacks on the civilian population; the only solution,

as they saw it, was to outlaw such threats by international cooperation, which would bring to an end the irresponsible expenditure of vast sums of money on armaments which was criminal in time of economic depression.[59]

Perhaps surprisingly, given their militant feminism, the radicals, like the more moderate feminists, were opposed to the creation of a Women's Party. They proposed rather that at elections there should be a 'women's list' composed of women from the various political parties in proportion to the parliamentary representation of the parties. This would, they claimed, have the result of giving women a larger representation and greater influence in the legislature than they had during the 1920s; but the radicals also felt that experience had shown that Germany's women were not yet sufficiently politically mature for their scheme.[60]

The German branch of the WILPF cast its net wide in trying to attract support for its views. Although most of its leadership regarded the Churches as bastions of reaction, it nevertheless realised that their influence was still considerable, and therefore tried to win their support for the disarmament campaign. The WILPF contacted Adam Stegerwald, a leading member of the Centre Party, and its representatives even obtained an audience with the Papal Nuncio, Pacelli; they then used their tenuous connection with these names to try to win over the Christian Trade Union organisation.[61] The German branch was also extremely active on the international scene, playing host to a full meeting of the League in Frankfurt in January 1929.[62] Three years later, another conference, of all international women's pacifist organisations, was held in Munich, under the chairmanship of the local WILPF leader, Constanze Hallgarten.[63] This meeting was reported by the Nazis under the title 'Pacifist scandal in Munich'.[64]

Besides disarmament, the other major issue which absorbed the energies of the radicals of the WILPF was the position of women in post-war Germany. The magazine of this group, *Die Frau im Staat*, founded in 1918 by Lida Gustava Heymann and Anita Augspurg, and edited by them,[65] devoted considerable space in every issue in the late 1920s and early 1930s to pointing out how little progress had really been made in winning equality of opportunity and equality of rights for women. It was here that they really felt themselves to be out of sympathy with the women of the BDF, who, not unjustifiably, were proud of the achievements they had made in the pre-war period, particularly in the field of education. The moderates were well aware that far less progress had been made during the 1920s than had been anticipated by both themselves and the radicals, in the euphoria of 1918-19 with the granting of the suffrage and the writing into the Constitution of many of their demands.[66] But although they realised that much had been left undone — especially with the Civil Code un-amended — they nevertheless gave the impression, to the radicals and to the young, who had not actually been involved in the struggles of the Imperial period, that they were complacent, always harking back to the things that they had achieved and to their contribution to the war effort.

At first sight the ground between the moderate and the radical groups in the middle-class feminist camp was not so very great. Both groups favoured improved opportunities for women at all levels and in all areas — economic, political, social, legal, cultural — and both were outspoken in their attacks on a male dominated society. In addition, the moderates came out strongly in favour of close international co-operation after the Peace Treaties had been signed. In a way, however, their motive was different from that of the radicals, who consistently and unconditionally supported disarmament and internationalism; the moderates worked rather from the premise that if Germany were dis-armed compulsorily then they would campaign tirelessly to achieve general disarmament.[67] But the moderates did genuinely believe that peace must be preserved, and that the international activity of women, whether generally in League of Nations' affiliates or particularly with women from other countries, was not merely desirable but actually essential.

Gertrud Bäumer, for one, was the German delegate to the League of Nations' committee on youth affairs, as well as being a representative at international disarmament discussions;[68] it was, after all, largely for her 'outspokenly pacifist and feminist outlook' that she was not only dismissed from public service by the Nazis in 1933, but even, from 1935 to 1937, denied the right to publish her writings.[69] Her friend Dorothee von Velsen, also a member of the DDP, and President of the *Allgemeiner Deutscher Frauenverein*, was a member of the committee of the World Union for Women's Suffrage, and was also in 1932 the Reich Government's representative for social matters and women's affairs in the German delegation to the League of Nations.[70] Marie-Elisabeth Lüders, a DDP Reichstag deputy throughout the 1920s, and a prominent member of the BDF and the *Deutscher Akademikerinnen-bund* — an association of professional women — was a member of three international committees, including the Society for a European Cus-toms Union, and was, in addition, a leading member of the German Society for the League of Nations.[71] The BDF itself became fully committed to working for universal disarmament, and in 1932 organ-ised a giant petition to gain support for this.[72]

The women of the BDF were also concerned with questions of youth welfare, employment prospects for girls in time of economic stringency, education of all kinds, and altogether anything which they felt was of interest to women. At their meetings they could call on representatives of the Land governments, for example Frau Zeisler from Saxony or Marie Baum from Baden, to report on policy in the different Länder. They could also call on representatives of some Reich ministries to explain the policies and the work of the central government; women in this category included, apart from Gertrud Bäumer at the Ministry of the Interior, Klara Mende in the Ministry of Economics and Käte Gaebel at the central office of the Employment Exchanges.[73] These women were themselves living examples of the progress that had been made in winning acceptance for the appointment of women to public office. This meant, however, that these women were necessarily associated with the policies of the governments for which they worked; since it was precisely these governments which were failing to introduce progressive legislation which would benefit women, the women associated with them came in for a share of the criticism heaped on them by the radicals. Naturally, the Reich governments were felt to have been particularly reprehensible since legislation was still wanting, after a decade, to implement the relevant clauses of the Constitution. As in all other matters, however, any Government was rendered ineffectual by its precarious coalition character, the growing succession of short-lived administrations serving only to increase Ministers' reluctance to introduce controversial measures.

The radicals understood this difficulty, and in the depression years they also appreciated that the Government's room for manoeuvre was negligible. Their argument, however, was that it should have been possible to achieve something more for women during the less troubled years of the 1920s, and that the blame for not agitating continuously to this end lay squarely with the women of the BDF, although they also condemned women in the SPD and the trade unions.[74] In an article entitled 'Women's Liberation', published in autumn 1932, Lida Gustava Heymann, in her pungent style, began with the words, 'Women's movement! How remote it sounds; it meant something once.' But even in the past, she felt, the BDF had been out of touch with reality, just as it assuredly was by 1930:

'Then, as now, the Bund lacked visible vitality; then, as now, the Bund had ossified; then, as now, it was involved in theoretical, soul-destroying discussions; then, as now, it possessed neither a militant spirit nor courage, neither initiative nor real enthusiasm.'

Given the real efforts of the BDF leaders in the pre-war period, this indictment was rather unjust; and yet, in relation to the 1920s it was not altogether without foundation. Indeed, Lida Gustava Heymann paid tribute to Luise Otto who, she believed, had had real aims and objectives which had been quietly ignored by the women's leaders from the end of the nineteenth century. For forty years, she claimed, the BDF had concentrated on securing for women a niche in social welfare activity and educating them for a trade or a profession; the undoubted practical value of this could not, she said, obscure the fact that it had only a very indirect bearing on the complete liberation of women, the aim of the radicals.[75]

It is clear, then, that the differences between the moderate and radical feminists were not merely minor ones of substance, but fundamental ones of spirit. The moderates aimed for equality of opportunity for women but accepted that women's physical strength, their biological role and their natural inclinations might mean that they would not in fact achieve positions fully equal with men.[76] As the radical Alice Rühle-Gerstel commented, in a spirit of criticism,

'The *Allgemeiner Deutscher Frauenverein* formulated the first point of its programme with a sarcasm obviously directed at the behaviour of many of its fellow women as follows: "The Women's Movement proceeds in the framing of its demands from the fact of the fundamental physical and spiritual difference between the sexes." '[77]

The radicals, on the other hand, denied that there were any differences so significant as to make complete equality of the sexes in every aspect of life impossible. They took this principle to extremes that seemed to many highly absurd, most notably in their opposition to labour protection for women, which they claimed was a device to justify paying women at a lower rate than men.[78] In this, they differed not only from conservatives and from the liberal women's movement, but also from both reformist and revolutionary socialists.[79]

The radical feminists believed that their campaign was one on behalf of the entire female sex, whereas the BDF was interested only in the affairs of professional, vocational and clerical women workers. The failure of the middle-class and working-class women's representatives to make common cause in the 1890s had led in fact to a division of functions with the middle-class feminists nominally representing the female sex but actually not representing its large working-class element, whose interests were the concern of the socialist parties, led as they were by men. The radicals had hoped to cross the class barrier and show working-class women that male chauvinism was as strong in the SPD as in non-socialist parties, and that one did not need to look to the Moscow dominated KPD to find representatives who wanted equality for all women, not just a privileged minority.[80] The charge that the moderate feminists were not interested in the mass of German women but worked only for the benefit of a few selfish 'female imitators of men' was useful ammunition for the Nazis in their attacks on the 'women's rightists'.[81] It was certainly true that most of the leading

25

feminists were spinsters, and could therefore be accused of being out of touch with the needs of the vast number of ordinary German wives and mothers. The radicals, at least, showed signs of appreciating some of the pressing problems of human relationships by campaigning for the repeal of the abortion law and the free dissemination of contraceptive advice,[82] but the reticence preferred by the BDF women on such matters was epitomised by Gertrud Bäumer's remark to a friend that 'I really hate the word "sexual".' [83]

The differences between the radical and moderate feminists were accentuated by an additional complicating factor, the generation problem. It was clear in the late 1920s and early 1930s that the BDF was not attracting young women, and this was a source of concern to the leadership. Naturally, some of the vitality had gone out of the movement once the aims of the pre-war campaign had been achieved; legal acceptance of women's suffrage, the admission of women to higher education and the professions, demonstrable improvement in senior schooling for girls, and the appointment of a small but significant number of women to prominent positions, meant that the big issues had been settled. The task now was one of comparative drudgery, the ironing out of the minutiae and the unspectacular working out of details to make the intentions expressed in the Constitution a reality. And economic and political circumstances ensured that issues which seemed more pressing took precedence over this work, so that by 1930 there was very little to show for what had been promised.

This gave point to the radicals' charge that the women's movement as it stood was becoming a meaningless anachronism, and that it could thus not expect to attract the young.[84] This was felt to be even more the case since the same old 'establishment' still ran the BDF as had been running it for twenty years, and that without an infusion of new blood it had become complacent and ossified. But the majority of BDF members seemed in favour of the long-serving committee, since it was returned again and again;[85] both the reason for and the result of this was undoubtedly that potential young adherents increasingly stayed away, in disgust. The radicals took obvious pleasure in publicising the BDF's 'generation problem' in *Die Frau im Staat*.[86] But they faced a similar problem in the WILPF, where the younger women felt that the methods and ideals of the older leadership were now out of date, but where they again failed to oust the old guard — in spite of their claim that they were anxious to stand down — and so the system remained unchanged in this camp, too.[87]

No doubt division, discussion and disputes were considered healthy inside the democratic forms of the Weimar Republic. The stalemate within the BDF, particularly, could probably have been resolved either by a determined takeover bid by the young within it, or else by its being eclipsed by a new, vital movement composed of the disaffected young. In a way, of course, it could be said that the latter did come about, with the attraction of even some feminists to the energetic radicalism of the National Socialist movement, although the majority of them were quite clearly against it. But, as Alice Rühle-Gerstel commented, 'Women as a whole have no single representative',[88] and the splits and divisions between and within the middle-class and socialist groups concerned with women's affairs were to prove critical, in undermining potentially effective opposition from women of all shades of feminist opinion, who could not, even in the face of a common danger, act in concert.

Further, it is clear that most groups in the feminist camp underestimated the Nazi threat. Indeed, the radicals were well aware of what a Nazi accession to power would mean for their campaign;[89] but Lida Gustava Heymann, writing in autumn 1932, showed how unrealistic she was by claiming that Hitler's party did not spell a real danger, since the cause of feminism was going from strength to strength. In any case, she added, 'Dictatorships never last long.'[90] A representative of the DVP, writing in the party's *Women's Review* early in 1932, was more pessimistic:

> 'The women's movement finds itself at the present time in a crisis of a kind which it has never in all its history experienced . . . The most threatening danger seems to lie in the political arena, since a movement with the great political momentum, which National Socialism currently has, has set itself decisively and unequivocally against the ideals and aims of the women's movement. The women's movement is portrayed in the party's press generally and without restraint as a manifestation of decadence.'[91]

The BDF, however, demonstrated how little it comprehended the nature of Nazism as late as March 1933. Its questionnaire, sent to all political parties, asking how many women candidates were being presented by each,[92] was clearly based on two assumptions: that elections still meant something in Germany, and that political parties still wielded influence and would continue to do so. Within a few months, both these assumptions were to be proved invalid, and the women's movement, in all its branches, effectively destroyed.

Even before all the parties were dissolved and the Nazis in unchallenged control of the state it was made clear that no branch of the women's movement was to be allowed to continue in existence. After all, every point on which the separate groups agreed was anathema to the NSDAP: pacifism, internationalism, feminism, individualism were the bogeys — along with the menace of 'Bolshevism', which for the Nazis covered the whole spectrum of left-wing thought — which they were sworn to destroy. The tragedy of the women's movement was, then, that its various warring factions could not temporarily sink their differences to present a united front to a party that was the enemy of all of them. The Nazis were able to pick off each group one by one, without any concerted protest. This process paralleled that taking place on the political front. Perhaps, given the skill, speed and good fortune of the Nazis even a united feminist movement could have achieved little; on the other hand, its chances of survival would no doubt have been considerably greater had there not been the disarray and the feeling of discouragement that were so obvious in feminist circles in the early 1930s.

The women's organisations associated with the KPD and the SPD were the first to go, naturally succumbing when their respective party and trade union movement were banned. Those who were not arrested and who refused to emigrate were at least temporarily hamstrung, although a left-wing underground organisation did develop quite rapidly. It was, however, a resistance movement of which some women — notably the lawyer, Hilde Benjamin (KPD), Joanna Kirchner (SPD),[93] and Eva Schulze-Knabe (KPD)[94] — were members, and not at all a specifically women's movement. There was, after all, only the one issue at this time, the need to overthrow the Nazi regime. The radical feminists were considered by the Nazis to be less dangerous, not being associated with a strong party machine, and so the Government contented itself with banning their publications and ridiculing their leaders in the Nazi Party's press.[95] But Nazi vindictiveness and greed were demonstrated when it was announced in February 1935 that

> 'On the grounds of the regulations concerning the confiscation of property of Communists and enemies of the state and the people, the property of the journalists Dr Anita Augspurg and Lida Gustava Heymann has been confiscated, to the benefit of the state of Bavaria.'[96]

This was the penalty to be paid by those denied the right to pursue their profession; they had seen their publications banned, their organisations dissolved, and in the end had seen no alternative to emigration, forfeiting in the process their personal possessions.

With the left-wing organisations outlawed and their leaders disgraced, the conservatives, who had long hated the women's movement in any of its manifestations, felt that their hour had come, and wholeheartedly pledged themselves to serve the new regime.[97] The *Ring Nationaler Frauenbünde*, an association of conservative women's organisations, wrote to Hitler in April 1933 welcoming the 'considerable efforts of the National Government to give strong leadership', and putting its organisations completely at his disposal.[98] Lammers replied that Hitler graciously acknowledged 'the willingness of the nationalist women to collaborate with the state'.[99] But it was soon to become apparent that the leadership of women's organisations, as of all others in the Nazi State, would be in the hands of party members, and that even the most compliant of conservative groups could no longer hope to retain its own identity.

A number of the conservative organisations hoped to save themselves by demonstrating their loyalty to the new regime in a concrete way; the Evangelical Women's Association, the National Association of German Housewives and the *Bund Königin Luise* (Queen Luise League), among others, at once joined the new Nazi association of women's organisations, the *Frauenfront*.[100] The leader of the *Bund Königin Luise*, Frau von Hadeln, was rewarded with the post of deputy leader of the *Frauenfront*, whose leader was an enthusiastic young Nazi, Lydia Gottschewski.[101] But early in 1934 a strong propaganda action was launched to bring about the dissolution of the BKL, and on 1 April 1934, this was effected.[102] Other groups lasted a little longer, but it was only a matter of time before a Nazi monopoly was enforced in this area, as in most others. At the end of October 1935, the *Deutscher Frauenbund*, the DNVP's leading women's organisation, was dissolved; the *Stahlhelmfrauenbund*'s turn came a week later; and in November 1936 the *Flottenbund deutscher Frauen* ceased to exist.[103] These organisations were allowed to survive so long because they were no threat to the Nazis, but their continued existence meant that there was diversity of a kind that the Nazis could not tolerate, and so they had, eventually, to be eliminated.

Of the organisations to which the Nazis had an intrinsic objection, the moderate feminist ones were treated with the least severity. Indeed their leaders suffered, in that they were promptly dismissed from positions they held in the public service, whether as civil servants, teachers, lawyers or lecturers, on grounds of 'political unreliability'; a law of 7 April 1933 permitted this, as it also made possible the dismissal of non-'Aryans' from the public service.[104] Thus, at a stroke, the Government purged vital areas of employment, particularly the highly sensitive teaching profession, which had been a stronghold of feminism. It was no doubt a severe blow to many women, to all those who held less exalted positions than Gertrud Bäumer, who was one of the first to suffer, but positions which gave them considerable interest and satisfaction nevertheless.[105] But they were, within the limits of Goebbels's censors, allowed to continue publishing their writings, and were deprived of neither their personal freedom nor their property, in contrast with the radicals and socialists.

In spite of the speed and ruthlessness with which the Nazis moved, the BDF's leaders still hoped that their organisations would be able to put up effective resistance to a complete takeover. But those which did make any show of resistance were summarily dissolved, so that Gertrud Bäumer and her associates quickly came to the conclusion that, for them and for the women they felt they still had a duty to represent, the most important thing was survival. Gertrud Bäumer still believed, in April 1933, that if the remaining women's organisations showed docility in joining the *Frauenfront*, and sacrificed some of their leaders to whom the Nazis chiefly objected, they would be able to carry on at least some of their former work, having accepted the supreme leadership of the Nazi organisation.[106] This mistaken belief was compounded by another: she also felt that the Nazi women's organisation would now be cast in the role of defender of the rights of women, and that a new women's movement would develop as a reaction to the Nazis' promised restrictions on women in public life, the professions and employment. This would be something in which, she confided to her close friend Emmy Beckmann, she would like to be able to participate. She maintained her optimism on this account throughout all the vicissitudes of the summer of 1933,[107] and even in May 1934 still believed that 'the new women's movement *is coming*'.[108]

But by this time the whole edifice of the movement built up over a period of almost seventy years had ceased to exist, and the continued publication of the chief magazine of the BDF, Gertrud Bäumer's *Die Frau*, was the only public reminder — apart from attacks on the 'women's rightists' in the Nazi press — that it had ever existed. On 15 May 1933, the leaders of the BDF had seen no alternative to the dissolution of their organisation; the taking over of many of its constituents by Nazi groups had left the BDF without a *raison d'être*, and its leaders could only advise the remaining groups to accommodate themselves to the new order as they saw fit.[109] The tactics of cooperation with the new regime did help to save one of the feminists' most valued organisations, the *Deutscher Akademikerinnenbund*, but only temporarily. Although, as Gertrud Bäumer admitted in November 1934, it had declared itself ready to make any concession necessary for survival,[110] it was finally dissolved just over a year later.[111] By this time it was in any case redundant, since the Nazis had established their own *Reichsbund deutscher Akademikerinnen*, which was safely under the leadership of a trusted official of the Nazi Teachers' League, Friederike Matthias.[112]

The dissolution of the various organisations, of a political, vocational, religious, charitable and purely social character, was one aspect of the change brought about in women's activities by the Nazi assumption of power and *Gleichschaltung* (coordination) in 1933. In addition, the establishment of a one party State in July of that year meant the end of what political power and influence women had had since 1918, however much it had been despised by the more militant feminists. The fundamental Nazi insistence that women should not be involved in politics and should not play a leading role in the party itself naturally brought an end to female representation in the Reichstag once the other parties had been either dissolved or outlawed. Thus, in a way, the situation could be said to have reverted to 'normal', since the only period in which women had been permitted to play a full part in politics had been one of scarcely more than a decade and that decade or so had been a period of instability and frustration for the majority of Germans. How much women lost in 1933 is perhaps questionable, given the relegation of the Reichstag to purely formal activities; but, at the same time, it was clear that all positions of power in the State, as in the Nazi Party, were, and would remain, in the hands of men. Gertrud Bäumer had not been wrong when she had detected signs of feminism within the Nazis' own ranks, but she had failed to appreciate that the exponents of feminist ideas within the party would be eliminated as effectively from the public eye as those outside the party had been, and given no opportunity to build up a viable base of support.[113]

But if women were, once again, to be denied a share in the political affairs of the nation this did not mean that they were also – as some had feared and others had hoped – to be excluded from all other positions and functions outside the realm of home and family. In the major areas of employment, higher education and the professions, the wilder Nazi predictions that in the Third Reich there would be a sharp reduction in the number of women admitted or allowed to continue in their position were not realised. Indeed there were some attempts to restrict women's activities in these areas, but as the 1930s progressed, with the build-up of an economy geared to the possibility of limited war, women were looked to increasingly to fill vacancies for which there was not an adequate supply of men, even in areas in which they had not formerly been well represented. This development, which was greatly intensified once Germany was at war, can no doubt be viewed as a retreat from policy which had been declared 'fundamental', even 'immutable'. But simply to say that is to accept the superficial and to fail to appreciate the essentially long-term view the Nazis themselves had adopted. In the 'thousand-year Reich' there had to be priorities, even among basic tenets of ideology, so that apparent inconsistencies emerge; in the long term, however, all the Nazis' principles were supposed to be compatible. The first priority was the securing for the 'Aryan' race of an impregnable position in the world, before which all others, including those regarding the nature and function of women, had to give way. But it is clear that the Nazis did expect that, once they had achieved this position, their other policies, including the return of women to their 'natural occupations', could be implemented.

In the meantime, there were indications during the 1930s of what this would mean. The insistence of the Nazis on the separation of the sexes allowed, for example, the creation of Nazi organisations for women which perhaps had little real power, but whose actual operation was in the hands of the women themselves, thus providing a limited amount of autonomy; this was permitted because the leadership of the organisations showed little inclination to step out of line.[114] There were developments within the realm of marriage and the family which were sometimes, in themselves, surprisingly close to what feminists and even socialists had called for in previous decades, although the Nazis introduced them for different motives: policy towards the unmarried mother and the reform of the divorce law are two examples of this. In other aspects, of course — notably the sensitive area of abortion — the Nazi view was diametrically opposed to what the radical feminists and the socialists had demanded.

These similarities and differences were the result of a fundamental difference between the ideologies — using the term loosely — of Nazis on the one hand and liberals and socialists on the other. The latter believed that the good of the individual, within society, was intrinsically worth pursuing, and that the State should protect and further the interests of its citizens. The Nazis, on the other hand, put the good of the State before the interests of its citizens, so that the State's demands always took precedence and the desires and needs of its citizens were, if it were found to be necessary, sacrificed. Much of Nazi policy was conditioned by a revulsion against the 'liberal individualism' of the Weimar Republic which, in the Nazi view, was one of the main causes of Germany's economic, political and social problems. The desire to make Germany great once more would therefore require the stamping out of all vestiges of this attitude. These points are fundamental to an understanding of Government policy towards women, with its apparent *volte-faces* at times, throughout the Nazi period.

NOTES

1.   For a detailed and fully documented account of some aspects of the feminist movement under the Empire, including the campaign for suffrage reform, see the unpublished D. Phil. thesis by Richard J. Evans, 'The Women's Movement in Germany, 1890-1919', Oxford, 1972; see also Katharine Anthony, *Feminism in Germany and Scandinavia*, New York, 1915.
2.   M. Greiff (ed.), *Bürgerliches Gesetzbuch*, Berlin and Leipzig, 1930, pp. 747-63.
3.   Figures from *Statistisches Jahrbuch (St. J.)*, 1914, pp. 14 and 16.
4.   E. Schuster, 'The German Civil Code (1)', *Law Quarterly Review*, 1896, p. 32.
5.   Lowie, *op. cit.*, p. 208.
6.   Schlesinger, *op. cit.*, p. 281.

7.   A good, brief account of these developments is to be found in Friedrich Paulsen, *Geschichte des Gelehrten Unterrichts*, Berlin and Leipzig, 1921, vol. 2, pp. 776-81.

8.   Figures from *St. J.*, 1914, pp. 322-5.

9.   Charlotte Lorenz, 'Die gewerbliche Frauenarbeit während des Krieges', in James T. Shotwell (general ed.), *Der Krieg und die Arbeitsverhältnisse*, Stuttgart, 1928, pp. 319-20.

10.   Gerhard Bry, *Wages in Germany, 1871-1945*, New York, 1960, p. 205.

11.   BDC, Gertrud Bäumer's file, 'Lebenslauf', undated (? 1936); Lorenz, *op. cit.*, p. 319; Evans, *op. cit.*, pp. 297-8, 324.

12.   Figures from *St. J.*; 1923, p. 318; 1924-5, p. 357; 1928, p. 509.

13.   Hugh W. Puckett, *Germany's Women Go Forward*, New York, 1930, p. 252.

14.   'Aus der Rede von Marie Juchacz als erste deutsche weibliche Abgeordnete, 11.2.1919', *Vorwärts*, 14 November 1968.

15.   Puckett, *loc. cit.*

16.   Report in *BF*, January 1933, p. 5.

17.   Lida Gustava Heymann: 'Deutsches Debacle', *Die Frau im Staat (FiS)*, November 1930, p. 2, and 'Frauenbefreiung', *FiS*, September/October 1932, p. 5.

18.   BA, *Nachlass* Katharina von Kardorff, no. 38, 1927-32, 'Brauchen wir eine Frauenpartei?', 22 January 1930, pp. 44-65; *ibid.*, no. 27, letter from Emma Ender to Katharina von Kardorff, 5 January 1931, p. 75.

19.   Report in *BF*, October 1932, p. 6.

20.   BA, *Nachlass* Katharina von Kardorff, no. 38, *loc. cit.*

21.   HA, reel 37, fol. 736, 'Mitteilungen des Reichsfrauenausschusses der DDP', 20 May 1930, 'Helene Lange †'.

22.   BA, R45 III/14, Protokoll über die Sitzung des Parteiausschusses der DDP, 25 May 1930, p. 44.

23.   BA, R45 II/62, 'Grundsätze der DVP 1919' (1931 reprint), Sammlungen . . . verschiedener Parteien, pp. 150-51.

24.   HA, *op. cit.*, 20 April 1930; BA, R45 II/64, DVP Reichsgeschäftsstelle, *Frauenrundschau*, 4 March 1932, 1141.

25.   HA, *op. cit.*, 20 January 1930.

26.   BA, R45 III/51, Protokoll über die Sitzung des Parteiausschusses der DDP, 7 July 1932, p. 109.

27.   BA, *Kl. Erw.*, no. 267, letter from Gertrud Bäumer to Emmy Beckmann, undated (? 1929).

28.   Reply by the DDP to a questionnaire sent to each party by the BDF on the eve of the March 1933 election, about the putting forward of women candidates, reported in *BF*, March 1933, p. 8.

29.   Reply by the DVP to the BDF's questionnaire, *BF*, *op. cit.*, p. 9.

30.   Elsa Matz's entry in *Reichstags-Handbuch*, Berlin, 1930, p. 417.

31.   BA, R45 II/64, *loc. cit.*

32.   Lida Gustava Heymann, 'Deutsches Debacle', *FiS*, November 1930, p. 2.

33.   Walter Kaufmann, *Monarchism in the Weimar Republic*, New York, 1953, p. 130.

34.   Reply by DNVP to the BDF's questionnaire, *BF, loc. cit.*

35.   Cuno Horkenbach (ed.), *Das Deutsche Reich von 1918 bis heute*, Berlin, 1930, p. 718.

36.   'Soziale Kundgebung des Deutschen Evangelischen Kirchentages, 14. bis 17.6.1924' and 'Aufruf des Deutschen Evangelischen Kirchenausschuss vom 25. Mai 1932', documents reproduced in *AfB*, 1932, no. 2, pp. 88 and 95-6.

37.   BA, *op. cit.*, *Frauenrundschau*, 6 April 1932, 'Zur Hindenburgwahl am 10. April', p. 1167.

38.   *Ibid., Frauenrundschau*, 28 January 1932, 'Deutsch-Evangelische Frauen für die Erhaltung von Ehe und Familie', p. 1111.
39.   BA, R45 II/62, 'Zentrum und Politische Neuordnung: Ein Programme', Sammlungen . . . verschiedener Parteien, p. 39.
40.   Quoted in Leo Zodrow, 'Die Doppelbelastung der Frau in Familie und Erwerbsberuf', *Stimmen der Zeit*, 1962-3, p. 376.
41.   BA, *Nachlass* Katharina von Kardorff, no. 34a, 'Papst contra Frau?', 1931, pp. 79-93.
42.   BA, R2/1291, letter from W. Rompel to Gärtner at the Reich Ministry of Finance, 10 April 1929.
43.   This 'working women's movement' was not so much a *women's* movement as a part of the socialist movement. There were women's groups within the SPD and the KPD, but these were composed of women who were full members of the respective party. See Alice Rühle-Gerstel, *Das Frauenproblem der Gegenwart. Eine Psychologische Bilanz*, Leipzig, 1932, pp. 142-3, and BA, R58/1146, RMdI/NsdL (see Glossary), 'Kommunistische Frauenbewegung', 5 March 1932.
44.   Thönnessen, *op. cit.*, pp. 84-98.
45.   G. G. L. Alexander, *Kämpfende Frauen*, n.p., 1924, pp. 3-4.
46.   Marie Juchacz's speech to the Women's Conference at the 1927 SPD Party Congress at Kiel, 27-29 May 1927, found in the published proceedings of the Congress, Berlin, 1927, p. 302.
47.   'Frauenarbeit und Gewerkschaften', *Gewerkschaftszeitung*, 11 January 1930, p. 22.
48.   Report of the SPD's 1927 Party Congress, pp. 303-4, 308.
49.   Thönnessen, *op. cit.*, pp. 100-2, 105, 118-9.
50.   Richard N. Hunt, *German Social Democracy, 1918-33*, New Haven, 1964, p. 81.
51.   Hermann Weber (ed.), *Völker hört die Signale*, Munich, 1967, pp. 22-3, 126.
52.   BA, R45/vorl. 10, RGO Referenten Materialien, October 1932, 'Die Arbeiterinnen in die Einheitsfrontaktion', pp. 12-13.
53.   BA, R58/1145, RMdI/NsdL, 6 February 1931, 'Kommunist-ische Frauenbewegung'.
54.   BA, R58/1146, RMdI/NsdL, 5 March 1932, pp. 5-13.
55.   Evans, *op. cit.*, discusses these differences in detail, as a consistent theme of his work.
56.   The BDF was a nationwide coordinating association of middle-class women's organisations of a charitable, vocational, professional and social nature.
57.   Rühle-Gerstel, *op. cit.*, pp. 137-8.
58.   'Zur Reichstagswahl', *FiS*, September/October 1930, p. 1.
59.   Report in *FiS*, April 1929, p. 8. The 1929 editions of *Die Frau im Staat* devoted a high proportion of their space to articles and reports on matters connected with war, peace and poison gas.
60.   'Frauenpartei? Nein, Frauenlisten', *FiS*, April 1931, p. 9.
61.   IfZ, MA 422, frame 5797, letter from Karl Genzler to Otte, General Secretary of the Association of Christian Trade Unions, 19 November 1928.
62.   *Ibid.*, frame 5794, 'Die modernen Kriegsmethoden und der Schutz der Zivilbevölkerung', proposals for the Frankfurt International Conference of the WILPF, 4-6 January 1929.
63.   'München: Kämpferin gegen den Krieg', *Süddeutsche Zeitung*, 15 September 1966. I am grateful to Mrs E. M. Robertson for this cutting.
64.   IfZ, MA 135, frames 136366-67, NS-Korrespondenz 2, 15 January 1932, 'Pazifisten-skandal in München'.
65.   Lida Gustava Heymann's entry in *Wer ist's?*, 1928, p. 656.

66.   Looking back over the 1920s, Dorothee von Velsen referred, in a letter to Gertrud Bäumer, to 'the disappointment at having achieved nothing'. BA, *Kl. Erw.*, no. 296-(1), letter of 8 March 1934, p. 31.

67.   See, e.g. report in *BF*, 15 January 1932, p. 1: 'Das ohnmächtige, waffenlose Deutschland . . . hat naturgemäss das allergrösste Interesse daran, dass das Ziel der Abrüstungskonferenz erreicht wird.'

68.   Gertrud Bäumer's entry in *Das Grosse Brockhaus*, 1967, vol. 2, p. 393; Emmy Beckmann (ed.), *Des Lebens wie der Liebe Band*, Tübingen, 1956 (letters of Gertrud Bäumer), letter to Emmy Beckmann, 14 September 1930, p. 40.

69.   BDC, Gertrud Bäumer's file, 'Aktenvermerk', 26 October 1937, p. 3.

70.   BDC, 8393, Dorothee von Velsen, 'Lebenslauf', October 1937.

71.   Horkenbach, *op. cit.*, pp. 709-10.

72.   Report in *BF*, 15 January 1932, p. 1.

73.   '17. Generalversammlung des BDF in Leipzig', *BF*, 15 October 1931, pp. 3-4.

74.   Lida Gustava Heymann, 'Frauen Heraus', *FiS*, March 1930, pp. 3-5.

75.   Lida Gustava Heymann, 'Frauenbefreiung', *FiS*, September/October 1932, pp. 5-7.

76.   Opitz, *op. cit.*, pp. 258-61.

77.   Rühle-Gerstel, *op. cit.*, p. 131.

78.   Lida Gustava Heymann, 'The Open Door Council', *FiS*, May 1929, p. 1.

79.   Thönnessen, *op. cit.*, pp. 165-6; report in *JADG*, 1930, p. 192; BA, R45/vorl. 10, RGO Referenten Materialien, October 1932, 'Die Arbeiterinnen in die Einheitsfrontaktion', pp. 12-13.

80.   Rühle-Gerstel, *op. cit.*, pp. 142-3.

81.   Rudolf Hess, quoted in *VB*, 27 May 1936.

82.   Auguste Kirchhoff, 'Siebenter internationaler Kongress für Geburtenregelung', *FiS*, November 1930, pp. 5-6.

83.   BA, *Kl. Erw.*, 258-(2), letter from Gertrud Bäumer to Marianne Weber, 17 December 1934; see also Evans, *op. cit.*, p. 232.

84.   Lida Gustava Heymann, 'Frauenbefreiung', *FiS*, September/October 1932, pp. 6-7; Rühle-Gerstel, *op. cit.*, p. 140.

85.   *Ibid.*, pp. 140-41.

86.   Lida Gustava Heymann, *op. cit.*, p. 7.

87.   'Die IX. Tagung des Deutschen Zweiges der Internationalen Frauenliga für Frieden und Freiheit', *FiS*, November 1929, pp. 6-7.

88.   Rühle-Gerstel, *op. cit.*, p. 142.

89.   Lida Gustava Heymann, 'Nachkriegspsychose', *FiS*, March 1931, pp. 1-2; Grete Stoffel, 'Die Arbeitslosigkeit und die Frauenarbeit', *FiS*, August/September 1931, p. 5.

90.   Lida Gustava Heymann, 'Frauenbefreiung', *FiS*, September/October 1932, p. 6.

91.   BA, R45 II/64, DVP Reichsgeschäftsstelle, *Frauenrundschau*, 4 March 1932, 'Nationalsozialisten und Frau', p. 1141.

92.   Report in *BF*, March 1933, pp. 8-9.

93.   Erich Stockhorst, *Fünftausend Köpfe: Wer war was im Dritten Reich*, Bruchsal, 1967, pp. 51 and 233.

94.   BDC, P262, Der Oberreichsanwalt beim Volksgerichtshof, 'Anklageschrift', 2 December 1941, pp. 37-40.

95.   F. Hamm, 'Lida Gustava Heymann "verteidigt" die deutsche Frau', *VB*, 12 July 1933.

96.   Report in *FZ*, 1 February 1935.

97.   See, e.g., Dora Hasselblatt (ed.), *Wir Frauen und die Nationale Bewegung*, Hamburg, 1933, which contains articles by non-Nazi women which are generally favourable towards Nazism.

98.   BA, R43 II/427, letter of ? April 1933 (exact date not given).
99.   *Ibid.*, letter of 12 May 1933.
100.   Clifford Kirkpatrick, *Women in Nazi Germany*, London, 1939, p. 57.
101.   BDC, Akten des Obersten Parteigerichts, 2684/34, letter from Walter Buch to Gottfried Krummacher, 20 September 1933.
102.   BA, *Sammlung Schumacher (Slg. Sch.)*, 230, Alton Gau-Verordnungsblatt 2/34, 1 March 1934.
103.   '5 Jahre Reichsfrauenführung', *Frauenkultur im Deutschen Frauenwerk (FK)*, January 1939, p. 4.
104.   'Gesetz zur Wiederherstellung des Berufsbeamtentums', *RGB*, 1933 I, 7 April 1933, pp. 175-7.
105.   Gertrud Bäumer wrote to Emmy Beckmann to commiserate with her after her own dismissal and then Emmy Beckmann's, from her position in the Hamburg education administration, agreeing with an earlier comment of the latter's that such a position was not just a job, but a source of interest and pleasure. Beckmann *op. cit.*, letter of 13 April 1933, p. 49.
106.   Beckmann, *op. cit.*, pp. 50-51.
107.   *Ibid.*, letter from Gertrud Bäumer to Helene König, 29 July 1933; BA, *Kl. Erw.*, no. 296-(1), letter from Gertrud Bäumer to Dorothee von Velsen, 23 October 1933, p. 20.
108.   Beckmann, *op. cit.*, letter from Gertrud Bäumer to Helene König, 2 May 1934, p. 68.
109.   Gertrud Bäumer, ' "Das Haus ist zerfallen" ', *Die Frau*, June 1933, p. 513; Evans, *op. cit.*, pp. 339-45, is most unsympathetic to the BDF leaders in their difficult situation in his account of these events.
110.   BA, *Kl. Erw.*, no. 296-(1), letter from Gertrud Bäumer to Dorothee von Velsen, 15 November 1934, p. 39.
111.   *FK, loc. cit.*
112.   'Aus dem NSLB', *Die deutsche höhere Schule*, 1935, no. 10, p. 10.
113.   A. Jill R. Stephenson, 'Women in German Society, 1930-40', unpublished Ph.D. thesis, Edinburgh, 1974, chapter 6, section B, pp. 352-64.
114.   *Ibid.*, section C, pp. 365-98.

2 MARRIAGE AND MOTHERHOOD

The one factor which has, above all, determined the role of women in society is their child-bearing function. The single or childless married woman has found her status to a great extent conditioned by the fact that most women, a small minority of them unmarried, become mothers at some time. The spread of contraceptive information has, however, led to the development of aspirations outside the home by mothers as well as childless women, and to a tendency to have fewer children than formerly, in a shorter period of time. In Germany, in the later nineteenth century, women began to reject their role as 'child-bearing machine' (*Gebärmaschine*), and to realise that fewer children could be afforded a better start in life, while a large family might mean long-term poverty.[1] In addition, women had sometimes chosen, and sometimes been compelled for financial reasons, to continue or resume working outside the home after marriage, particularly from the 1870s. These factors, together with the spread of ideas about female emancipation, led to a slowing down of the birth rate after the abnormally high level of the 1870s and, to a lesser extent, the 1880s and 1890s. Although an unprecedentedly large number of children was born in the first decade of the twentieth century, with the figure around two million every year, the actual rate of births was declining steadily, amid growing official concern.[2]

The huge human losses in the war and at the peace settlement, serious enough in themselves, were compounded by a disastrous slump in the wartime birth rate,[3] and made the formulation of a positive policy to encourage procreation — a 'population policy' — highly desirable, even, thought some, essential. The problem was heightened by the increase in the surplus of women in the population, from 800,000 before the war to 2.8 million after it, as a result of military casualties.[4] Many potential mothers would therefore fail to find a husband, and while unmarried motherhood remained socially unacceptable this suggested that the birth rate would continue to decline.

The Great War and its aftermath also had a profound impact on the marriage relationship and family life. The liberal atmosphere of the post-war years, which had, in the first flush of enthusiasm, led to licence,[5] indeed facilitated open discussion of population policy, but it also conditioned the attitudes with which people entered marriage, and made the provisions of the Civil Code appear irrelevant. The experimenting with the marriage relationship, for example with trial marriage and companionate marriage, was perhaps practised by a small minority, but it was important because of the reactions it generated. Moderate feminists, like Katharina von Kardorff, felt uneasy about the 'new morality', including the greater emphasis on sexual satisfaction for both partners,[6] while the higher rate of divorce in the post-war than in the pre-war years[7] was regarded by the Churches and the conservative majority in the middle class as a clear symptom of decadence.

But in spite of the changes which had taken place in the position of women during and after the Great War, the legal basis of marriage described in the Civil Code remained unaltered. Article 119 of the Weimar Constitution, which recognised that it should be reformed, remained a dead letter, although resolutions were put forward for its implementation.[8] At a time when marriage was felt by many to be on the defensive, it is hardly surprising that there was reluctance to alter its traditional form. Agitation for reform came chiefly from the radical feminists; but it was Marie-Elisabeth Lüders, a conservative in many respects, who proposed a radical change in the divorce law. In the Civil Code, the sexes were indeed set on an equal footing, and various grounds for divorce — including adultery, bigamy, insanity and undefined 'cruelty' — were specified.[9] Now, in the 1920s, Dr Lüders represented those who believed that the concept of 'guilt' associated with these grounds should be abolished, and the 'irretrievable breakdown' of a marriage made the sole ground for divorce.[10] But this, like other proposals for amendments to the Civil Code, came to nothing; in marriage, at any rate, the man retained the rights of decision and authority delegated to him in 1896 until, in the Federal Republic, a new declaration of intent in the Basic Law was given substance by the Equal Rights Law of 18 June 1957.[11]

By 1930, many different groups believed marriage and family life to be in crisis, and attributed to this the steeply declining birth rate.[12] The conservatives blamed the permissive society of the Republic; Communists and radical feminists retorted that the bourgeois conception of marriage was irreconcilable with both reality and social justice; and the Nazis claimed that the 'system' was destroying marriage and family life, with politicians standing idly by while the German nation died out.[13] A more sober writer came to the conclusion that the family as an institution was perfectly sound, although many individual families were struggling for existence in the depression.[14] And, indeed, in spite of the imbalance between the sexes, the marriage rate in the later 1920s was marginally higher than it had been just before the war, so that even in the depths of the depression marriage seemed as popular as ever.[15]

With the marriage rate steady and the incidence of illegitimate births declining from the mid-1920s,[16] it was clear that the sinking birth rate was the result of married couples' choosing to have smaller families or to remain childless. This indication of personal choice created a dilemma for liberals and socialists: on the one hand, they wished to see the Draconian abortion law mitigated, even repealed, and contraceptive advice made freely available; on the other hand, they were as anxious as the conservatives to reverse the decline in the birth rate. These conflicting priorities contributed to a situation where the 1920s went by, with the birth rate plummeting, without any serious attempt being made by governments to formulate a national population policy.[17]

But there was a Reichstag Population Policy Committee, on which Gertrud Bäumer was the DDP's representative,[18] and at last in January 1930 Severing, the Reich Minister of the Interior, demonstrated his concern by calling a conference to discuss the problem and to try to find possible remedies. The result was a national Standing Committee on Population Policy, which at its meetings discussed proposals for tax incentives to encourage procreation, protection for the pregnant woman and special care for infants. The guiding principle was to be 'protection and aid for women who want children', so that the pronatalist motive was encouraged but not aggressively propagated. Clearly, this was a real attempt to resolve the conflict between the growing individual desire to limit families and the national need for more children. The formula was also sufficiently undefined so that the political and ideological differences between the groups favouring a population policy would not prevent the search for a solution.[19] There was growing urgency about this, since the renewed decline in the birth rate in the later 1920s had come at a time when the number of women of childbearing age had actually been steadily increasing.[20] According to an official report, even worse was in store: it was estimated that there would be a continued rise in the number of marriages – and, it was hoped, a rise in the number of births – until 1935, but there would then be a decline as the generation of the lean wartime years of birth reached the age at which they were most likely to marry and reproduce; thus, from the later 1930s an even sharper decline in the birth rate could be expected.[21]

If there was no national population policy, the individual parties had been developing some ideas. The women's committee of the DDP, for example, drew up a basic document for discussion in the party's local groups. The central point of concern was less the size than the quality of the population, quality in 'biological, social and mental' terms, which was to be achieved by positive means including improved social welfare and the encouragement of physical education in schools. Negative measures, such as the discouragement of certain categories of people from procreating, were not mentioned. The DDP women were characteristically moderate, favouring tax reform to encourage large families but opposing the more blatant artificial incentives — which the Nazis would offer — which might be striven for *per se*, without a genuine desire for more children.[22]

Moderation was also shown by a writer in the DVP's *Women's Review*, who put Germany's declining birth rate in its European perspective: the other countries of northern Europe, as well as Switzerland and the United States, she pointed out, were experiencing a similar trend; and the decline was less disastrous than might at first appear, she continued, since it was partially offset by the lower mortality rate among infants and children in the 1920s, as a result of medical advance and improved hygiene.[23] Nevertheless, the low birth rates in the countries of northern and western Europe were a source of general anxiety, not least in Britain, particularly in relation to the rapidly growing populations of eastern European countries.[24] But it was only the Nazis in Germany who saw this as a real threat to the west's future, and to Germany, with her strategic position in the centre of Europe, particularly.

Continuing concern about the birth rate contributed to the intensification of interest in the health and care of pregnant women and mothers in the late 1920s and early 1930s. Investigation revealed that, for example, full-time employment was a considerable strain on married women, which was reflected in the 'remarkable increase in the frequency of illness during the years of sexual activity'.[25] This was a source of deep concern, as was the possibly deleterious effect on young girls' reproductive capacity of employment in unhealthy occupations.[26] Standards of hygiene in childbirth were also criticised, and the more thorough training of doctors and midwives in the conduct of a confinement and post-natal care were warmly recommended.[27] But proposals that the Government itself make financial provision for expectant and nursing mothers came to nothing;[28] the Government was in no mood to incur new commitments when it could barely meet existing ones in the depression.

In addition to their strident demands that every effort be made to reverse the decline in the German birth rate, the Nazis claimed to want to promote marriage and maintain the family; it was hardly to be expected that they would consider changing the relative legal positions of men and women within them. But the encouragement they gave applied strictly to those whom they regarded as valuable citizens, from the points of view of race, heredity, health and politics. Hans Frank expressed his party's view thus: 'There is no area of State policy which does not have its foundations in the realm of the family.'[29] This was felt to justify the intervention of the State in the marriage relationship: 'marriage is not merely a private matter, but one which directly affects the fate of a nation at its very roots', explained a spokeswoman.[30]

Here, then, is the motive behind a number of measures instituted by the Government which were euphemistically termed 'laws for the protection of marriage'.[31] The first priority was to prevent marriages taking place between 'Aryan' Germans and non-'Aryans', especially Jews. Not everyone went as far as Hans Schemm, who claimed to have found scientific backing for the theory of Julius Streicher that intercourse with a Jew would poison the blood of an 'Aryan' woman, so that she would not be able to bear 'Aryan' children.[32] But the Nuremberg Laws of September 1935 forbade not only the marriage of an 'Aryan' with a Jew, but also sexual intercourse between them.[33] This opened the way for other measures, and for a general reappraisal of both the marriage and divorce laws, with a view to reforming them.[34]

Heredity was felt to be as vital a factor as race, and so the 'Marriage Health Law' was passed in October 1935 with the purpose of actually prohibiting a person from marrying under certain circumstances. These included illness which might affect either a potential spouse or any offspring; the illness could be physical, mental, or some other described in the 'Law for the Prevention of Hereditarily Diseased Offspring' of July 1933. To ensure that the law was enforced, it was decreed that an engaged couple must obtain a certificate from the local health office affirming that both had been medically examined and were, by the definition of the law, fit for marriage.[35] Marriages contracted abroad in order to circumvent the law would be invalid, and the contracting of a marriage without a certificate was punishable by imprisonment for at least three months, although the penalty would be imposed only if the marriage was declared null and void as the result of an eventual examination.[36]

It became clear that the examination did not, however, always reveal hereditary defects, even when an SS doctor, trained in understanding the genealogical tables which applicants for marriage had to provide, carefully scrutinised the family history. Investigation showed that men and women whose forebears had suffered from tuberculosis, alcoholism and even insanity were slipping through the examination, because the SS doctors, particularly in the cities, were not familiar with the applicants' case and family history.[37] The Party's Racial Policy Office launched a campaign to draw attention to its 'Ten Commandments for Choosing a Spouse', to try to alert the 'racially and hereditarily healthy' to the dangers of choosing a partner who was not 'equally valuable'; having outlined the qualifications required in this respect, the Commandments stipulated another, which would not necessarily be compatible with them — 'marry only for love!'.[38] The motive here was that a loving couple would be more likely to provide a stable home, and, so it was thought, many children.

Not only were the Nazis anxious to prevent marriages which they did not feel to be in the interests of the State from taking place; they were also concerned to facilitate the dissolution of 'unsuitable' marriages which had already been contracted. Hans Frank made it clear that his party did not take divorce lightly; equally, he was at pains to point out that it could not support a view which forbade the dissolution of a marriage which had patently broken down. The new divorce law, over whose constitution he was presiding, would be designed to reflect these views, he said.[39] The present law was felt to be in such urgent need of reform that the Family Law Committee of the Academy of German Law had decided at its opening meeting in Munich in March 1934 to devote its energies towards a reframing of the divorce law as its first priority.[40] The most difficult question here was whether guilt should continue to be apportioned to one or both parties in a divorce. The Committee was of the opinion that this was sometimes an obstacle to divorce, even where the maintenance of a marriage was neither desired by the two partners nor to the benefit of the community.[41] The chief consideration here was that an estranged couple was unlikely to contribute to the birth rate, while the dissolution of their marriage would enable each to enter into a new and more fruitful partnership.[42]

The result of the exertions of the Family Law Committee was the Marriage Law of 1938, which incorporated the new divorce law. The existing restrictions on marriage were reiterated and slightly augmented; but the most sweeping provisions related to divorce. The clauses of the Civil Code concerning it were revoked and replaced by a new definition of grounds for divorce. These included the formalising of a practice already begun, by which a partner might sue for divorce if his or her spouse refused, without good cause, to allow the begetting or conceiving of offspring; in addition, a divorce might be granted if either partner resorted to illegal means to try to prevent a birth — a clear reference to abortion.[43] As early as December 1935 it had been reported that a county court had dissolved a marriage and named the wife as the guilty party because she had refused to have children. The explanation given was that she was directly contravening the current view of the nature of marriage.[44] The 1938 law was indeed intended to spell out the Nazi view of the nature of marriage, which, as in this case, included an indication of what constituted an unacceptable marriage.

Adultery remained a ground for divorce; and premature infertility became one, provided that there were no 'hereditarily healthy' children of the marriage. But the most interesting, and indeed revolutionary, provision was 'paragraph 55', which stated that either partner might apply for a divorce if the couple had lived apart for three years and the marriage seemed to have broken down irretrievably.[45] This clause thus permitted the dissolution of a marriage without the apportioning of blame, and without the need for the existence — or manufacture — of

42

the traditional kind of 'grounds'. If this was seen chiefly as a means of enabling citizens to enter a new union, which would be more likely to provide the nation with children, it nevertheless also permitted the dissolution of an irreparable marriage, in a manner which was at last regarded as humane and sensible in England and Wales (but not in Scotland) in 1969.[46]

Ironically, this new provision was very similar to what liberals and radicals had been campaigning for in the 1920s, but for rather different motives; then, the happiness of the individual was seen as a good reason for trying to revise the law.[47] In Nazi Germany, however, it was made clear that this policy was designed not so much to accommodate the private individual as to allow the interests of the nation to take precedence, by upholding 'valuable' marriages and allowing the dissolution of those which had no value for the community.[48] But individuals did benefit: Erich Hilgenfeldt, leader of the Nazi welfare organisation, had his marriage dissolved in 1940, under 'paragraph 55', in order to remarry; his first marriage had long since broken down, his wife and he having separated in 1932 or 1933.[49]

The new divorce law was demonstrably popular: in 1939, the first full year of the law's operation, there were almost 62,000 divorces, 21.6 per cent of which were granted under 'paragraph 55'. The official view, which seems reasonable, was that a substantial number of people whose marriage had indeed broken down, but who had no grounds for divorce under the Civil Code, at once took advantage of this new provision; certainly, 50 per cent of the divorces granted under 'paragraph 55' had been contracted twenty or more years earlier. In 1940 the number of divorces dropped to below 50,000, but still 15.5 per cent were granted under 'paragraph 55', and almost half of these were marriages of long duration.[50] Clearly, the new measure would continue to relieve estranged couples of the legal ties of a marriage which had in reality ceased to exist. And, more important from the Government's point of view, it would also permit the regularising of relationships already entered into by nominally married persons, and therefore the legitimising of offspring of the new union.

If 'paragraph 55' seemed reasonable to many, there was doubt about another aspect of the new divorce law, that relating to the support of a divorced spouse. It was laid down that the 'guilty' husband, in cases where guilt still applied, must support his former wife in the manner to which she had been accustomed, if she did not have sufficient income from property and could not reasonably be expected to earn her own living; equally, the 'guilty' wife was obliged to pay maintenance to her former husband if he was unable to support himself. This was, in fact, almost an exact repetition of a paragraph in the Civil Code.[51] But the 1938 law went on to add that the new responsibilities of the partner liable to pay maintenance — if he entered a new marriage, especially — should be considered when the amount of alimony was settled.[52]

This broad definition of responsibility led to demands for further clarification, and in 1939 Dr Gürtner, the Minister of Justice, tried to explain it. It was not intended — as some people claimed — he said, that a man declared 'guilty' would no longer be required to support his former wife, simply because she was capable of working; after all, she might have children to look after. But beyond this all the Minister would say was that the condition of the labour market could influence a divorced wife's duty to take a job.[53] Again, the needs of the State were to have full priority: by 1939 Germany needed to tap every available reserve of labour; and for pro-natalist reasons men were to be relieved of the need to pay maintenance, if possible, so that they would be enabled to enter a new marriage and start a new family.

Nazi legislation affecting marriage and divorce led in the later 1930s to growing friction between the regime and the Catholic Church. The Vatican was quick to register its disapproval of the 1938 law with the German Ambassador,[54] and, on the other side, Himmler repeatedly attacked the Church for its narrow minded view of marriage and morality.[55] In reports by his secret service agents the Catholic Church was habitually referred to under the heading 'opponents'.[56] Certainly, priests had spoken out against what they saw as a relaxing of moral standards. Perhaps more surprisingly, early in 1940 the Catholic bishops in Germany criticised a law passed just before the outbreak of war which removed the requirement that an intending couple submit to a medical examination to assess their fitness for marriage.[57] The bishops argued that couples ought to spend time seriously considering the nature of marriage and preparing themselves for it.[58]

The Government's intention was that conscripts should be allowed to marry — and, it was hoped, beget a child — before going to the front, whereas the provisions of the Marriage Health Act would have forced many to wait, perhaps indefinitely. But it was soon discovered that 'hereditarily unsound' persons were taking advantage of the quicker procedure.[59] Himmler congratulated himself early in 1940 on the success of his 'population propaganda' which, he claimed, was leading to the contracting of large numbers of marriages in wartime,[60] and indeed the marriage rate was higher in 1939 than it had been for some years.[61] But how many of those marrying after August 1939 would have married in previous years but for the new 'race and heredity' legislation was something Himmler did not consider. Although the extent of this can only be surmised, it is reasonable to suppose that a backlog of unregistered marriages built up in the later 1930s which would be regularised at the first opportunity. Thus in their anxiety to promote one of their pro-natalist objectives the Nazis vitiated the measures they had taken to achieve another, and people who were 'unsuitable' were again given the chance to marry and to produce children who would not, in the Nazi view, be 'hereditarily valuable'.

It was to protect the 'hereditarily valuable' children of the nation that the Nazi Government made a considerable effort to improve the maternity and child welfare services. In June 1935, a law was prepared for the provision of increased maternity benefit and post-natal care; characteristically, it was to be the insurance funds, and not the State, which would shoulder the burden of extra expenditure.[62] In addition, the various midwives' organisations were centralised into one national organisation, and their education and professional status improved.[63] There was, similarly, the centralisation of all maternity advice centres into the 'Mother and Child' branch of the Nazi welfare organisation, the NSV. Its bureaux provided care and assistance, in cooperation with the local health offices, and gave advice on, and even sometimes aid for, financial problems. Homes were provided for single women, 'to serve the campaign against abortion', and in 1935 Frick, the Minister of the Interior, ordered that every pregnant woman should attend an advisory centre,[64] no doubt to prevent or detect any resort to abortion, and to try to ensure that every desirable pregnancy was noted and supervised. It was claimed in mid-1938 that the NSV had 25,000 advice centres in its 'Mother and Child section' throughout the country, and that more than ten million women had so far attended them.[65]

But anxiety at the rising number of premature births in the mid-1930s, and the high rate of mortality connected with them[66] suggested that the care afforded by the NSV was not fully adequate, and so the Midwives' Law was passed in 1938. This stated that 'every German woman has the right to the assistance of a midwife' and 'every pregnant woman has the duty to call in a midwife promptly'.[67] Nazi anxiety about the well-being of women before and during childbirth was simply based on the needs of the State, as they saw them; healthy parents were more likely to have healthy children, and strong children would make healthy parents for the next generation. In this context a woman was indeed, as one writer put it, 'arbiter over the life and death of her nation'.[68] Further, she was seen not merely as a childbearing machine − as the Nazis' opponents claimed − but as the 'first educator of the new generation',[69] the person responsible for the healthy upbringing of her children, in both physical and moral terms, to be valuable citizens and parents.[70] This was perhaps a hazardous situation for a dictatorship to encourage: the Nazis had therefore not only to exhort women to bear children, but also to give them a feeling of self-importance which would foster gratitude towards the regime which had, apparently, upgraded the status of mothers in the family and in society.

The first positive incentive to procreation came with the introduction of the Marriage Loan scheme, as part of the 'Law to Reduce Unemployment' of 1 June 1933. This provided that a couple intending to marry would be given a tax-free loan of up to RM 1,000[71] — in vouchers for household goods, not cash — to help them to set up house at this difficult time. Repayment was to be at the rate of 1 per cent per month, and was to begin three months after the loan had been made. The money for the loans was to be raised by a tax on all single persons — except those with children — who were eligible to pay income tax, at a rate of between 2 per cent and 5 per cent of their income, according to its size.[72] Within three weeks it was further decreed that the birth of a child would lead to the cancellation of 25 per cent of the loan repayments, and to a moratorium of one year on repayments after the birth.[73] Thus, the childless were to be penalised for not contributing to population growth, while loan holders were to be encouraged to have a child as quickly as possible, and to follow that one with three more in a short space of time in order to have the maximum possible of the repayments cancelled. Dorothee von Velsen described in 1939 how a neighbour had told her that 'now I just need another baby and I shan't have to pay back any more'.[74] This was the conclusion the Government hoped its 'Aryan', healthy, 'politically reliable' citizens would draw; those who did not fit this description were, naturally, excluded from this scheme for state supported marriage and procreation.[75]

The marriage loan scheme was reasonably popular, although the majority of couples either did not fall into the relevant categories or did not make application for a loan. The requirement that the wife give up work[76] was undoubtedly a deterrent to many. In the last four months of 1933, when the scheme was first operational, 37 per cent of the marriages contracted were loan aided, with an above average figure in Prussia and a lower than average figure in Bavaria, a relative position which continued for some years.[77] Part of the reason for this difference was probably that in rural Bavaria working wives were not in the category where they could be replaced by paid labour, as in industry; it would not have been worthwhile for a small farmer to pay a wage to a male labourer, hired to replace his wife who had retired, in order to obtain a loan. The revoking of the employment prohibition in the autumn of 1937[78] resulted in a sharp rise in the number of applications for loans in both absolute and relative terms, so that in 1939 42 per cent of all marriages contracted were assisted by loans, the highest percentage since the scheme began,[79] and a marked revival from the nadir of 24 per cent, the figure for 1935.[80]

Two other factors helped to increase the popularity of the marriage loan scheme in 1939; the relaxation of the restrictions on marriage at the end of August and the outbreak of war immediately after together led to an increase in hastily contracted marriages, for a large number of which loan applications were made.[81] The outbreak of war also led to requests for a moratorium on loan repayments by conscripts; since the burden of making them was bearing heavily on those receiving only their army pay. To help spin out the loan, it was further suggested that the stipulation that only new furniture could be bought with the loan vouchers be rescinded since, in any case, industry could not supply the demand and already had indefinite waiting lists of customers.[82]

The main purpose of the marriage loan scheme was, of course, the raising of the birth rate, and loud boasts were made about the success achieved in this direction. At the 1936 Party Rally, Reinhardt, the Secretary of State whose brainchild the scheme was, announced that so far 620,000 marriages had been assisted by loans, and that already 425,000 children had been born to these marriages. Nevertheless, he went on to warn that these children were very largely the first born in their family, and that at least another three children would have to follow each of them if the scheme were to be really worthwhile.[83] He still showed optimism in the following year when he claimed that now 550,000 children had been born to loan aided marriages, which was, he said, proportionately twice as many as to the other marriages contracted during the same period.[84] But still in 1938 it was reported that up to June of that year almost one million loans had been made altogether, and 840,000 children born to achieve partial cancellation of them.[85] This was a considerable rise in births compared with the previous year, but hardly an impressive figure considering that the scheme had been in operation for almost five years.

Allowing for the time lag of nine months between conception and birth, so that a proportion of the loans made by any given time could not have been partially cancelled by a birth, the impression remains that on average only one child was being born to each couple who had received a loan; for most people, the incentive of partial cancellation of the loan for each child was clearly not sufficient to encourage large families quickly. The granting of a loan could not disguise the fact that children would be a long term financial burden. The number of births to couples in receipt of loans did rise, as a proportion of all live births, from a modest 11 per cent in 1934 to 17.5 per cent in 1937, and to 20.5 per cent in 1939. In the first full year of the war, the figure rose even further, to 22 per cent.[86] But with loan aided marriages on the whole constituting over 30 per cent of all marriages from autumn 1933, and over 40 per cent at the end of the decade, it is obvious that the marriage loan scheme failed to have the sharp impact on the birth rate which had been anticipated when it was introduced in 1933.

The marriage loan scheme was only one tactic used to try to provide incentives to Germans to have large families. Other schemes were based on either direct cash benefits or the elevation of mothers to the status of national heroines, or a combination of both. It was reported in March 1934, for example, that the local authorities in Darmstadt were already making rent rebates to large families and were now proposing to issue cards to their 1,500 mothers with three or more children which would allow them to go to the theatre free of charge on certain evenings.[87] This set an example to other authorities, so that in Camburg, near Halle, it was announced that the twenty-four large families in the area would have to pay only half of the normal water rate; it was also hoped to charge them half price for the use of electricity.[88] On the other side, the *Völkischer Beobachter* announced that Honour Cards were to be presented to all mothers with at least three children under the age of ten. The cards were to carry on the reverse a request to all offices and shops to give the holder preferential treatment, while on the front there would be a picture of a mother surrounded by small children with the legend: 'The most beautiful name the world over is Mother.'[89]

The exhortation seems not to have had the desired effect, however, since there were complaints from parents that preferential treatment was not being given to large families and to mothers with small children in shops and offices. The chief offenders seem to have been the Government's own departments, since it was claimed that parents were often told at Employment Exchanges or welfare offices that having several children was no reason for receiving special treatment. The order therefore went out again that it was the duty of every civil servant who dealt with those in need of aid or advice to discriminate in favour of large families.[90] Three or four children were considered more or less sufficient for the term 'large family', although it was constantly stressed that this sort of figure should in no way be considered an upper limit; after all, in compensation for every childless marriage the nation needed a family of six or more children, if the declining birth rate of the previous twenty years were to be reversed. The Nazis' aim was to achieve a return to the large family of the later nineteenth century, and to the prosperity and expansion which had accompanied the high birth rate of that period.[91]

The concessions made to large families, and especially to their mothers, by local authorities had the twin virtues of costing the central government nothing, while furthering its policy, and providing favourable propaganda. They could not, however, be a real substitute for direct governmental action in the Nazi State to achieve the desideratum of national uniformity. Accordingly, the first general measure came in September 1935, with the provision that large families should receive a bonus from the funds accumulated for the marriage loan scheme if they applied for it.[92] The conditions were that the family have four or more children under sixteen living in the parental home and that — in addition to the now inevitable clauses pertaining to 'racial health' and physical and mental fitness — the family be in financial straits.[93] It was claimed that up to the end of 1935 alone about 300,000 children benefited from the bonus, which amounted to RM 100 for each child.[94] Then, in March 1936, it was announced that, instead, large families would be afforded recurrent State support;[95] and further benefits followed in the next few years.[96] The financial incentives had to be accompanied by a propaganda campaign to try to persuade women, particularly, that large families were not — as the liberals of the 1920s were alleged to have insisted — 'stupid and needy',[97] although the Nazis did have to admit, at least privately, that there were large families which were 'antisocial' which, naturally enough, were not to be supported by the State.[98]

The propaganda aspects of the incentives to women to procreate particularly commended themselves to the Government since they were inexpensive.[99] Accordingly, there was a campaign to elevate motherhood to a position of the highest esteem in the nation. The Nazis had already turned Mother's Day — a moveable feast generally held about 10 May — into a festival of national celebration of 'how fine and noble it is to be a mother, and how wonderful a thing it is to have a mother', as Frick sentimentally put it in his message for the appropriate day in 1935.[100] Hitler made periodic references to the importance of motherhood in speeches which were designed to refute foreign propaganda about the 'enslavement' of women in Nazi Germany as well as to encourage German women to fulfil their own instinctive desires, as well' as the nation's needs, by having children. At the 1935 Party Rally he made his famous remark 'The woman, too, has her battlefield', the battle being that of the birth rate,[101] while two years later, again at Nuremberg, he spoke thus:

'If to-day a female lawyer achieves great things and nearby there lives a mother with five, six, seven children, all of them healthy and well brought up, then I would say: from the point of view of the eternal benefit to our people the woman who has borne and brought up children and who has therefore given our nation life in the future, has achieved more and done more!'[102]

This was, in fact, a two pronged attack, since Hitler's opposition to the practice of law by women had only a month earlier been demonstrated in an order restricting it.[103]

The Honour Cards issued in 1934 to prolific mothers were, it transpired, only the first step in providing symbols of the esteem in which the nation held its mothers. At the end of 1938 it was announced that on Mother's Day in 1939 three million prolific mothers of good 'Aryan' stock would be presented with the new Honour Cross of the German Mother by Party notables. The legend on the reverse of the cross was to be: 'The child ennobles the Mother!'[104] Hess explained that mothers of good character who had at least four children were eligible for the cross, which would be awarded in three grades, according to the actual number of children.[105] How far this promoted the institution of the Order of Glorious Motherhood in the Soviet Union in 1944 for particularly fecund women as one of a number of incentives at this time to encourage rapid population growth,[106] is uncertain, but the parallel is indeed striking.

In their anxiety to promote procreation, and to avoid excessive Government expenditure in the process, the Nazis went to lengths which can only be considered absurd. Presenting an Honour Cross to prolific mothers was perhaps peculiar, but positively eccentric was the order that members of the Hitler Youth must salute women wearing the cross.[107] No doubt it was intended to impress on the young that these women were living examples of what they should themselves aim to achieve, in addition to enhancing the national esteem for mothers in a demonstrable way. Certainly Himmler believed in the value of this kind of activity. In August 1940 he told Kersten, his masseur:

> 'After the war we'll have an entirely new system of honours and titles . . . The Mother's Cross is the best of all; one day it'll be the greatest honour in Greater Germany. Sentries will have to present arms to a woman with the Mother's Cross in gold . . . You'll find that a delegation of women with the Mother's Cross will have precedence on parade over the Führer's bodyguard — and just consider the effect of that!'[108]

Part of the motive for all this was, of course, the immediate need in wartime to raise the spirits of German women when they had a husband or son risking his life at the front. As he awarded a new batch of Honour Crosses in October 1939, Hess extolled the mothers, thanking them for giving Germany their children, paying special tribute to those who were mourning the death of a son in the field. His purpose was, however, to strengthen their will to accept whatever the Government might demand of them in the future, and it was to this end that his flattery and encouragement were primarily directed.[109]

The measure of the success of all the encouragement and incentives given to promote procreation lies in the trend in the birth rate after 1933. At first, certainly, there was apparent endorsement of Nazi policies as early as possible, in 1934: the nadir of 59 live births per 1,000 women of childbearing age in 1933 was followed by a dramatic rise to a figure of 73 in 1934 and 77 in each of the following three years, and in 1938-40 the figures were as high as 81, 85 and 84, respectively.[110] That this upward trend was achieved by persuading married couples to procreate is illustrated by the continuing decline in the incidence of illegitimate births, in the years 1933-9 at any rate.[111] But the rise in the birth rate was, if encouraging, much less spectacular than the Nazis had hoped to achieve, and less than their propaganda boasted. Indeed, in comparison with the abnormally low birth rate of the late 1920s and early 1930s the years after 1933 showed a marked improvement; but they failed to match even the 1922 figure of 90 births per 1,000 women of childbearing age, far less the 1910-11 rate of 128 which, coming at a time when the birth rate had been steadily falling, must have been the minimum the Nazis hoped to achieve.[112] No doubt the imbalance between the sexes in the age group most likely to provide parents contributed to the failure to achieve a better result; but with an increase in the marriage rate after 1933 it seems as if couples were deliberately choosing to have small families.

Indeed the 1934-9 birth rate showed a marked improvement over that for the years 1929-33; but the comparison between these two periods — which the Nazis liked to make — is hardly valid, given the economic recession in 1928 followed by the effects of the depression from 1929. It is clear that the political stability which the Nazis brought, in spite of the repression, and the economic revival in the 1930s, although there was not actual prosperity, were factors which created a climate in which potential parents felt more secure, and therefore more inclined to bring children into the world. But the encouragement and the incentives were clearly not sufficient to persuade people to have several children. Women had increasingly become accustomed to being able to choose the size of their family, and were, on the whole, not convinced by propaganda designed to portray a lifetime devoted to childbearing and rearing as idyllic. The discovery by women before the war, intensified by experience after it, that the female of the species, too, could have aspirations outside the home and family, could not be reversed. Even if women were not obliged to work and did not want to work after marriage and the birth of children, the sole alternative was not bringing up a large family, but rather having few children in a short space of time and enjoying a more independent social life outside the home, and more leisure generally.[113]

NOTES

1.   K. M. Bolte and Dieter Kappe, *Struktur und Entwicklung der Bevölkerung*; Opladen, 1964, pp. 30-31; J. Peel, 'The Manufacturing and Retailing of Contraceptives in England', *Population Studies*, 1963-4, p. 117.
2.   The number of live births per 1,000 of the population was: 1870s — 39; 1880s — 37; 1890s — 36; 1900s — 33; 1911-14 — 28. Calculated from figures in

St. J.: 1911, p. 22; 1933, p. 27; 1934, p. 27.

3.   The birth rate dropped to around 14 live births per 1,000 inhabitants in 1917 and 1918, i.e. to half of the already diminished pre-war level. Figures from *St. J.*, 1933, p. 27.

4.   The population of Germany by sex in 1910 and in October 1919 was:

	1910	1919
men	32,040,166	29,011,216
women	32,885,827	31,887,368

Figures from *St. J.*: 1919, p. 1; 1920, p. 1.

5.   Stefan Zweig, *The World of Yesterday*, London, 1943, pp. 238-9.

6.   BA, *Nachlass* Katharina von Kardorff, no. 34a, 'Papst contra Frau?', 1931, p. 92.

7.   The number of divorces per 100,000 inhabitants was: 1913 — 26.6; 1920 — 59.1; 1923 — 55.0; 1929 — 61.6; 1932 — 65.0. Figures from *St. J.*: 1924-5, p. 51; 1926, p. 37; 1934, p. 50.

8.   W. Knorr, 'Die Frau im Recht', *FiS*, October 1931, pp. 5-7.

9.   Greiff, *op. cit.*, pp. 824-39. See also Julius Hirschfeld, 'The Law of Divorce in England and Germany', *Law Quarterly Review*, 1897, pp. 396-405.

10.   Puckett, *op. cit.*, pp. 265-6.

11.   Karl Larenz, 'Einführung', *Bürgerliches Gesetzbuch*, Munich, 1970, p. 19.

12.   The birth rate rose to between 20 and 25 for the years 1919-25, but then dropped every year, to reach 15 in 1932. Figures from *St. J.*, 1933, p. 27.

13.   Käthe Braun-Prager, review of Rosa Mayreder, *Die Krisis der Ehe*, *FiS*, November 1929, p. 12; Karl Fiehler, 'Sozialgesetzgebung', *Nationalsozialistisches Jahrbuch*, 1927, pp. 122-3.

14.   Anneliese Kasten, 'Frau, Familie, Staat', *Archiv für Frauenkunde (AfFr)*, 1932, no. 4, p. 280.

15.   In each of the last few years before the Great War there had been about 7.7. marriages per 1,000 of the population; in the years 1927-31 a rate of 8 or 9 was consistently maintained, and even in 1932 the figure was 7.9. Figures from *St. J.*: 1920, p. 28; 1930, p. 30; 1932, p. 24; 1936, p. 37.

16.   See below, Chapter 3, p. 58.

17.   Bolte and Kappe, *op. cit.*, p. 44.

18.   HA, reel 37, fol. 736, 'Mitteilungen des Reichsfrauenausschusses der DDP', no. 5, 11 August 1929.

19.   'Reichsausschuss für Bevölkerungsfragen', *Archiv für Bevölkerungspolitik (AfB)*, 1931, pp. 62-5.

20.   Information from figures in *St. J.*, 1932, p. 29.

21.   Report in *Wirtschaft und Statistik (WuS)*, 1930, no. 24, p. 972.

22.   BA, R45 III/43, Reichsfrauenausschuss der DDP, 'Grundsätze einer deutschen Bevölkerungspolitik', 23 April 1930, pp. 52-4.

23.   BA, R45 II/64, *Frauenrundschau*, 25 February 1932, 'Zerfall der Familie?', p. 1133; the decline in the incidence of infant mortality in Germany was as follows: in 1905, 20 per cent of babies born alive died in infancy; in 1913 the figure was 15 per cent; in 1930 it was 8.5 per cent. The rate was always higher among illegitimate than among legitimate children. Figures from *St. J.*: 1934, p. 48; 1935, p. 56.

24.   'Internationaler Kongress für Bevölkerungswissenschaft' *Der Öffentliche Gesundheitsdienst*, 5 December 1935, pp. 645-80.

25.   Franz Goldmann and Alfred Grotjahn, 'The German Sickness Insurance Funds', *ILO Studies and Reports*, Series M, no. 8, Geneva, 1928, pp. 40-2, 64.

26.   Hugo Sellheim in *AfFr*, 1931-2, p. 189.

27.   'Bericht über die 22. Tagung der deutschen Gesellschaft für Gynäkologie,

Frankfurt-am-Main, 27.-30.V.1931', *AfFr*, 1931-2, pp. 156-7.
28. BA, R2/18554, Reichstag motions of 22 November 1930 and 15 October 1931.
29. BA, R61/172, Hans Frank's speech to the Academy of German Law's Family Law Committee, December 1935 (exact date not given).
30. Else Vorwerck, 'Gedanken über die Ehe im nationalsozialistischen Staat', *NS-Frauenbuch*, Munich, 1934, p. 146.
31. BA, *loc. cit.*
32. Report in *Fränkische Tageszeitung*, 30 January 1935.
33. 'Reichsbürgergesetz' and 'Gesetz zum Schutze des deutschen Blutes und der deutschen Ehre', *RGB*, 1935 I, 15 September 1935, pp. 1146-7.
34. 'Vorschläge zur Eherechtsreform', *FZ*, 12 January 1935.
35. 'Gesetz zum Schutze der Gesundheit des deutschen Volkes (Ehegesundheitsgesetz)', *RGB*, 1935 I, 18 October 1935, p. 1246.
36. 'Eheverbote in gewissen Fällen', *VB*, 20 October 1935.
37. IfZ, MA 387, frames 5183-85, 'Ausbildungsbrief Nr. 3 des SS-Sanitätsamtes', 31 May 1937.
38. IfZ, MA 47, frames 8005272-73, 'Zehn Leitsätze für die Gattenwahl', Rassenpolitisches Amt, Gau Baden, reproduction of an article of June 1937 in the *Festschrift für das R.d.K.*
39. BA, R61/172, *loc. cit.*
40. BA, R61/173, Academy of German Law, 'Vorschlag zur Neugestaltung des Deutschen Ehescheidungsrechtes', August 1935.
41. BA, R61/174, Academy of German Law, Family Law Committee, 'Stellungnahme betreffend Neugestaltung des deutschen Ehescheidungsrechtes', 29 September 1936.
42. Report in *WuS*, 1939, no. 23, p. 755.
43. 'Gesetz zur Vereinheitlichung des Rechts der Eheschliessung und der Ehescheidung im Lande Österreich und im übrigen Reichsgebiet', *RGB*, 1938 I, vol. 2, 6 July 1938, pp. 807-22.
44. Report in *FZ*, 1 December 1935.
45. *RGB, op. cit.*, pp. 812-13.
46. J. L. Barton, 'Questions on the Divorce Reform Act of 1969', *Law Quarterly Review*, 1970, p. 348.
47. Puckett, *loc. cit.*
48. Report in *WuS, loc. cit.*
49. BDC, SS file on Erich Hilgenfeldt. Hilgenfeldt's association with the Nazi women's organisation is discussed in Stephenson, *op. cit.*, chapter 6, section B, pp. 358-63.
50. Report in *WuS*, 1942, no. 1, pp. 22-3.
51. Greiff, *op. cit.*, p. 839.
52. *RGB, op. cit.*, pp. 814-5.
53. 'Der Unterhalt geschiedener Frauen', *FZ*, 14 May 1939.
54. BA, R43 II/1523a, letter from the Foreign Office to Lammers, Kerrl, Gürtner *et al.*, 31 July 1938.
55. IfZ, MA 387, frame 5194, 'Verein "Lebensborn" e.V.', 31 May 1937. Felix Kersten, *The Kersten Memoirs*, London, 1956, pp. 154-6, 176-7.
56. Heinz Boberach (ed.), *Meldungen aus dem Reich*, Munich, 1968, e.g. pp. 34, 47, 61, 87.
57. 'Verordnung zur Durchführung des Gesetzes zur Verhütung erbkranken Nachwuchses und des Ehegesundheitsgesetzes', *RGB*, 1939 I, 31 August 1939, p. 1561.
58. BA, R58/147, *Meldungen aus dem Reich (MadR)*, 15 January 1940, 'Gegner: Katholische Hirtenbrief über die Ehe'.

59. IfZ, MA 441/1, frame 2-750525, *MadR*, 27 December 1939.
60. BA, R58/147, *MadR*, 17 January 1940.
61. The marriage rate rose from 7.9 marriages per 1,000 of the population in 1932 to 9.7 in 1933 and 11.2 in 1934. From 1935-8 it fluctuated between 9.1 and 9.7, again reaching 11.2 in 1939. Figures from *St. J.*: 1934, p. 27; 1937, p. 37; 1939-40, p. 42; 1941-2, p. 66.
62. BA, R2/18554, letters from Seldte to Lammers, 8 June 1935 and from Schwerin von Krosigk to Seldte, 20 June 1935.
63. BA, R36/1884, correspondence for 1934; *ibid.*, letters from the Governor of East Prussia to the Deutscher Gemeindetag, 3 March 1937, and *vice-versa*, 11 March 1937.
64. Egon Farrensteiner, 'Schwangerenfürsorge und Geburt', doctoral dissertation for Rostock University, 1939, p. 7.
65. BA, NSD17/RAK, July 1938, 'Deutschlands Kinderschutz vorbildlich!', pp. 1-2.
66. Josef Brunn-Schulte-Wissing, 'Die Frühgeburten – ihr Lebensschicksal in den ersten zehn Tagen und ihre bevölkerungspolitische Bedeutung', doctoral dissertation for Rostock University, 1937, p. 13; Karl Heinz Grasshoff, 'Das Schicksal der häuslichen Frühgeburten und ihre bevölkerungspolitische Bedeutung', doctoral dissertation for Rostock University, 1937, p. 9.
67. 'Hebammengesetz', *RGB*, 1938 I, 21 December 1938, pp. 1893-6.
68. Eva Kriner-Fischer, *Die Frau als Richterin über Leben und Tod ihres Volkes*, Berlin, 1937, pp. 3, 12-13.
69. Annemarie Bechem, 'Die deutsche Mutter als Erzieherin', *NS-Frauenwarte*, April 1937, pp. 695-6.
70. Erich Siegel, *Die Deutsche Frau im Rasseerwachen*, Munich, 1934, pp. 16-17.
71. BA, NSD17/RAK, November 1936, Werner Hüttig, 'Massnahmen zur Steigerung der deutschen Bevölkerungszahl', p. 3, states that the average amount of the loans made so far had been RM600. Bry, *op. cit.*, pp. 457-60, gives the average weekly earnings of women in twenty-two industries in 1936 as ranging between RM 15 and RM 27 per week; the average marriage loan therefore was equivalent to between about six and ten times the average monthly wage for these women, although it would be less attractive to, say, female bank employees, whose average monthly earnings in February 1934 were RM 176, according to *St. J.*, 1934, p. 278.
72. 'Gesetz zur Verminderung der Arbeitslosigkeit', *RGB*, 1933, I, 1 June 1933, pp. 326-9.
73. 'Durchführungsverordnung über die Gewährung von Ehestandsdarlehen (ED-DVO)', *RGB*, 1933 I, 20 June 1933, p. 379.
74. BA, *Kl. Erw.*, 296-(1), letter from Dorothee von Velsen to Gertrud Bäumer, 10 March 1939, p. 55.
75. *RGB, op. cit.*, p. 377; '2. DVO über die Gewährung von Ehestandsdarlehen' *RGB*, 1933 I, 26 July 1933, p. 540.
76. 'Gesetz zur Verminderung der Ärbeitslosigkeit', *RGB*, 1933 I, 1 June 1933, pp. 326-7.
77. Information from *St. J.*: 1936, p. 42; 1937, p. 44; 1938, p. 48.
78. 'Drittes Gesetz zur Änderung des Gesetzes über die Förderung der Eheschliessungen', *RGB*, 1937 I, 3 November 1937, pp. 1158-9.
79. BA, NSD30/1836, *Informationsdienst . . .* , November 1938, 'Ehestandsdarlehen in der neuesten Statistik'; report in *WuS*, 1942, no. 2, p. 52.
80. *St. J.*, 1936, p. 42.
81. *WuS, loc. cit.*
82. IfZ, MA 441/1, frame 2-750356, *Bericht zur innenpolitischen Lage (BziL)*,

29 November 1939.
83.   BA, NSD17/RAK, November 1936, Werner Hüttig, 'Massnahmen zur Steigerung der deutschen Bevölkerungszahl', p. 3.
84.   *Ibid.*, July 1937, Fritz Reinhardt, 'Deutschland treibt Familienpolitik', p. 2.
85.   BA, NSD30/1836, *Informationsdienst* . . . , November 1938, 'Ehestandsdarlehen in der neuesten Statistik', p. 14.
86.   Figures from *St. J.*: 1936, p. 42; 1938, p. 48; 1939-40, p. 53; 1941-2, p. 75.
87.   'Theaterfreiplätze für kinderreiche Mütter', *FZ*, 6 March 1934.
88.   Report in *FZ*, 28 September 1934.
89.   'Ehrenkarte für Mütter', *VB*, 18 November 1934.
90.   'Bevorzugte Behandlung Kinderreicher', *Fränkische Tageszeitung*, 5 November 1934.
91.   'Aufruf des Ehrenführrringes des Reichsbundes der Kinderreichen', *VB*, 12 December 1935.
92.   'Verordnung über die Gewährung von Kinderbeihilfen an kinderreiche Familien', *RGB*, 1935 I, 15 September 1935, p. 1160.
93.   'Durchführungsbestimmungen zur Verordnung über die Gewährung von Kinderbeihilfen an kinderreiche Familien', *RGB*, 1935 I, 26 September 1935, p. 1206.
94.   Wilfrid Bade, 'Der Weg des Dritten Reiches', Lübeck, 1936, p. 14.
95.   'Verordnung zur Änderung der Verordnung über die Gewährung von Kinderbeihilfen an kinderreiche Familien', *RGB*, 1936 I, 24 March 1936, p. 252.
96.   E.g., 'Ausbildungsbeihilfen für Kinderrreiche Familien', Alfred Homeyer, *Die Neuordnung des höheren Schulwesens im Dritten Reich*, Berlin, 1943, p. F6.
97.   Report in *NS-Frauenwarte*, 1936-7, p. 730.
98.   BDC, *Slg. Sch.*, 212, Kreisleitung Marktheidenfeld-Karlstadt, 'Rundschreiben an alle Ortsgruppenleiter der NSDAP', 24 January 1941.
99.   The *Reichsbund der Kinderreichen* exemplifies this. All 'racially pure' parents of four children were encouraged to become full members, while those with three could have probationary status. But the RdK gave no aid to large families; they were merely gathered together as good examples for the rest of the nation to emulate. See BDC, *Slg. Sch.*, 212, and Chapter 3, pp. 60-61.
100. 'Reichsminister Dr Frick zum Muttertag am 12. Mai', *VB*, 11 May 1935.
101. Domarus, *op. cit.*, vol. 1, p. 531.
102. BA, NSD17/RAK, October 1936, 'Der Führer Adolf Hitler über die Aufgaben der deutschen Frau', p. 1.
103. BA, R43 II/427, letter from Bormann to Gürtner, 24 August 1936. See below, Chapter 9, p. 170.
104. 'Das Ehrenkreuz der Deutschen Mutter', *VB*, 25 December 1938.
105. 'Welche Mutter erhält das Ehrenkreuz', *VB*, 27 December 1938; BA, NSD3/5, *Verfügungen, Anordnungen, Bekanntgaben*, vol. 1, 'A. 37/39 vom 15.2.39. – Verleihung des Ehrenkreuzes der deutschen Mutter. Merkblatt für die Auslese der Mütter, die . . . vorgeschlagen werden sollen', p. 346.
106. Schlesinger, *op. cit.*, pp. 371-2.
107. BA, NSD17/RAK, June 1939, 'Ehrenkreuz für kinderreiche deutsche Mütter', p. 3.
108. Kersten, *op. cit.*, p. 54.
109. BA, *op. cit.*, October 1939, Rudolf Hess, 'Das Mutterkreuz ist das Ehrenzeichen der Heimatfront der deutschen Frauen', p. 4.
110. Figures from *St. J.*: 1932, p. 29; 1938, p. 47; 1941-2, p. 77.
111. See below, Chapter 3, p. 58.

112. Figures from *St. J.*, 1933, p. 32.
113. Hermann Ahrens, 'Untersuchungen zur Soziologie der Familie in systematischer Absicht', doctoral dissertation for Rostock University, 1931, pp. 88-97.

3 BIRTH CONTROL AND UNMARRIED MOTHERHOOD

Within the realm of marriage, the family and the birth rate, the most contentious subjects were abortion, contraception and the status of the unmarried mother. Before the Great War, the radical feminists had campaigned on these issues, demanding the repeal of the harsh penalties provided in the Criminal Code for anyone attempting to procure or perform an abortion, the free dissemination of contraceptive advice, and an end to discrimination against the unmarried mother.[1] The SPD, too, had called for reform of the abortion law, and this remained party policy after the war.[2] During the Empire only one concession was made in this area: on 4 August 1914, the Reichstag voted in favour of providing State support for all mothers of children whose fathers were serving soldiers, regardless of marital status.[3] But although the Weimar Constitution stated that illegitimate children should have full equality with those born in wedlock, legislation proposed during the 1920s to effect this demonstrated that the reformers' concern was with the position of the child, and that any benefit which might accrue to the unmarried mother from their schemes would be incidental.[4] If liberals envisaged no radical change in the position of the unmarried mother, and were satisfied to see her continue to be outcast from society, conservatives were even less inclined to help a fallen woman: the Evangelical Church, for example, firmly maintained its hard line attitude against 'any pre-marital or extra-marital sexual intercourse'.[5] The placing of legitimate and illegitimate children, of married and unmarried mothers, on an equal footing in the Soviet Union[6] was seen as an example of the kind of evils which would result from any relaxation of moral standards.

Equally frightening from the conservative point of view was the precedent of legalised abortion in the Soviet Union,[7] which provided a model for the policy of the KPD. To Communists, population policy was a nationalist irrelevance, another way of perpetuating the misery of the working class. Accordingly, the KPD campaigned for an end to all restrictions on abortion and the spread of contraceptive advice, as well as equality for the unmarried mother. The KPD bitterly attacked the SPD for failing to take decisive legislative action while in government, particularly with regard to the abortion law; but, at the same time, the KPD implicitly pointed to the chief reason for this failure by attacking the Churches and the Centre Party for their implacable opposition to toleration of abortion.[8] Indeed the SPD had soft pedalled its policy of favouring radical reforms, in its new found respectability as a party of government; but given the pathological fear of its one constant coalition partner, the Centre Party, of any relaxation of moral standards,[9] this was prudent if reform in any area were to be achieved.

Throughout the Weimar period, the lot of the unmarried mother remained hard, particularly if she lived alone and was obliged to work; little progress was made in finding an effective way of making the father support his child.[10] Nevertheless, the Civil Code left the unmarried mother with no legal rights over her child. Goldmann and Grotjahn found that a large proportion of those in need of relief were unmarried mothers 'who', they believed, 'must be accepted in Germany because of the surplus of women over men'. In 1925, they reported, 33 per cent (133 out of 406) of the mothers insured with the sickness fund of the AEG in Berlin were unmarried, a similar proportion occurring in several other funds.[11] This was during a period when illegitimate births had been rising consistently, from 8.5 per cent of all live births in 1905 to 11.4 per cent in 1920 and 12 per cent in 1925; there had, further, been a much higher figure in the abnormal circumstances of 1918, with 13 per cent being reached for the only time between 1905 and 1939. From the mid-1920s, however, the illegitimacy rate declined steadily, again dropping to 8.5 per cent in 1934, and then falling even further to remain at 7.7 per cent or 7.8 per cent for the rest of the 1930s.[12] Thus, Nazi claims of restoring morality after the decadence of Weimar were belied by the downward trend in illegitimacy figures from 1926; equally, allegations that the Nazis encouraged widespread procreation outside marriage to boost the birth rate must be questioned for the years 1933-9, although the situation changed dramatically after the outbreak of the Second World War.[13]

The one tangible improvement made in the 1920s was — surprisingly, given the Centre's intransigence — in the abortion law. In May 1926, the Draconian Imperial penalties were modified to bear less heavily on the woman seeking or undergoing an abortion, while still allowing, under paragraph 218 of the Criminal Code, the severe punishment of anyone discovered performing an abortion for payment.[14] Then in 1927 a test case permitted for the first time abortion on medical grounds where, especially, the health or life of the woman would be endangered if the pregnancy ran its course.[15] The compromise resulting from these decisions partially satisfied reformers without driving the Churches, especially, into hysteria; but it was seen by both the KPD and the radical feminists as a feeble and inadequate outcome.

Particularly in the depression years, the KPD waged a massive campaign against 'paragraph 218', chiefly through its auxiliary group the ARSO (Association of Social Policy Organisations), which operated in conjunction with affiliated groups working for sexual reform, including the League for the Protection of Mothers and the Workers' Union for

Birth Control.[16] There was also the Freethinkers' Society, another KPD auxiliary, whose purpose was to combat the influence of the Churches, regarded as the chief defenders of 'paragraph 218' and of the capitalist system generally.[17] The KPD therefore tried to attract women to the class war by publicising its campaign against the abortion law, as the Ministry of the Interior's Information Service reported:

'The sexual organisations affiliated to the ARSO, like all fringe groups of the KPD, have as their primary aim the recruiting and educating of new fighters for the proletarian revolution by exploiting their particular grievance or distress.'[18]

The propaganda of the KPD and the ARSO indeed gave the impression that millions of working-class women were suffering untold distress as a result of 'paragraph 218'.[19] Certainly, with between half a million and a million abortions performed in Germany annually[20] the issue was one of national importance, particularly since the result of driving desperate women — more of them married than single — into the hands of back street abortionists was that there were perhaps 100,000 cases of serious illness each year attributable to crude techniques.[21] Then there was the additional hazard of prosecution. *Die Frau im Staat*, calling for the abolition of 'paragraph 218', reported in autumn 1930 the case of a miner's wife who had been sentenced to three years' imprisonment for having performed abortions, although she had never, in 140 cases, caused illness or taken payment.[22] On the last point she may well have been exceptional: generally, abortions cost money, and in 1932 a Breslau woman doctor insisted that the availability of abortion had become 'purely a matter of cash'.[23]

The tenacity and enthusiasm with which Communists and radical feminists campaigned for 'abortion on demand' did not mean that they regarded abortion as intrinsically good. They saw it, rather, as a necessary evil, as an emergency measure which was less evil than forcing a woman to bring into the world a child who was not wanted and who probably could not be cared for adequately. The better solution, they felt, was an end to the restrictions on the spread of contraceptive advice.[24] Although birth control organisations existed freely, some being commercial ventures, some run on a charitable basis, and some provided as part of the insurance funds' service,[25] there was a legal ban on the public advertisement of contraceptives, so that those most in need of help had only a limited chance of learning about it. To combat this, the KPD created another auxiliary group, the AMSO (Association of Marxist Social Workers), to agitate for freely available contraceptive advice. Its main complaint was that the law was invoked only against proletarian organisations for sexual reform, and in January 1933, in order to highlight this anomaly, the AMSO seriously considered bringing a case against the Berlin Police Sports Union's magazine, which habitually carried frank advertisements for contraceptives, but which had never been prosecuted.[26]

If the KPD and the radical feminists were in a minority in campaigning for the legalisation of abortion, they were in much larger company in promoting the spread of contraceptive advice and sex education. Birth control organisations had existed before the war, and they multiplied greatly after it. The expansion was above all in those groups appealing to the working class, and in July 1928 a number of these amalgamated in the National Association for Birth Control and Sexual Hygiene, a non-profit-making organisation with 12,000 members. Although it addressed itself to working-class women in the language of the political left, it deliberately remained non-partisan, to appeal to as wide a clientele as possible. Organised activity intensified in the late 1920s and early 1930s, when economic hardship made freedom from an unwanted pregnancy even more important to many. In 1930, to meet the needs of the capital, three doctors founded the first marriage advisory centre in Berlin, and their example was followed elsewhere.[27] And in January 1931 the German Central Office for Birth Control was created to facilitate the exchange of information among the various groups, and to look at sexual matters in a social, legal, eugenic and ethical context; it was also hoped to make contact with birth control groups abroad.[28]

The Churches were rightly seen by socialists and radicals as the chief bastions of resistance to any reform in this area. The Evangelical Church favoured large families and opposed 'any limiting of births on grounds of selfishness, convenience or pleasure';[29] it regretted that economic problems were leading to an erosion of family life as the Church understood it.[30] The Roman Catholic Church's attitude was summed up in the Papal Encyclical 'Casti Conubii' of 1930, in response to a situation which had, from the Church's point of view, rapidly deteriorated during the 1920s. Abortion was and is anathema to Catholics, and contraception — this 'shameful and intrinsically immoral . . . criminal abuse' as the Pope called it — was to be stamped out by a concerted campaign by Catholics everywhere.[31] To counter the advisory centres established by the advocates of birth control, both Churches opened their own 'Marriage Advisory Centres', which merely gave clients the Christian view of marriage and sexual life, with no medical or physiological advice whatsoever.[32]

The Churches were not alone in their opposition to the birth control groups. Concern about the declining birth rate before and during the war had led to the founding of pro-natalist organisations which propagated the view that large families were intrinsically desirable as well as nationally necessary. In 1923 these groups coalesced into the *Reichs-*

bund der Kinderreichen Deutschlands zum Schutz der Familie (RdK), based in Berlin. A meeting held by it in Bochum in 1927 was estimated to have attracted 5,000 participants;[33] but this was unimpressive beside the organised support for the birth control groups, which had 70,000 members by 1931 in the lay organisations, in addition to those run by the medical profession.[34] The population certainly demonstrated its preference, as the birth rate steadily declined. No doubt the depression affected people's desire for children; but if choice was the chief element, the real reason was clearly the more widespread use of contraceptives as a result of the greater activity and success of the birth control organisations around 1930, compared with the RdK.

This could be true only in a political climate which permitted freedom of choice and of association. Once the Nazis established themselves in power in 1933 the remnants of democracy and freedom were eliminated, and the views of the Party on procreation became national policy. Hitler had written, 'it must be considered as reprehensible conduct to refrain from giving healthy children to the nation', which suggested that abortion would be stamped out, contraceptives banned, and the birth control organisations dissolved. On the other hand, Nazi theories about race and heredity suggested that in certain cases methods of birth control would be positively encouraged. Again, Hitler had provided the guidelines: ' . . . there is only one infamy, namely for parents that are ill or show hereditary defects to bring children into the world'.[35] To ensure that the fittest survived, only the fit should procreate. For the first time, then, there was to be an official population policy, with coercion as the corollary of the incentives previously mentioned.

It was as typical of the Nazis to introduce compulsion as it had been of Weimar governments to shun it. But the closing of the birth control centres served the new regime's political as well as its pronatalist aims, since several of the organisations providing contraceptive advice were, of course, run by the KPD. The 'Law for the Protection of the People and the State', passed on 28 February 1933, enabled the police authorities in Dortmund, Hamburg and Liegnitz, for example, to ban birth control organisations on the grounds of their association with 'Marxist groups', while in Thuringia all the birth control groups were dissolved on the same pretext.[36] Other groups survived, but had to conduct their activities in the greatest secrecy, which was bound to be counterproductive to a campaign so dependent on propaganda. Even so, assiduous police activity often resulted in the detection of groups which had disguised their purpose: in April 1933 it was reported that the apparently acceptable League for the Protection of Mothers was not only a welfare concern but also a front for illicit KPD meetings.[37]

The League was continuing to campaign as effectively as possible, under the circumstances, against 'paragraph 218' and also against two measures which it feared were imminent, the prohibition of all birth control organisations and the restricting of the distribution of contraceptives to chemists, which would mean the end of free contraceptives and the putting of prices beyond the means of working-class women. Already, as a sign of the Government's earnest intent, the number of prosecutions for abortion was increasing.[38] And in May 1933 a law reintroduced paragraphs 219 and 220 of the Criminal Code, in a new form which provided a punishment of up to two years' imprisonment or a fine for anyone offering abortion facilities, unless there were permitted medical circumstances.[39] To try to prevent doctors from using their position to perform abortions freely, a campaign was launched to detect and dismiss those felt to be suspect. In Berlin, on the day after the law was passed, the Mayor reported to a police chief that certain persons, including some doctors, had been dismissed from municipal employment because of their connection with the 'Red Welfare' organisation of the KPD. The AMSO was still managing to survive, but by now the authorities were keeping a close watch on its activities.[40] Amazingly, a few of the groups did manage to stay in existence; Hodann reported in 1935 that Marxist groups for sexual reform were still active in Germany, in spite of their being known to the Gestapo.[41]

Meanwhile, it was apparent that the Nazis were prepared to approve abortion in certain cases. The Hereditary Health Court in Hamburg, in a test case in March 1934, gave a judgement which declared — as a matter of fundamental principle — that abortion on grounds of racial health was not an offence. The 'medical indication' had been made a ground for legal abortion in 1927; now the 'eugenic indication' permitted the termination of a pregnancy if the health of the nation might be endangered by the birth of an 'hereditarily unhealthy' child, with the mother's acquiescence.[42] This was a corollary to the Sterilisation Law of 14 July 1933, and the same definition of 'hereditary health' applied, namely the absence of mental illness and those physical ailments which might conceivably be heritable. Alcoholism was also regarded as an 'hereditary risk',[43] since it was claimed that women alcoholics generally gave birth to mentally or physically handicapped children, or to future delinquents or prostitutes; it was also believed that the wife of an alcoholic, who did not herself suffer from the disease, might bear maladjusted children.[44]

Although some who were by no means Nazi supporters welcomed the law, since it gave a woman more control over her reproductive capacity in certain circumstances,[45] it was evident that the interests of the State and the Nazis' obsessive racial theories were the dominant motives behind this measure. The announcement in 1938 that Jews would not be prosecuted if they resorted to abortion since this could only benefit the German people[46] followed the same logic. Equally, Himmler regarded homosexuality among men as sabotage, and contemplated tolerating it in non-'Aryans' while punishing most severely German 'Aryan' homosexuals.[47] Female homosexuality was treated simply as undesirable but not particularly damaging, since it was believed that lesbians were also often heterosexual and therefore much less likely than homosexual men to fail to contribute to the birth rate.[48]

Partly because the unmarried mother could also be considered a wasted asset from the population point of view — since she would normally have only the one child — Nazi attitudes to her were, at first, generally unfavourable. Further, the Nazis associated unmarried motherhood with the licentiousness which they claimed Marxists propagated. A Labour Front publication carried a most censorious article on the subject in August 1934, claiming that women who had a child out of wedlock tended to be emotionally unstable, were often heavy drinkers, psychopaths or mentally ill, and would therefore often bear children who could not be considered of value to the nation. There was a particular risk, it was said, with those women who had two or more children by different fathers, and in any case National Socialism was fundamentally opposed to moral laxity since it threatened the family, the base of society. Thus, concluded the article, the nation might show compassion to those 'racially valuable' women who, in a moment of weakness, conceived children out of wedlock, but their irresponsible behaviour could not be condoned.[49]

There was some confusion within the Party, with the scruples of the puritans obviously in conflict with the desire of others to encourage and support all 'racially valuable' children. The result was that in the 1930s, as in the 1920s, little of material value was done to solve the problems or raise the status of the unmarried mother. From 1933, though, she received tax relief on her earnings to help to maintain her child, and when a tax on single persons was introduced to finance the marriage loan scheme it specifically did not apply to single women with children.[50] This would benefit not only unmarried mothers, but also single women — like Lea Thimm, the women's representative in the Nazi doctors' organisation[51] — who adopted children. No doubt in order to allay fears that immorality was being encouraged by these meagre concessions, it was explained that if the State afforded aid to the unmarried mother this did not denote approval of what she had done.[52] But in spite of the moral indignation exhibited in some publications on the subject, it became apparent that, at last, official attitudes towards the unmarried mother were softening.

One indicator of this was the attempt to settle the contentious question of whether women who bore an illegitimate child were fit to be public employees. In summer 1936 Frick called a meeting of interested parties to consider both individual cases which had arisen and general policy on the matter.[53] One case concerned a dispute between the Minister of Posts — who had fined an unmarried female employee for having a child, and who favoured severity because of the immoral act which had led to it — and Hess, who advocated leniency and was campaigning against the punishment of Fräulein Wagner, the lady concerned. This case raised two points of principle: namely, should a woman be punished for having an illegitimate child, and, if so, should the penalty be dismissal from or ineligibility for public employment?[54]

No decision was reached at this meeting, nor at another held in October 1936, which was attended by representatives of Reich Ministers and by Hess and Himmler in person, but to which Gertrud Scholtz-Klink was not invited,[55] although as National Women's Leader she should surely have been considered an interested party. The matter was felt to be particularly sensitive from the population point of view, and a committee of Ministers, Gauleiters and population pundits was appointed to consider it in this context.[56] As an interim measure, Hess, with the approval of Frick,[57] asked to be consulted in every case where proceedings were being contemplated against a woman official who had an illegitimate child, before a decision was given, so that he might influence it if he chose.[58] Given the stand Hess had taken on Fräulein Wagner's behalf, it was probable that he would generally intervene in favour of the woman concerned.

Himmler, too, was clearly emerging as a champion of the unmarried mother because, he said, she should be given credit for contributing to the population. No doubt he hoped that if there were a change in attitude she might be encouraged to have more children, whether out of wedlock and supported by the State, or in marriage as she became a more acceptable partner. But Himmler was extremely sensitive to suggestions that he was positively in favour of unmarried motherhood, and tried to refute rumours that his *Lebensborn* (Fount of Life) Association was directed at encouraging illegitimacy. At the same time, he pointed out that greater tolerance

'does not bring down the married mother to a certain level, but raises the unmarried mother to her proper place in the community, since she is, during and after her pregnancy, not a married or an unmarried woman but a *mother*.'

The unmarried mother, said Himmler, was a particularly vulnerable member of society whose legal interests required special protection; therefore he had decided to assume legal guardianship of illegitimate children where this seemed necessary, provided, of course, that they were 'racially and hereditarily valuable'. On the same basis, the *Lebens-*

born homes for expectant and nursing mothers also admitted married women,[59] and indeed one of their chief functions lay in assisting the wives of SS men whose financial position was precarious.[60] Even in May 1944 Himmler insisted that the ratio of legitimate to illegitimate babies born in the homes was 'about 50-50, more likely 60-40 in favour of the legitimately born babies'.[61]

The Government realised that opinion in the country and within the Party itself was conservative on this issue,[62] and it was therefore prepared to move only cautiously in improving the position of the unmarried mother. The first tangible sign of the direction in which official policy was moving came in May 1937, with an order by Gürtner that unmarried women could elect to be called 'Frau' instead of 'Fräulein', with a special provision that unmarried mothers must be addressed as 'Frau' in all official business if they opted for this designation.[63] Ironically, this was exactly what the radical reformers had long demanded,[64] and among even the moderate feminists it had been customary to use the designation 'Frau' for mature women, regardless of marital status.[65] With the provision of a single title for all women, if they so chose, and the improvement in the status of unmarried mothers that this implied, the Nazis were in line with the progressives of the past whom they so castigated, and with radical opinion some thirty years later. Even so, the difficulty in reaching agreement on a fundamental change of policy was such that in 1940 it had to be admitted that after seven years of Nazi rule not the slightest change had been made in the legal position of the unmarried mother; the relevant clauses of the Civil Code still obtained, although the SS, at least, clearly felt that they were out of date. There had indeed been lengthy discussions, particularly within the Nazi Lawyers' Association, and several proposals had been made, but the variety of these was felt to be an indication of how difficult a problem it was to solve.[66]

A decision was reached, however, within the restricted area of public employment. Early in 1939 the Minister of Justice pronounced that the bearing of an illegitimate child should not of itself ever be made a reason for dismissal, although he would be inclined to a stricter attitude if the circumstances leading to the pregnancy — if intercourse had taken place on official premises, for example — gave the impression that the woman had abused her position and was likely to bring her office into disrepute.[67] The National Institute for Youth Welfare wrote to Frick to press for tolerance, since, it claimed, the current climate of opinion, and the Government's population policy, made it desirable that women to whom there was no objection other than that they had had a child out of wedlock should be acceptable in public service positions.[68] On receipt of this letter, Frick issued a statement to the Land governments in the sense of the Minister of Justice's earlier remarks, asking that it be transmitted to the relevant authorities that the circumstances of a conception, rather than the event itself, be the basis for any decision as to the advisability of employing or dismissing an unmarried mother.[69]

The population aspects of all matters concerned with birth control and unmarried motherhood assumed clear predominance once Germany was at war, in September 1939, and there was the prospect of carnage among young men. The failure to stamp out abortion had already been recognised in 1937, with the SS aware that the number of abortions taking place annually 'must still, incredibly, be estimated as high', and anxious that it be reduced. But in spite of the sanctions, the practice continued.[70] Himmler's agents reported an increase in miscarriages in December 1939, which they attributed partly to the increased burden of heavy work on the land for women whose husbands had been called up, and partly to women's anxiety at the danger their husbands might be facing. But in addition to this they believed that some miscarriages were being deliberately induced. This was particularly noticeable in Danzig, where German troops had been in occupation for the two or three months most likely to elapse between conception and resort to abortion. But also in Karlsruhe a gynaecologist reported that almost every week he had to treat miscarriages which showed all the signs of having been caused by attempted abortion.[71]

In wartime, unmarried women who became pregnant faced a particular hazard which might encourage them to seek abortion more urgently: the father of the child, who normally might have been persuaded to marry the mother, might very well be in mortal danger at the front. Hess spotlighted this problem in December 1939 when he sent Frick a copy of a long letter he had sent to the pregnant fiancée of a soldier killed in action, with a request for a prompt regulation of the legal position of women who found themselves in this position, and Frick complied by calling an urgent meeting to discuss the matter.[72] Already, however, Hess had unilaterally announced that the NSDAP would be prepared to assume the guardianship of children whose fathers perished in the war since

'considerations which are justifiable in normal times must for the present be overlooked . . . What use is it if a nation is victorious, but through the sacrifices made for that victory it dies out?'

Thus, men and women — of pure racial descent — who created a new life were giving the nation in time of war the next most precious thing to their own life, and should be honoured accordingly. Hess added that he was convinced that the German people would soon come to share his view, and would in future be prepared to treat as equal with married mothers those 'who, perhaps outside the bounds of bourgeois morality and custom, contribute to compensation for the blood sacrificed in the war . . . for . . . the life of the nation comes before all principles thought up by men, all conventions which carry the mark of recognised custom but not of morality, and before prejudice. The highest service a woman can render to the community is the gift of racially healthy children for the survival of the nation.'[73]

Hess had turned a message of comfort to a girl in most distressing circumstances into barely veiled encouragement for procreation outside marriage. This was welcomed by the SS weekly, *Das Schwarze Korps*, which went on to quote Himmler as saying that in wartime no soldier could go to the front, possibly to die, in peace of mind if he had not left heirs behind him. Therefore the names 'wartime father' and 'wartime mother' would signify that in time of national emergency there were those who served their country not only in the field or in the factory, but by their contribution to the future of the nation by begetting and bearing children. Thus, girls who refused to serve their country in this way, even if unmarried, could be compared with army deserters, while those who had illegitimate children could be confident that the State would welcome and support them.[74] The tone of this article was nothing short of revolutionary, and the response it evoked vindicated those who had urged caution in legislating to promote legal and social equality for the unmarried mother.

It was, for example, hardly surprising that the Roman Catholic Church strongly attacked the new morality proposed by Hess and the SS. At the festival of — appropriately enough — the Holy Family in January 1940, the bishops' pastoral letter, which in recent years had concentrated on attacking the Sterilisation Law, criticised particularly Hess's much publicised letter and Himmler's utterances supporting extra-marital procreation. Cardinal Faulhaber insisted that the view of the Church on the sanctity of marriage and the sinfulness of unchastity remained what it had always been, and that the war could not alter it. Himmler's agents reported that the Church was so incensed that in some areas priests were telling their congregations that the war was God's punishment for the moral depravity currently encouraged by the nation's leadership.[75]

Others were less sweeping in their opposition: Gertrud Bäumer pointed out that the proposals now suggested for a regularising of the position of illegitimate children were not dissimilar from those for which she and her associates had campaigned. But she also believed that there was a sharp difference between fathering a child and regarding fatherhood as a continuing commitment within a family.[76] Her friend Dorothee von Velsen was horrified by the article in *Das Schwarze*

Korps, and also frustrated at being unable to criticise it openly.[77] Gertrud Bäumer took comfort from the fact that although she could not publish her views, open opposition to the article had been voiced by the leaders of the Nazi women's organisation, who had called SS officers to a meeting to face questions about it.[78] But the lack of real influence that the Nazi women's organisation had[79] meant that it was in no position to challenge the new morality, particularly since it was proposed at a time of national emergency.

The SS was unrepentant, and its paper led demands for legal action in favour of those 'considered up till now "illegitimate" '. Financial aid for the unmarried mother was seen as a top priority, and it was suggested that the needy might be paid a monthly sum to enable them to support a child. In addition there should, said *Das Schwarze Korps*, be full medical facilities for the confinement, a ban on the dismissal or demotion of the mother from work, and a prison sentence for any who besmirched the good name of an unmarried mother.[80] But this policy raised financial problems which Himmler and his men had apparently not foreseen. In summer 1940 Himmler reported to Keitel that

> 'as a result of extensive troop movements illegitimate pregnancies have reached an unprecedented height since the beginning of the war . . . The fathers of 90 per cent of the illegitimate children born in *Lebensborn* homes are serving soldiers.'

Accordingly, the initial system, by which the homes had been financed by a levy on SS men and used specifically for their children,[81] was inadequate now that the homes had been opened to a far wider circle, and so Himmler asked that Keitel try to interest the army in the work of *Lebensborn* and, more important, to put some of the funds at the disposal of the army towards the upkeep of the homes.

Part of the motive in opening the homes to women unconnected with the SS was to encourage them to have their child rather than resort to abortion. Himmler was deeply concerned that official statistics showed that there were still about 600,000 abortions annually, a figure comparable with that estimated for the years between 1918 and 1933.[82] The heavy pro-natalist propaganda and the sanctions used as instruments of Nazi policy seem therefore to have had little effect, although the penalty of imprisonment was freely imposed on offenders.[83] There was, perhaps surprisingly, no formal decree before the war against the production and sale of contraceptives, no doubt because the condom served also as a protective against the spread of venereal disease; it was one of the Nazis' constant preoccupations that venereal disease could lead to sterility, and Lenz, one of the Party's chief population pundits, estimated that more than 100,000 children were lost annually as a result of infection.[84] But although the spread of venereal disease in the peculiar situation of the war — not least among teenage girls who hung around railway stations soliciting among soldiers — was a source of deep concern,[85] the Himmler Police Ordinance of January 1941 categorically banned the production and distribution of contraceptives. The growing hysteria about the need to replace the fallen with an increased birth rate finally led to the introduction in 1943 of the death penalty for anyone found to have performed an abortion.[86] This still, of course, applied only to the 'racially and hereditarily valuable'; in wartime it was considered particularly vital to prevent as far as possible the birth of children deemed to be 'unfit' by sanctioning abortion where at least one parent had an 'hereditary defect', and where — so Frick believed — racial grounds made the continuation of the pregnancy undesirable.[87] The grotesque lengths to which this view was taken during the war were revealed only when Nazism was finally defeated.

In trying to persuade unmarried women to accept a pregnancy and let it run its course, rather than resort to abortion, the Party's contribution was to award a cash grant to full-time single women employees who had a child on the same basis as to a married man who had a legitimate child.[80] And the Government agreed to provide grants for unmarried mothers who required support. But it awarded them grudgingly, carefully vetting each case to ensure that the claimant was indeed needy, and also of good character.[89] In the case of Helene Richter, however, a grant of RM 125 was recommended although she had previously been jailed for assisting with abortions. It was said that her character was otherwise good, and that she seemed thoroughly 'politically reliable'.[90] But in approving the grant an official in the Chancellery wrote to Helene Richter to emphasise that grants could only be made in exceptional cases,

> 'since the means for them are small. I therefore ask you not to acquaint others with the fact that you have been given aid, so as not to encourage the submitting of applications which are hopeless, and can result only in disappointment.'[91]

The idealism of the SS caused dismay among the bureaucrats who were well aware that the Government could not suddenly assume financial responsibility for illegitimate children and their mothers on the scale which Himmler, his men and Hess were encouraging.

Himmler continued to be obsessed with overcoming 'middle-class convention' and 'defying existing laws and explaining to my men that children are always a great blessing, legitimate or not'. He admitted to Kersten that he had already, discreetly, given notice that women anxious to have children could have 'racially pure' men provided as 'conception assistants'; only a few women had responded so far, but

Himmler hoped to extend the scheme greatly after the war, even to make it compulsory, eventually, for women of 'good stock'. Together with Bormann, he also had plans for encouraging bigamy, 'to safeguard and improve the racial qualities of the Greater German Reich' at a time when there would, after the war, be a surplus of women.[92]

Nazi attitudes to birth control and unmarried motherhood were a curious mixture of repression and apparent enlightenment; after all, it cannot be disputed that more tolerant and humane treatment of the unmarried mother than was customary in most parts of inter-war Europe was thoroughly desirable. But the motives of Hess, Himmler and the SS were completely indefensible. The provision of children for Germany was the criterion, and any considerations of either morality or personal happiness were secondary. Further, the 'new morality' was nothing short of a revolution, which would drastically alter the nature, if not threaten the existence, of the family unit which the Nazis had originally pledged themselves to protect and promote. Any benefit which may have accrued to the unmarried mother was, as in the Weimar period, purely incidental, not to the welfare of the child as an individual but to the naked power ambitions of the Nazi leadership.

With birth control, the motives were similar: the 'racially and hereditarily undesirable' were to be encouraged, perhaps even compelled, not to 'pollute' the German nation with 'inferior' offspring, while healthy 'Aryans' were to be severely punished if they attempted to deprive the *Volk* of 'valuable' future citizens, soldiers and mothers. The chief result of Nazi attempts to stamp out abortion and drastically reduce the practice of contraception seems to have been to hinder the development of a liberal policy towards birth control in the Federal Republic. The Himmler Ordinance remained in force in most Länder until 1961, while the near suppression of the former birth control movement meant that a new campaign had to start virtually from scratch, again in the face of strong opposition from the Churches.[93] Once again, the legal barrier is 'paragraph 218', the 1926 abortion law.[94]

In the Third Reich, it is clear that the Nazi aim of completely eliminating abortion among the 'valuable', and of reducing contraceptive practice as far as possible, was not realised. Certainly, the measures the Nazis took were piecemeal, and the loop holes they left seem unaccountable, in the light of their obsession with the population issue. But the real reason must be that the German people, in this matter as in so many others, did not make an open demonstration of their opposition, but rather continued to follow their own desires quietly, in deep secrecy if necessary. Even with a huge army of spies and informers, the Nazis could not watch all of the people all of the time; they were not even able to stamp out the last vestiges of birth control organisations, although they came close to it. The long history of birth control in Germany, with widespread resort to abortion if contraception had been unavailable, or had failed, could not be eliminated from popular consciousness by a few laws and even a mass of propaganda, so that in this area the Nazi aim of creating a fully totalitarian state which controlled every aspect of the life of its people was, inevitably, frustrated. Repression could only drive these practices underground, where popular demand ensured that, somehow, they survived.

NOTES

1.   Evans, *op. cit.*, pp. 174-86 and 192-221 discusses the radicals' campaigns.
2.   Bolte and Kappe, *loc. cit.*
3.   P. Krische in *AfFr*, 1931-2, pp. 72-3.
4.   See, e.g., BA, R36/1438: parliamentary question no. 1706 by Marie-Elisabeth Lüders *et al.*, 23 June 1922; letter from Mohrmann, of the Archiv Deutscher Berufsvormünder e.V., to Oberbürgermeister Mitzlaff, 15 January 1926; letter from Mende, of the Deutsches Archiv für Jugendwohlfahrt e.V., to the Deutscher Städtetag/Preussischer Städtetag, received 13 April 1929.
5.   'Aufruf des Deutschen Evangelischen Kirchenausschuss vom 25. Mai 1932', document in *AfB*, 1932, p. 96,
6.   Halle, *op. cit.*, p. 106.
7.   *Ibid.*, pp. 38-9.
8.   'Richtlinien der KPD zur Frage der Geburtenregelung', document in *AfB*, 1931, pp. 60-61; BA, R58/, RMdI/NsdL, 'Private Wohlfahrt und Reformismus', Rote Wohlfahrt publication, 21 September 1932, p. 251; BA, R58/(fol. 1), RMdI/NsdL, 'Politische Resolution beschlossen auf dem Reichskultur-Kongress, Leipzig, 14. und 15.3.1931', 13 April 1931.
9.   Klaus Epstein, 'The Zentrum Party in the Weimar Republic' (review article of Rudolf Morsey, *Die deutsche Zentrumspartei 1917-1923*, Düsseldorf, 1966), *Journal of Modern History*, 1967, p. 162.
10.   Krische, *op. cit.*, p. 72.
11.   Franz Goldmann and Alfred Grotjahn, *op. cit.*, p. 69.
12.   Figures from *St. J.*: 1934, p. 27; 1937, p. 37; 1939-40, p. 42; 1941-2, p. 66. Since there was a higher rate of dead births among illegitimate than legitimate children, the proportion of unmarried women who carried children was higher than the figures suggest; equally, the rate of infant mortality was higher among the illegitimate, and so a smaller proportion of women than that suggested by the figures had to bring up an illegitimate child.
13.   Official statistics, which had consistently given the illegitimate birth rate along with other population statistics since 1882, do not provide figures for the number or rate of illegitimate births in 1940, although they continue to give those for marriages, deaths, live births, etc., in *St. J.*, 1941-2, p. 66. It is tempting to conclude that the figures were deliberately concealed because they were so high.
14.   Bolte and Kappe, *loc. cit.*; Hans Harmsen, 'Notes on Abortion and Birth Control in Germany', *Population Studies*, 1949-50, p. 402. Paragraphs 219 and 220 of the Criminal Code were repealed, leaving an altered paragraph 218, which became the symbol as well as the reality of what those in favour of legalising abortion opposed.

15.　Bolte and Kappe, *loc. cit.*; 'Eugenische Indikation und Paragraph 218', *FZ*, 23 January 1935.

16.　BA, R58/1148, RMdI/NsdL, 19 December 1932, 'Arso'.

17.　BA, R58/1146, RMdI/NsdL, n.d., ? April 1932.

18.　BA, R58/1148, *loc. cit.*

19.　Numerous examples of such propaganda material may be found in the BA, R58 files, e.g., R58/ , RMdI/NsdL, 'Proklamation zur kulturellen Befreiung des werktätigen Volkes', *Kampfbereit*, December 1931, p. 14, and R58/1148, RMdI/NsdL, 19 December 1932, 'Arso'.

20.　The estimates vary: D. V. Glass stated that 800,000 to one million was the most common estimate for the years after 1918 (*Population Policies and Movements*, London, 1940, p. 279); Dr Clara Bender, in *Archiv für Frauenkunde*, 1932, p. 282, estimates an annual figure of ½ million to 1 million; O. Jean Brandes, 'The Effect of the War on the German Family', *Social Forces*, 1950-51, p. 166, n. 3, reports the 1928 Congress of German Physicians at Eisenach as estimating that there were 500,000-800,000 abortions each year.

21.　Again, estimates vary: a book reviewer in *FiS*, May 1929, p. 11, puts the figure at somewhere between 61,000 and 100,000; Clara Bender, *loc. cit.*, states that abortions led to 4,000-5,000 deaths and at least 100,000 cases of serious illness each year. It is possible that a greater resort to abortion during the depression years partly explains this discrepancy.

22.　'Unsere Buchstaben-Justiz', *FiS*, September/October 1930, pp. 16-17.

23.　Clara Bender, *loc. cit.*

24.　'Richtlinien der KPD zur Frage der Geburtenregelung', document in *AfB*, 1931, pp. 57-9; BA, R58/ , propaganda leaflet of ? early January 1933, gives the KPD slogan as 'Nicht abtreiben, sondern verhüten!'; Auguste Kirchoff, *op. cit.*, pp. 5-6.

25.　Glass, *op. cit.*, pp. 276-7.

26.　BA, R58/336, RMdI/NsdL, 6 January 1933.

27.　Hans Lehfeldt, 'Die Laienorganisationen für Geburtenregelung', *AfB*, 1932, pp. 62-8.

28.　Report in *AfB*, 1931, p. 84.

29.　The wording here is strikingly similar to that of a resolution adopted by the Anglican Church at the Lambeth Conference in 1930: 'The Conference records its strong condemnation of the use of any methods of conception control from motives of selfishness, luxury, or mere convenience.' Quoted in Flann Campbell, *op. cit.*, p. 136.

30.　'Aufruf des Deutschen Evangelischen Kirchenausschuss vom 25. Mai 1932', document in *AfB*, 1932, pp. 95-6.

31.　Campbell, *op. cit.*, p. 138.

32.　Max Hodann, *History of Modern Morals*, London, 1937, pp. 167-8.

33.　Glass, *op. cit.*, pp. 272-4.

34.　Report in *AfB*, 1931, p. 84.

35.　Adolf Hitler, *Mein Kampf*, Munich, 1936, p. 338.

36.　'Verbot der Laienorganisationen für Geburtenregelung', *AfB*, 1933-4, p. 55.

37.　BA, R58/ , typewritten memo, 14 April 1933.

38.　BA, R58/ , 'Kampf gegen das drohende Verbot der Sexualorganisationen', *Die Warte*, ? March/April 1933 (covering letter, as above, dated 14 April 1933).

39.　'Gesetz zur Änderung strafrechtlicher Vorschriften', *RGB*, 1933 I, 26 May 1933, p. 296.

40.　BA, R58/ , letter from the Mayor of Berlin to the head of a section of the Berlin police force, 27 May 1933.

41.　Hodann, *op. cit.*, pp. 165-6.

42.   'Eugenische Indikation und Paragraph 218', *FZ*, 23 January 1935.
43.   'Gesetz zur Verhütung erbkranken Nachwuchses', *RGB*, 1933 I, 14 July 1933, p. 529.
44.   Gertrud Kaetzel, *Volksgift und Frauenpflichten*, Munich, n.d., pp. 4-10.
45.   'Die Eugenische Indikation', *FZ*, 28 June 1935; Glass, *op. cit.*, p. 283.
46.   BA, NSD30/vorl. 1836, *Informationsdienst* . . . , March 1939, 'Anwendung nur auf das deutsche Volk'.
47.   Kersten, *op. cit.*, p. 57.
48.   Gertrud Schubert-Fikentscher, 'Zum Problem der Weidlichen Homosexualität', *Die Frau*, November 1939, pp. 373-5.
49.   'Klarheit!', *Der Deutsche*, 11 August 1934.
50.   'Gesetz zur Verminderung der Arbeitslosigkeit', *RGB*, 1933 I, 1 June 1933, p. 327; 'Gesetz über die Einkpmmenbesteuerung für 1933', *RGB*, 1934 I, 21 December 1933, p. 3.
51.   BDC, Lea Thimm's Reichsärztekammer membership card, and answers to a questionnaire for the Journalists' Association, 10 January 1934.
52.   Alice Rilke, 'Die ehelose Mutter im nationalsozialistischen Staat', *VB*, 30 August 1934.
53.   BA, R43 II/443, letter from Pfundtner to Lammers, 12 August 1936.
54.   *Ibid.*, notes by Seel at the Ministry of the Interior, 15 August 1936.
55.   *Ibid.*, circular from Pfundtner to nine Ministers and Secretaries of State, 13 October 1936.
56.   BA, R43 II/1523, circular from Pfundtner to eighteen leading people in Party and State, 31 May 1937.
57.   BA, R43 II/427, letter from Pfundtner to the Reich Ministers, 13 December 1938.
58.   *Ibid.*, letter from Gramsch, the Prussian Prime Minister, to the Minister of the Interior, 4 January 1939.
59.   IfZ, MA 387, frames 5189-95, 'Verein "Lebensborn" e.V.', 31 May 1937.
60.   IfZ, Fa 202, letter from an SS officer on behalf of the Governing Council of *Lebensborn* to SS officer Pohl, 21 June 1938.
61.   R. Manvell and H. Fraenkel, *Heinrich Himmler*, London, 1965, pp. 93-4. C.f. Richard Grunberger, 'Lebensborn', *Bulletin of the Wiener Library*, July 1962, p. 52, who states that between 50 and 80 per cent of the babies born in the homes were illegitimate. Kersten reports Himmler as saying in May 1943 that married women accounted for 50 per cent of the confinements (*op. cit.*, p. 180).
62.   See, e.g., Else Vorwerck, 'Gedanken über die Ehe im nationalsozialistischen Staat', *NS-Frauenbuch*, Munich, 1934, pp. 147-8.
63.   BA, R22/41, order of the Minister of Justice, no. 2697, 'Führung der Bezeichnung "Frau" durch unverheiratete weibliche Personen', *Reichshaushalts- und Besoldungsblatt*, no. 18, 21 June 1937, p. 201.
64.   Anthony, *op. cit.*, pp. 108-11, describes the campaign of the *Bund für Mutterschutz* to eliminate the title 'Fräulein', particularly to protect unmarried mothers.
65.   See, e.g., correspondence between Gertrud Bäumer and the friends and acquaintances who were, like her, unmarried, in Beckmann, *op. cit.*, and BA, *Kl. Erw.*, no. 296-(1).
66.   IfZ, Fa 202, letter from the staff of *Lebensborn* to Himmler's office, 15 February 1940.
67.   BA, R43 II/427, letter from Freisler to the Reich Ministries, 13 January 1939.
68.   *Ibid.*, letter from the Deutsches Institut für Jugendhilfe e.V. to the Ministry of the Interior, 11 July 1939.
69.   *Ibid.*, letter from Stuckart to the Land governments and the chief

Government officials, 14 July 1939.
70.   IfZ, MA 387, frames 5193-94, *op. cit.*; IfZ, MA 306, frame 593008, letter from Wangemann, on Himmler's staff, to Himmler, 7 February 1938.
71.   BA, R58/146, *MadR*, 13 December 1939, 'Zunahme der Fehlgeburten'.
72.   BA, R43 II/1286, letter from Frick to Lammers, 24 December 1939.
73.   *Ibid.*, letter from Hess to the fiancée of a dead soldier, n.d. (covering letter, above, dated 24 December 1939).
74.   'Der Sieg der Frauen', *Das Schwarze Korps*, 4 January 1940.
75.   BA, R58/147, *MadR*, 15 January 1940; IfZ, MA 441/1, frame 2-750508, *MadR*, 22 December 1939, reports a Roman Catholic priest as saying publicly that Germany will lose the war if the current increase in immorality is not reversed.
76.   BA, *Kl. Erw.*, no. 296-(1), letter from Gertrud Bäumer to Dorothee von Velsen, 4 April 1940.
77.   *Ibid.*, letter from Dorothee von Velsen to Gertrud Bäumer, 31 March 1940.
78.   *Ibid.*, letter from Gertrud Bäumer to Dorothee von Velsen, 4 April 1940.
79.   Stephenson, *op. cit.*, pp. 365-70.
80.   'Ein Frau hat das Wort', *Das Schwarze Korps*, 11 April 1940.
81.   IfZ, MA 387, frame 5189, *op. cit.*
82.   IfZ, Fa 202, letter from Himmler to Keitel, n.d., ? late July 1940. See above, p. 59 and p. 72, n. 20.
83.   BA, R43 II/1286a, letter from the Hanover Chief of Police to the Reich Chancellery, 13 March 1941.
84.   August Mayer, *Deutsche Mutter und deutscher Aufstieg*, Munich, 1938, pp. 17-18.
85.   IfZ, MA 441/1, frame 2-750184, *BziL*, 3 November 1939.
86.   Bolte and Kappe, *op. cit.*, p. 45. Hans Harmsen, *op. cit.*, p. 403, says that during the war the military authorities succeeded in exempting the condom from the Himmler Ordinance, to prevent the spread of venereal disease.
87.   IfZ, MA 47, letter from Frick to Reichsstatthalter, Land governments, health offices *et al.*, 19 September 1940.
88.   IfZ, MA 135, frames 136153-54, letters from the Kreisleitung Erkelenz to its DAF and NSV officials, 3 February 1941, and the Gauschatzmeister of Cologne to his Kreisleitungen, 30 January 1941.
89.   BA, *op. cit.*, letter from Ehrich, in the Chancellery, to the Gauleitung in South Hanover-Brunswick, 12 February 1941.
90.   *Ibid.*, letter from the Hanover Chief of Police to the Chancellery, 13 March 1941.
91.   *Ibid.*, letter from Meerwald, in the Chancellery, to Helene Richter, 25 July 1941.
92.   Kersten, *op. cit.*, pp. 176-82; Hans-Jürgen Lutzhöft, *Der nordische Gedanke in Deutschland 1920-1940*, Stuttgart, 1971, pp. 395-6.
93.   D. V. Glass, 'Family Planning Programmes in Western Europe', *Population Studies*, 1966, p. 229; Bolte and Kappe, *op. cit.*, p. 46.
94.   Hans Harmsen, *op. cit.*, p. 402; 'Abtreibung: Massenmord oder Privatsache?', *Der Spiegel*, 21 May 1973, pp. 38-58.

4 WOMEN'S EMPLOYMENT: EXPANSION AND OPPOSITION

The Great War, with its heavy toll of male casualties, and the inflation consequent upon the war, were important in increasing the scope and extent of women's employment outside the home beyond the considerable dimensions they had reached before 1914. It was, however, the rationalisation of industry and business, following the stabilisation of the currency in 1924, which had the most profound impact on this development: mechanisation, one of its major characteristics, led directly to a fundamental change in the demand for various types of labour. Tasks which had previously been performed by skilled workers — and this meant almost exclusively by men — could now be carried out much more efficiently by machines, for whose operation cheaper semi-skilled or even unskilled labour sufficed. It rapidly became apparent to employers that women were far preferable to men for this kind of work, for two reasons: first, and most obviously, women were cheaper to employ, with even skilled women paid at a lower rate than unskilled men; but at least as important was the discovery that women actually tended to be better machine operators than men. This was the case not only in wage earning occupations; the real revolution was in white collar jobs, where the increasing use of the typewriter and the calculating machine facilitated the replacement of men with skills which had formerly been essential by women whose dexterity and acceptance of monotonous work only enhanced their advantage, already strong from the financial point of view.[1]

The 1925 census showed that about one third of the 3.5 million employees in white collar occupations were women,[2] which Kracauer attributed to the need for more women than formerly to support themselves after the war.[3] This view was confirmed by an inquiry carried out in 1929 which revealed that 93 per cent of the sample of women interviewed were unmarried, and that their age distribution indicated that for many employment was not merely a temporary stage in their life but a career.[4] About a quarter of a million white collar workers were members of unions in the later 1920s,[5] and these led a campaign to try to achieve equal pay for women in clerical jobs.[6] In fact, women employees were paid on average between 10 per cent and 15 per cent less than men in the same grade of job; and on the whole women were to be found in the lower grade, poorly paid positions.[7] When the depression came, it hit white collar workers as a group much less severely than it hit industrial workers, although there were many areas of individual hardship among them.[8] Men and women in offices and shops suffered to a similar extent: women accounted for 41.3 per cent of the unemployed in these positions in 1932,[9] while the 1933 census showed that they constituted 42.2 per cent of all employees in these areas.[10]

In industry, the fields in which women had traditionally been chiefly employed were textiles and clothing, which together accounted for about half of all women in industry in the first quarter of the twentieth century. In 1925, over 1.5 million women, out of a total of 2.9 million in industry, were employed in these two areas. The food, drink and tobacco industries came third, with over 400,000 women between them.[11] But in the 1920s women were also beginning to figure in industries in which they had formerly been represented either negligibly or not at all; for example, in the metal industry some works recorded the employment of women for the first time in the 1925 census return.[12] In the later 1920s this trend gradually intensified, partly as a result of the rationalisation process generally, and partly because employers saw the use of cheaper female labour as the only way of keeping down costs at a time when wages generally had risen since the war. Women were therefore once more, as in wartime, being increasingly employed in work, particularly with heavy machinery, which was extremely unsuitable for them.[13] There was growing anxiety about this, particularly when young girls were involved, since it was becoming apparent that their physical development was suffering, so that their ability to bear healthy children was being diminished by work where there was extreme heat and dirt, and by the need to stand continuously for hours to work a machine.[14]

To try to combat the worst effects of industrial work on women and young people a piecemeal scheme of labour protection had been built up in the later 19th century. Article 157 of the Weimar Constitution had promised the introduction of a unified system of labour legislation to protect all workers as far as possible from danger and damaging conditions at work, but this was yet another pious hope which came to nothing in the political and economic difficulties of the 1920s. Women, however, benefited from a law, operative in 1927, which brought Germany into line with the Washington Convention of 1919 in the matter of employing women before and after childbirth.[15] This provided for up to twelve weeks' leave around the confinement, during which time maternity benefit was payable by the sickness funds, dismissal was illegal, and on returning to work a nursing mother was to be allowed time for feeding her baby.[16] The Free Trade Unions admitted that this was a real improvement, but pointed out that it was only the first step towards a proper, comprehensive labour protection system.[17] The depression, however, put their demands beyond the realm of possibility in the short term, as they acknowledged at the end of 1930, accepting that it was hard enough for the exchequer to find money even to operate the 1927 law.[18]

In spite of the economic difficulties, however, the Government continued to demonstrate interest in labour protection, with the reintroduction in 1930 of earlier measures, repealed during the war, to protect women working in glassworks, rolling mills and foundries.[19] Medical investigations into the effects of certain industries on women's physiology — particularly from the gynaecological point of view — were carried out which showed, for example, that women working in tobacco factories were highly susceptible to nicotine poisoning which contributed to a high rate of miscarriages among them and infant mortality among their offspring[20] — a serious finding for a nation with a declining birth rate. Even in the textile industry, where large numbers of women had been employed for long enough, conditions were found to be poor, with inadequate lighting and ventilation in factories and an insufficiency of seating and toilet facilities.[21] Clearly, much was still left to be desired in German labour legislation, but equally clearly the growing interest in conditions at work suggested that further legislation would be contemplated in an improved economic situation.

The two largest trade union groupings, the Free and the Christian unions, were unequivocally in favour of special protection for women at work,[22] no doubt at least partly because of the relative strength of their women's sections.[23] Although numbers — and women's share — dropped in the 1920s after a peak in 1920, when women's share in both combines was about one fifth, the total membership revived modestly with the depression biting, so that in 1930 there were altogether 4.7 million members of the Free unions and three quarters of a million in the Christian unions. But the decline in women's share to 14 per cent in both groups[24] seemed to confirm the view that women were readier to give up union membership in times of high unemployment.[25] The Free unions undertook a massive campaign, led by Gertrud Hanna, to attract more women,[26] and support for improved conditions at work was no doubt regarded as good propaganda for this purpose.

But there were those who saw labour protection as a way of putting women at a disadvantage on the labour market, and who suspected — not without some justification — that the male dominated trade unions promoted it for precisely this reason. In June 1929 the Open Door International for the Economic Emancipation of the Woman Worker was founded in Berlin, for the following purpose:

'To secure that a woman shall be free to work and protected as a worker on the same terms as a man, and that legislation and regulations . . . shall be based upon the nature of the work and not upon the sex of the worker; and to secure for a woman, irrespective of marriage or childbirth, the right at all times to decide whether or not she shall engage in paid work, and to ensure that no legislation or regulations shall deprive her of this right.'[27]

The aim of the Open Door, then, was to achieve complete, literal, and even absurd equality for women. Its chief supporters in Germany were to be found among the radical feminists,[28] who felt that special protection for women robbed them of the right to choose the kind of work they would do.[29] The trade unions were completely opposed to the Open Door, regarding it on the one hand as an embarrassment and on the other as a threat to the development of further protective legislation, even if it could not undo what had already been achieved.[30] On the whole, the new organisation made little impact in Germany, seeming largely irrelevant in the economic crisis, but it did continue to hold international conferences abroad during the 1930s.[31]

The expansion of women's employment after the Great War would have been desirable if the German economy had also been expanding, as it had done before the war. But in a situation where it was jobs, and not labour, that were in short supply, a situation intensified by mechanisation on a large scale, the influx of an increased number of women onto the labour market was potentially serious. With recession setting in, in late 1927, to be compounded in 1930 by deep depression, it became a real problem. The reason for the increase in the female labour force was attributed by Agnes von Zahn-Harnack, President of the BDF, to technical improvements in the home and to smaller families, which had made the occupation of wife and mother a less full-time one than formerly;[32] but she must have been referring only to her own constituency, the middle class. It was a much more widely held view that working-class women worked almost exclusively out of necessity.[33] This double burden of a full-time job and a family to care for after work was oppressive to many, and led a commentator to remark: 'The working-class wife is the tragic figure of our age.'[34]

In addition to factors which forced or encouraged women to take a job in the 1920s, there was another reason for the vast increase in the number of women in employment, from 8.5 million in 1907 to 11.5 million in 1925. In 1907, only about half of the very large number of Germans born since the founding of the Empire were of working age, while in 1925 almost all of those born in the decades of the high birth rate before the Great War were of working age. Even given the losses in the war, the number of men in employment had risen between 1907 and 1925, although the overall result had been to increase women's share in the labour force by 2 per cent, to almost 36 per cent of the total.[35] A change in the supply of labour would, however, become apparent, but not until about 1935, when those born in the 1870s began to retire, to be only partially replaced by those born in the lean war and post-war years of birth.

For the present, then, the absolute number of people of working age continued to grow. But the increase was greater among men than among women after 1925: in 1929 and 1930 the total number of women in the labour force actually declined, by 25,000 and 94,000 respectively, while men's numbers still increased. Most significantly, the decline in women's numbers was due solely to a drop in the number of single women in the labour force, from 1927, while the number of married women showed a net rise every year, even in 1930, when there had been a reduction of 25,000 in the total work force compared with 1929.[36] These figures would not be known to the mass of the population, and even those writing about the situation in the early 1930s generally based their comments on the 1925 census returns; but the situation represented by these figures must have created the general impression that more and more married women were working, at a time of rising unemployment.

As jobs became ever scarcer, employers had the pick of the labour market, and often they chose to employ women, as cheaper labour, while men lost their jobs; the result was that in many cases a wife would have to work to support the family, on a wage lower than that previously earned by her husband, because she could find work and he could not.[37] In spite of the narrowing of the differential between men's and women's wages, as a result primarily of the war but also of the 1923 inflation,[38] women were left with take home pay which was considerably lower than men's. Even in the textile industry, a female stronghold where women tended to do the same kind of work as men, women spinners in 1930 received only two thirds of the hourly wage rate paid to men, although women weavers fared rather better, with 83 per cent of men's rates.[39] This was, however, exceptionally high; across a broader spectrum of industry it was found, in 1928, that skilled and semi-skilled women — unfortunately, classed together — earned about 63 per cent of a skilled man's wage, while unskilled women earned 52 per cent. Unskilled men, by contrast, earned 78 per cent of a skilled man's wage. In 1932, after the wage cuts introduced by the Government to try to combat the depression, the relative positions remained broadly the same.[40] It was, therefore, still advantageous to an employer to take on a skilled woman, to whom he could pay a lower wage than that payable to an unskilled man.

But their relative inexpensiveness was not the only reason for women's continuing to work as men were laid off. Even more important was the fact that women were chiefly to be found in those sectors of the economy which were less severely affected by the depression. Women were predominantly employed in the consumer goods indus-

79

tries, which maintained a reasonable level of output during the crisis: although employment in relation to total labour capacity in this area dropped to 48 per cent throughout the second half of 1932, it remained above 60 per cent most of the time in the food, textile and luxury industries,[41] in which, together, women constituted almost half of the labour force. By contrast, women's share in industry as a whole was less than a quarter.[42] On the other hand, the production goods industries suffered much more, with employment in relation to total capacity as low as 35 per cent throughout 1932. The area affected worst of all was the building trade, which could reach a figure of only 23 per cent in summer 1932, with figures catastrophically low — at 12 per cent at the start of 1932 and 14 per cent at the start of 1933 — as its seasonal character compounded the effects of the crisis.[43] The building trade — accounting for 9 per cent of all unemployment in 1932 — was overwhelmingly a male preserve,with women less than 2 per cent of its labour force. The other area hit disastrously was the metal industry, where women comprised less than 4 per cent of the work force.[44]

These details contributed to a picture where women, as 35 per cent of all employed Germans, accounted for just under 20 per cent of the registered unemployed in 1931 and 1932, the worst years of the crisis.[45] But many unemployed women did not register at an employment exchange, and the extent to which women actually suffered in the crisis can be gauged by comparing the figure of 2.9 million women classed as industrial workers in the 1925 census with the 1.1 million women who had a job in industry in the early months of 1933. In 1925, however, women had been classed as 23 per cent of industrial workers, whereas early in 1933 30 per cent of all employed persons in industry were female.[46] Thus it would appear that women survived the economic crisis somewhat better than men, largely because a reasonable level of demand was maintained in the industries in which they chiefly figured, while they were employed in relatively insignificant numbers in the industries which bore the major burden of the unemployment. But whatever the reason, the impression was growing that women, by occupying jobs, were keeping men out of work: the response to this was a growing campaign from the autumn of 1930 to replace women who had jobs by unemployed men.

The 1925 census had shown that 68 per cent of all employed women were single, widowed or divorced;[47] these would probably have to support themselves, and perhaps also dependents — almost always on a lower income than men, as a radical feminist pointed out.[48] Nevertheless, in December 1930 the Economics Party proposed that the employment of women generally — and particularly of women holding what they termed 'men's positions' — should be restricted, unless they had absolutely no other means of support. This clear attack on the wives and daughters of employed men reinforced an attack made by a right-wing white collar union on the daughters of wealthy families who had a job and therefore 'increased the misery of those who have no-one to provide for them'.[49] It was certainly true that girls from prosperous middle-class families were to be found in clerical jobs, working for pocket money rather than for subsistence,[50] but they were only a tiny minority of employed women. However, those who attacked the employment of women in time of depression often did so for ideological reasons rather than because they believed that the removal of women from jobs would solve the unemployment problem. The Churches, with their view of the place of women in family life, were a case in point.[51] And the Nazis, in their anxiety about the birth rate, claimed that the present situation degraded women, prevented their devoting themselves to family life, and deprived 'fathers of families' of the right to work.[52]

If there were some generalised attacks on the employment of women as a group, the main burden of complaint was against the married woman who had a job, who, it was claimed, was giving some families an extra wage, over and above that earned by the actual bread-winner, the father, while in other families — as a consequence, it was implied — the breadwinner was without work. These women, the *Doppelverdiener*, were felt to be not only depriving able men of work, but were even threatening the very existence of whole families. It was thus against them that the full force of official concern and widespread unofficial propaganda was directed.

Early in 1931, the Minister of Employment, Stegerwald, asked a commission to consider the possibility of legislation to restrict the *Doppelverdiener*; but it was on the basis of the commission's report that he decided against such a course. Instead, he instructed the Employment Exchanges that where they had to place applicants for jobs, they should take the social circumstances of candidates of equal suitability into account. In addition, he announced that he would write to employers to ask them to cooperate by making their choice of labour — for firing or hiring — at least partially dependent on whether the person involved was or would be bringing a second income into a home. Stegerwald was convinced that, for psychological reasons, the exchanges would have to be seen to be taking some action to restrict the employment of the *Doppelverdiener*.[53] It was clear that this measure was indeed directed primarily against married women, since the Minister added that it should not be applied to young people living with their parents, lest their long term career prospects suffer.[54] The Brüning Government, then, was anxious to take action, and to be seen to be taking action; but even in this emergency it was unwilling — or perhaps unable — to legislate.

The attacks on employed married women were met by defence of her position from a number of quarters. Although many men trade unionists were prepared to join in the attacks, the large and influential socialist federation of unions, the ADGB (General German Trade Union Association) repeatedly reminded its members that its position was clear, namely that it opposed the campaign against the employment of married women since it infringed their rights and would not achieve its aim — of eliminating unemployment — anyway.[55] By 1930, the ADGB had decided that the only way to prevent women from being given preference over men simply because they were cheaper to employ would be to launch a campaign to achieve better wages for women.[56] But this of itself would not solve the problems of families where the man's wage was so low that the wife had to work, to help to feed and clothe her children, not to buy them luxuries.[57] This situation, said the Communist Party, was a natural result of the capitalist system, where in a crisis the employers still managed to come out on top, by reducing wages and pocketing the amount they saved. Women, 'the weakest part of the proletariat', were paid miserable wages because employers believed them to be more docile.[58] Alone of political parties the KPD unequivocally demanded the abolition of wage differentials altogether, and the upholding of a woman's right to work on equal terms with men.[59]

The many women who jumped to the defence of their own sex did not, however, tend to argue that women should have equal rights with men in the employment market in time of depression; they concentrated on trying to disprove the case that the dismissal of the *Doppelverdiener* would solve the unemployment problem. Even the radical feminist Grete Stoffel affirmed the priority of men with families to support, although she did suggest that any 'double earnings' rule should equally allow for the dismissal of the husband of a woman who owned a business.[60] Gertrud Hanna, leader of the ADGB's women's section, pointed out that the vast majority of wives classed in 1925 as employed were still working in 1931, in spite of the mounting campaign against them, because 'it could not be otherwise'. Her analysis of the distribution of the 3.7 million married women listed as employed showed that the vast majority, some 77 per cent of the total, were classed as 'assisting family members', who worked full-time, but not for a fixed wage, in their husband's business; and three quarters of these, or slightly more than two million, were engaged in agriculture. Gertrud Hanna claimed, rightly, that these women could only in very exceptional circumstances be replaced by unemployed men, who would have to be paid a fair wage; in addition, if these women were obliged to give up their job, many would have to dismiss paid help from the household, which would certainly be harmful to the labour market.[61]

A few months later, Maria Hellersberg gave a similar analysis in the relatively conservative magazine *Die Bayerische Frau*, and went on to point out that a further two categories of working married women could be eliminated from consideration as *Doppelverdiener* who could be dismissed. The 309,000 women with their own business could hardly be replaced by men, for obvious reasons, she said; presumably this was because their jobs would not have existed without them. In addition, the 44,000 married women in domestic service might be replaceable 'in individual cases' by unemployed single women, but certainly not by men. That left the wage earning, salary earning and professional married women, and Maria Hellersberg whittled their numbers down to half a million by eliminating about 276,000 women in the textile, clothing and food industries in areas where, she pointed out, only a very few men had ever been employed.[62] Marguerite Thibert subtracted another large group, arguing that children's nurses, dressmakers and milliners could hardly be replaced by unemployed men. The highest number of working married women who, she estimated, were in jobs which men could do equally well was 200,000, a figure already suggested by Else Lüders in the Employment Ministry's official gazette.[63] And these 200,000 women could hardly, as Marguerite Thibert somewhat drily remarked, be replaced by the four million or more men who were unemployed in 1931-2.[64]

Given the mounting opposition to the employment of married women, particularly in the depression, it might have been expected that they would find it harder than men to obtain unemployment benefit. The institution of what amounted to a household means test before emergency relief would be granted, in 1930,[65] was one way in which a wife – or a daughter, for that matter – could find her chances of receiving State support much reduced. But at the worst of the crisis women were still receiving benefit more or less to the same extent as men: in 1932, women's share among the recipients of the two main kinds of support, unemployment benefit and emergency relief, was 19.9 per cent and 19.4 per cent respectively, at a time when their proportion among the registered unemployed was 19.9 per cent.[66] Thus it is clear that the number of unemployed women, including married women, who were found not to be in need of support was very small indeed, reinforcing claims made before and during the depression that most married women worked out of dire necessity. Not only did women generally withstand the depression better than men; they also had an even chance with men of obtaining support from public funds. If this was because women's needs was as great as men's, it was nevertheless hardly likely to mollify those who believed that there should be positive discrimination in favour of men.

In fact men did benefit marginally more than women from the work creation programme begun tentatively by Brüning before his dismissal. The Labour Service, for which public funds were provided by a law passed in July 1931,[67] was largely a male concern, with only 5,000 of the 175,000 places available in January 1933 allotted to women.[68] But these numbers were minute compared with the problem the Labour Service was supposed to be helping to solve. Nevertheless, hardship was greatly eased in a few individual cases; for example, the DVP's *Women's Review* described glowingly how redundant women office workers could be given work mending clothes and cooking in return for Labour Service remuneration.[69] Much of the time women were used for similar domestic purposes; while the men were gathered together in camps to work in agriculture or in public works schemes, in return for board, lodgings and pocket money,[70] the women were generally put to work cooking and cleaning for them.[71] On a smaller scale, the Red Cross in Bremen was paying subsistence wages to twenty-five unemployed girls, who were brought together to make and repair garments for needy citizens.[72] All these activities were completely voluntary; the Nazis attacked them because they favoured a compulsory system,[73] the Communists and radical feminists because they saw Labour Service as exploiting women and girls, particularly, and as a potential strike breaking weapon.[74] But most other parties and groups — including the Churches — supported the Labour Service, in the hope of alleviating the misery of some of the unemployed.[75]

It was partly the failure of the democratic parties and of the more authoritarian governments in the early 1930s to find a way out of the crisis into which Germany had sunk that provided the opportunity for Hitler to form a government at the end of January 1933. Thus he became responsible for solving the economic problems of the country. But, although it seemed as if some measure of success in this area would be essential if he were to retain power, and if he were to be able to pursue the aggressive foreign policy which was his basic aim, the introduction of a vigorous economic policy was not his first priority. He was determined to consolidate his political power first and attempt to deal with economic problems once he felt politically secure. He was fortunate in two respects: from January into the summer there is a general seasonal improvement in unemployment figures; and, as was not yet fully apparent, the depression had reached its nadir before the end of 1932, and an upturn had begun before his Government took office. These two factors, combined with loud and optimistic propaganda, gave the impression that Hitler's Government was at last bringing recovery to Germany, when all it had done was to continue the piecemeal work creation projects of the previous administrations. But at last on 1 June 1933, the 'Law for the Reduction of Unemployment' was passed; this included measures which seemed to reflect the Nazi view of the place of women in society.[76]

It was a fundamental part of the Nazi *Weltanschauung* that the man was the guardian of and provider for the home and family; an unemployed man, however, would be unlikely to be able to fulfil this function. If he were married, a man might be put in the degrading position of having his wife support him, and possibly a family in addition, on the meagre wage she could earn; if he were single, he could not afford to marry and have children.[77] Either way, severe unemployment was a major obstacle to a healthy rate of population growth. In addition, the increased employment of women, sometimes at the expense of men, was driving women into occupations which, in the view of a Social Democrat like Judith Grünfeld, as well as in the Nazi view, were unsuitable for them.[78] To remedy these problems, women would have to be taken out of heavy industry, to protect them physiologically – or, as the Nazis preferred to say, 'biologically' – since they were the actual or potential mothers of the nation.[79] For this reason, young girls were a source of particular concern, as they had been to doctors and factory social workers for some years.[80] The Nazis promoted the desirability of farm work and domestic service for girls because they hoped to provide cheap labour in areas which were now unpopular with women; but it was as high a consideration that this kind of work would be much less damaging to adolescent girls than work in a tobacco or chemicals factory.

The Nazis' intention was not, as was often claimed,[81] to remove women completely from the labour market. They did aim to persuade married women to leave work, to devote their full attention to their family, or to start a family if they were childless or add to it if they had followed the post-war pattern of a one or two child family. This would, they believed, create a situation in which single women could be found work in occupations suited to the female physique and the feminine nature. The number of these women was, however, expected to be greatly reduced by the fact that the job security afforded to men by the withdrawal of married women from work would enable and encourage more single men to marry.[82] But the Nazis did not oppose the employment of women root and branch; in fact, they firmly believed that women had an essential role to play in social work of every kind, particularly nursing, primary teaching and welfare services. In addition, Hitler had recognised that women would continue to be the comrades of men in the factory and the office, so that it is clear that the Nazis did not aim to eliminate women from those white collar and even manual jobs which caused no harm to the female frame. When there were enough jobs to go round, there would no longer be the unseemly rivalry for positions which had characterised the post-war period, and which disturbed the harmony of the nation.[83]

It was this situation which the law of 1 June 1933, set out to achieve. It provided, in the first place, considerable sums of money to be spent on public works, and, in addition, introduced some rather dubious expedients, including work sharing and the use of manpower for work previously done by machines.[84] Then there were two provisions which specifically affected women: in the first place, a tax concession was announced for those who employed a female domestic servant.[85] This dealt with a genuine problem, since in the contracted economy there had been severe unemployment among domestic servants.[86] But there had also been a voluntary exodus of women from this kind of work since the war, in favour of jobs which were less restricting and better paid,[87] and it was to try to reverse this trend, since domestic work was deemed particularly suitable for women by the Nazis, that the measure was partly geared. Above all, perhaps, work done by maidservants was not, on the whole, work that a man would expect, or would be expected, to do, and so domestic service could provide jobs for women without taking them away from men.

The other section of the law which had special relevance to women was headed 'Promotion of marriages', and dealt chiefly with the marriage loan scheme.[88] From the employment point of view, the important feature was that it was a condition of receiving a loan that the bride-to-be had held paid employment for at least six months out of the two years preceding the passage of the law — that is, in the depths of the crisis — and that she now undertake to relinquish her job on marriage; in addition, she was not to resume employment until the loan was repaid, unless her husband's income fell below a certain level. In recognition of the essential part played in family concerns, particularly in agriculture, by wives as 'assisting family members', this category of employment was not counted as falling within the provisions of the law;[89] this meant, however, that families living on the land and depending on the labour of the wife would not benefit from the marriage loan scheme, which was hardly in line with the Nazis' obsession with encouraging the growth of a healthy 'peasant' class. But it was consistent with the Nazi view that agriculture, like domestic service, was a particularly suitable area of employment for women.

The scope of the scheme was soon extended, to include those who had married in the year before the publication of the law, if the wife had been working for at least six months and was now prepared to retire. In addition, the period during which the wife had worked was now to fall between 1 June 1928 and the date of the marriage, thus bringing in the entire period of the depression, and much of the recession before it.[90] Thus it was clear that the encouraging of married women to give up work was a major priority in this law, of perhaps less long term significance than the population aims behind the marriage loan scheme, but certainly of pressing importance in mid-1933. The general idea behind the scheme was not a new one; the giving of an attractive lump sum as severance payment to married women to give up work, particularly in the public service, had been suggested in the early 1920s, and such a sum had been prescribed in the law passed by the Brüning Government in 1932 to permit the dismissal of married women civil servants under certain conditions.[91] The marriage loan scheme, however, had a much wider application, and was intended to serve several purposes at once — increasing the number of marriages, raising the birth rate, freeing jobs for men, giving orders to factories producing the household goods on which the loan had to be spent — and gave the impression of being an incentive rather than a bribe.

Minor modifications were made to the marriage loan laws during the remainder of 1933 and in 1934. It was, for example, stipulated that the Minister of Finance should be able in exceptional cases to authorise the granting of a loan even if the applicant had not complied with all the provisions of the original act; this provided the loop hole which the Nazis so often allowed themselves in seemingly categorical regulations. At the same time, the loan scheme was made applicable in the case of 'assisting family members', where the wife who gave up work was replaced by someone to whom a full wage was paid.[92] This was sensible from the points of view of both employment and population policy, but it was unlikely that many people would be affected, since it would almost always be more expensive to hire paid labour in place of a wife who did not receive a wage as such. But this measure was included no doubt merely to make it possible for the rural population, particularly, to be brought into the scheme somehow, and to find even a few positions for unemployed persons. It was not, however, stipulated that these persons must be male, so that there was the possibility of an unemployed woman benefiting from the withdrawal of a wife from work. The situation clearly was still desperate in winter 1933-4, with another amendment stating that a husband had to be indigent, not merely poorly paid, before a wife in a loan aided marriage was entitled to take a job.[93]

Explaining the marriage loan scheme, the *Völkischer Beobachter* was completely open about the fact that 'in the campaign against unemployment one of the most important tasks of our economic policy is to send women back to the home from the workplace', adding the qualification 'wherever that is suitable'. The paper went on to report what it saw as the shining example of the Reemtsma cigarette company which was supporting the purpose of the marriage loan scheme by replacing the women who retired by men, and, in addition, was making the scheme even more attractive by giving every female employee who entered it a substantial cash payment. By November 1933, 122 women workers had already benefited from this offer by giving up work to marry, and these had carried their celebrations to the incredible length of having a huge combined wedding ceremony! The *Völkischer Beobachter* found this entire episode thoroughly admirable, and expressed the expectation that other employers would emulate Reemtsma before long.[94] This was precisely the kind of 'voluntary' initiative which the Nazis encouraged, so that an objective which they saw as important could be achieved by money contributed privately, thus saving the Government expense. At any rate, it seems that by the end of 1934 some 360,000 women had given up work as a result of receiving a loan,[95] and if this was a reasonably pleasing outcome for the Government, it cannot be doubted that many women were glad to be able to give up their job, in return for official approval and financial benefit.

The marriage loan scheme could not, of course, bring about the elimination of all, or even most, married women from employment, since only those who had married since June 1932 were eligible for it. To deal with the remainder, it must have been eagerly anticipated by some; just as it was feared by others, that the Nazi-led Government would take the earliest opportunity to legislate against the *Doppelverdiener*, the Party having been active in the campaign against her before 1933. But the only measure passed in this area was the law of 30 June 1933, which extended the Brüning law of 30 May 1932, and thus allowed for the dismissal of married women from the civil service on a larger scale.[96]

Nevertheless, the general attitude of the Government to the *Doppelverdiener* was hostile, and this encouraged some employers and authorities to demonstrate their loyalty to the new regime by dismissing married women. The Government, however, soon discovered that these local initiatives were having undesirable effects; in the first place, they were causing considerable unrest among employees in the concerns affected, and, in addition, the result was by no means always in the interests of the families they were supposed to benefit. To try to clarify the position, the Minister of Employment issued instructions in November 1933 which explained that the campaign against the working married women had so far shown that a lack of discrimination could be detrimental to productivity since 'it is actually often the best and most industrious people who try, by bringing a second income into a home, and by extra effort, to provide a higher standard of living for themselves or a better education for their children'. Preventing those who were eager to work hard for certain objectives from doing so turned out, it was admitted, in many cases to be counterproductive, and so in future careful consideration would have to be given to each individual case.[97]

Faced with the chance to take real action against the *Doppelverdiener*, action which the last governments before Hitler's had been unwilling, but probably unable, to take, the Nazis discovered that what the apologists of the working married woman had maintained was true, namely that an intensive campaign against the employment of married women would not solve Germany's economic problems, and also that most of the married women who worked did so out of necessity. The term *Doppelverdiener*, which had been so widely used in the years 1930-33, almost exclusively in a pejorative sense, is still to be found in use in 1934, but to a rapidly decreasing extent; after 1934, it was used only to describe something which had existed in the past. The Government might maintain that this was because the problem had been eliminated by decisive action; the reality was that the Government discovered that this problem was very largely a red herring.

Although it had taken little direct action to remove women from the productive process, by 1935 the Government seemed, at first sight, to have achieved its aim of discriminating in favour of men. An official publication confidently asserted that,

> 'since the assumption of power, women's employment has once again been reduced. The decisive factor in this has been above all the fundamental nature of National Socialist population policy.'

In new appointments, continued the article, men had been given preference, while the Employment Exchanges had been particularly at pains to find work for family men, and then to help single men, to give them the chance to marry and start a family.[98]

Other tactics included the banning of women from certain categories of heavy work, for example in any kind of work underground, in mining, salt works, and coking plants,[99] in rolling mills or foundries.[100] If these were not areas in which women figured greatly it was the employment of women for the first time in them in the 1920s which had caused concern then, and which was justified only by the extremists of the Open Door International. In other industries, for example in brickworks, shoe making, and certain areas of the glass industry, the introduction of equal pay for women was intended to discourage employers from taking on women, when men were actually better suited to the work.[101] But equal pay for women was not an end in itself, and it was introduced in only a small minority of cases where it was felt that women had been used as labour only because they could be paid at a lower rate than men.

The result of these measures indeed appeared to be a reduction in the employment of women. Official figures showed that whereas in the first three months of 1933 women's proportion in the industrial labour force had been around 30 per cent, there had been a decline to 25.5

per cent for the last four months of 1934. But this was not a true reflection of the overall situation: it had to be admitted – albeit with a singular lack of emphasis – that in absolute terms the number of women in industry had actually risen by 300,000 in the same period, to a total of 1.4 million.[102] Thus, far from achieving its stated aim of cutting drastically the size of the female labour force, the Nazi Government had not been able, apparently, to prevent there being a net rise in it. The reason behind this is obvious: the real remedy for the massive unemployment of the early 1930s was the creation of more jobs, not the provision of work for some people at the expense of others, nor widespread work sharing, the expedients to which the Nazis turned at the start.

Men had perhaps found job opportunities less available because of female competition, but the crucial factor in the depression was that the traditional strongholds of men's employment had been those most catastrophically hit by the crisis. To achieve a genuine improvement in men's employment prospects, these areas, in the production goods industries, had to be revived; and this process was also a vital part of Nazi aims in foreign policy, which would require not only a return to pre-depression capacity in heavy industry, but a considerable expansion of it beyond that. Thus, the decisive factor affecting women's proportion in the labour force was not the few measures designed to encourage them to leave work, to make way for men, but rather the entire direction of the Government's work creation programme, whose purpose was to raise production in the capital goods industries; this would have the effect of creating new jobs for men, and would therefore not work to the disadvantage of women.

Women would continue to be employed in those consumer goods industries where they had traditionally had a substantial representation, although the restricting of domestic demand would prevent their expansion on a scale comparable with that urgently planned for the capital goods industries. But it is obvious that the return of men to employment would lead to a lowering of women's share in industry as a whole, restoring the balance which had been distorted in women's favour by the unnatural circumstances of the depression. And yet, in the first two years of Nazi rule, women's unemployment was reduced at a rate similar to that of men's, so that by the end of May 1935, 93 per cent of available women employees had jobs, the comparable figure for men being 88 per cent. It was estimated that, just as the progress made since the 1870s had depended on the participation of women in industry, so any further expansion of the economy would not be possible unless the remaining reserve of female labour were tapped, for industry and business as well as for agriculture and domestic service.[103]

Instead of eliminating women from employment, the Nazis were increasingly to try to encourage them to go out to work, even before Germany was at war in 1939, and more urgently in wartime. The poor results of official persuasion and threats of compulsion reinforce suggestions[104] that while the Nazi regime was indeed dictatorial, it was unable to force its will on the German people when there was confusion and disagreement in the upper echelons of the Party and Government, and when there was deep rooted opposition to its policies.

NOTES

1.   Judith Grünfeld, 'Frauenarbeit im Lichte der Rationalisierung', *Die Arbeit*, 1931, no. 12, pp. 911-13, 922; Ludwig Preller, *Sozialpolitik in der Weimarer Republik*, Stuttgart, 1949, pp. 115, 125, 136.

2.   Report in *WuS*, 1930, no. 13, p. 558.

3.   Siegfried Kracauer, *Die Angestellten*, Frankfurt, 1930 (reprinted by Verlag für Demoskopie, Allensbach and Bonn, 1959), p. 5.

4.   Report in *FiS*, January 1930, p. 10.

5.   Figures may be found in *St. J.*: 1927, pp. 511-12; 1928, pp. 592-3.

6.   Maria Hellersberg, 'Die soziale Not der weiblichen Angestellten', *Schriftenreihe des Gewerkschaftsbundes der Angestellten*, Berlin, 1928, pp. 22-3.

7.   *Ibid.*; Kracauer, *op. cit.*, p. 7; Herta Schmidt, 'Die Berufsarbeit der Frau', *FiS*, May 1931, p. 6.

8.   Kracauer, *op. cit.*, pp. 38-9, vividly describes examples of this.

9.   Calculated from figures in *St. J.*, 1933, p. 291.

10.   Figures from *Statistik des Deutschen Reiches (St. D. R.)*, vol. 451, part 3, p. 40.

11.   Figures from *St. J.*, 1933, p. 22. For comparison, the 1925 census also recorded that there were a million female domestic servants (*op. cit.*, p. 23).

12.   A. Vallentin, 'The Employment of Women since the War', *International Labour Review (ILR)*, vol. 25, 1932, pp. 493-4.

13.   Judith Grünfeld, *op. cit.*, pp. 912-17.

14.   *Ibid.*, p. 921; Hildegard Jüngst, *Die Jugendliche Fabrikarbeiterin*, Paderborn, 1929, pp. 36-8.

15.   'Arbeiterinnen- und Mutterschutz', *JADG*, 1927, p. 204.

16.   Johannes Feig, 'The New Labour Protection Bill', *ILR*, vol. 15, 1927, p. 190.

17.   *JADG, op. cit.*, pp. 205-7.

18.   Report in *JADG*, 1930, p. 194.

19.   *Ibid.*; 'Verordnung über die Beschäftigung von Arbeitern unter achtzehn Jahren und von Arbeiterinnen in der Glasindustrie', *RGB*, 1930 I, 26 March 1930, p. 105.

20.   S. M. Klein in *AfFr*, 1931-2, pp. 34-43; M. Sserdjnkoff in *AfFr*, 1932, pp. 264-5.

21.   Annemarie Hermberg, ' "Mein Arbeitstag – Mein Wochenend" ', *Die Arbeit*, 1931, no. 2, p. 168.

22.   *JADG*, 1927, *op. cit.*, p. 205; IfZ, MA 422, frames 5-455196-97, letter from Mina Amann to the leaders of unions in the Christian Trade Union movement, 23 June 1931.

23.   Marguerite Thibert, 'The Economic Depression and the Employment of

Women', *ILR*, vol. 27, 1933, p. 461, states that Germany had a much larger women's membership in the trade unions than many countries.
24. Figures from *St. J.*: 1921-2, p. 458; 1923, p. 436; 1928, pp. 594-5; 1931, p. 558; 1932, p. 557.
25. Marguerite Thibert, *op. cit.*, p. 462.
26. 'Frauenarbeit und Gewerkschaften', *Gewerkschaftszeitung*, 11 January 1930, pp. 21-2.
27. Report of the Third Conference of the Open Door International, Prague, 24-8 July 1933, p. 43. The ODI's headquarters were in London.
28. Lida Gustava Heymann, 'The Open Door Council', *FiS*, May 1929, p. 1.
29. Thönnessen, *op. cit.*, p. 166.
30. Report in *JADG*, 1930, p. 191; IfZ, *loc. cit.*
31. After the Prague Conference in 1933, conferences were held in Copenhagen in 1935 and Cambridge in 1938. See the reports of these conferences.
32. 'Das Berufsschicksal der weiblichen Jugend', *BF*, November 1931, p. 2.
33. Agnes Karbe, *Die Frauenlohnfrage*, Rostock, 1928, pp. 88, 130; Gertrud Hanna, 'Vom Kampf gegen die verheirateten erwerbstätigen Frauen', *Die Arbeit*, 1931, p. 259; E. E. Schwabach, *Revolutionierung der Frau*, Leipzig, 1928, p. 95.
34. *Ibid.*, p. 132.
35. Figures from *St. J.*, 1930, p. 23. The 1907 figures are given in adjusted form, taking the loss of population in 1919 into account, to give comparability; A. Vallentin, *op. cit.*, p. 492, comments on the relationship between the growth of the population and that of the labour force; Renate Bridenthal, *op. cit.*, pp. 149-50, regards this as a poor result in the context of the 'economic liberation' of women. She ignores the fact that for very many women employment meant anything but 'liberation'.
36. Report in *WuS*, *loc. cit.*
37. Karbe, *op. cit.*, p. 113.
38. Bry, *op. cit.*, p. 96.
39. Calculated from figures in *St. J.*, 1933, p. 272.
40. Calculated from figures in 'The General Level of Wages in Mines, Industries and Transport', *ILR*, 1938, vol. 37, p. 105.
41. Figures from *St. J.*, 1933, p. 309.
42. The 1925 census showed that women's share in the three industries mentioned was 46 per cent, while that in industry as a whole was 23 per cent. Figures calculated from information in *St. J.*, 1930, p. 88.
43. Figures from *St. J.*, 1933, *loc. cit.*
44. Calculated from figures in *St. J.*, 1930, *loc. cit.*
45. Figures from *St. J.*, 1933, p. 291.
46. Figures from *St. J.*: 1930, *loc. cit.*; 1933, p. 22. And from *WuS*, 1935, no. 13, 'Beschäftigung, Arbeitszeit und Arbeitseinkommen', p. 8, 'Die Anteil der Frauenarbeit in der Industrie'.
47. Calculated from figures in *St. D. R.*, no. 451, part 3, p. 76.
48. Herta Schmidt, *loc. cit.*
49. Gertrud Hanna, *op. cit.*, p. 260.
50. Kracauer, *op. cit.*, p. 65.
51. Grete Stoffel, 'Die Arbeitslosigkeit und die Frauenarbeit', *FiS*, August/September 1931, p. 6; Leo Zodrow, *loc. cit.*; report in *VB*, 4 April 1934.
52. Karl Fiehler, *loc. cit.*; Report in *VB*, 4 April 1934.
53. Report in *RAB*, 1931 I, no. 15, 25 May 1931, pp. 101-2.
54. Report in *RAB*, 1931 I, no. 18, 25 June 1931, p. 137.
55. Report in *JADG*, 1930, pp. 193-4.
56. *Gewerkschaftszeitung*, *op. cit.*, p. 23.
57. Judith Grünfeld, *op. cit.*, pp. 921-4; Karbe, *op. cit.*, pp. 88, 130, 136.
58. BA, R45 IV/10, 'Die Auswirkungen der Papennotverordnung für die

Frauen', pp. 1-2.
59.   BA, R2/18554, Reichstag motion no. 1201, 15 October 1931, signed by Communist deputies.
60.   Grete Stoffel, *op. cit.*, p. 5.
61.   Gertrud Hanna, *op. cit.*, p. 254.
62.   Maria Hellersberg, 'Die Berufsarbeit der Frau', *BF*, February 1932, p. 2. Maria Hellersberg was a leading member of a white collar union, the *Gewerkschaftsbund der Angestellten*.
63.   Else Lüders, 'Die Erhaltung der Familie in der Gegenwart', *RAB*, 1931 II, no. 7, 5 March 1931, p. 108.
64.   Marguerite Thibert, *op. cit.*, p. 622.
65.   'Verordnung über die Krisenfürsorge für Arbeitslose', *RGB*, 1930 I, 11 October 1930, pp. 463-4.
66.   Calculated from figures in *St. J.*, 1933, p. 299.
67.   'Verordnung über die Förderung des freiwilligen Arbeitsdienst', *RGB* 1931 I, 23 July 1931, pp. 398-400.
68.   Maria Burgstaller, 'Der Deutsche Frauenarbeitsdienst', *NS-Frauenbuch*, Munich, 1934, p. 26.
69.   BA, R45 II/64, DVP Reichsgeschäftsstelle, *Frauenrundschau*, 13 January 1932, 'Erwerbslosenhilfe durch freiwilligen Arbeitsdienst', p. 1103.
70.   This is described in detail in Hans Freising, 'Entstehung und Aufbau des Arbeitsdienstes im Deutschen Reich', doctoral dissertation for Rostock University, 1937, pp. 21-32. See also P. W. van den Nieuwenhuysen, *De Nationaalsocialistische Arbeidsdienst*, Louvain, 1939, pp. 26-7.
71.   Toni Saring, *Die Deutsche Frauenarbeitsdienst*, Berlin, 1934, pp. 74-5.
72.   IfZ, MA 422, frame 5-455891, *Deutscher Arbeitsdienst*, 'Mädels im Arbeitsdienst', April 1932.
73.   BA, *Slg. Sch.*, 262, Reichsleitung, 'Rundschreiben Nr. 14a', 5 October 1932.
74.   BA, R58/ , RMdI/NsdL, 17 March 1932, 'Kampf der Arbeitsdienstpflicht', p. 20; BA, R45 IV/vorl.10, RGO Reports, October 1932, 'Frauen im "freiwilligen" Arbeitsdienst', p. 8; 'Zwangsarbeit für Frauen', *FiS*, December 1932, p. 6.
75.   Wolfgang Benz, 'Vom freiwilligen Arbeitsdienst zur Arbeitsdienstpflicht', *Vierteljahrshefte für Zeitgeschichte (VjfZ)*, 1968, pp. 323, 326-7.
76.   'Gesetz zur Verminderung der Arbeitslosigkeit', *RGB*, 1933 I, 1 June 1933, pp. 323-7.
77.   Engelbert Huber, *Das ist Nationalsozialismus*, Stuttgart, pp. 123-4; Friedrich Lenz, 'Arbeitslosigkeit und Rassenhygiene', *VB*, 25/26 June 1933.
78.   Judith Grünfeld, *op. cit.*, pp. 913-21.
79.   'Nachprüfung der industriellen Frauenarbeit', *VB*, 7 February 1934.
80.   See above, p. 76.
81.   See e.g. Hilda Browning, *Women under Fascism and Communism*, London, 1935, pp. 8-9. M. Lode, 'Women under Hitler's Yoke', *The Communist International*, November 1938, pp. 42-3. This article was kindly pointed out to me by Professor V. G. Kiernan.
82.   *WuS, loc. cit.*
83.   Paula Siber, *Die Frauenfrage und ihre Lösung durch den Nationalsozialismus*, Berlin, 1933, pp. 26-7; Huber, *op. cit.*, p. 123.
84.   *RGB, op. cit.*, p. 323; T. W. Mason, 'National Socialist Policies towards the German Working Classes', unpublished Oxford D. Phil. thesis, 1971, pp. 141, 148-9.
85.   *RGB, op. cit.*, p. 326.
86.   BA, *Nachlass* Gothein, Georg Gothein, 'Streiflichter der Arbeitslosigkeit', *Deutsche Wirtschafts-Zeitung*, 15 October 1931, p. 987.

87.   Otto Michalke, 'Die Frauenarbeit', *Jahrbücher für Nationalökonomie und Statistik*, 1935, p. 437.
88.   For the population aspects of the marriage loan scheme, see Chapter 2, pp. 46-7.
89.   *RGB, op. cit.*, pp. 326-7.
90.   'Zweite Durchführungsverordnung über die Gewährung von Ehestands-darlehen', *RGB*, 1933 I, 26 July 1933, p. 540.
91.   See Chapter 8, especially pp. 150, 153-5.
92.   'Dritte Durchführungsverordnung über die Gewährung von Ehestands-darlehen', *RGB*, 1933 I, 22 August 1933, p. 596.
93.   'Gesetz zur Änderung des Gesetzes über die Förderung der Eheschlies-sungen', *RGB*, 1934 I, 28 March 1934, p. 253.
94.   'Die Frau in den Haushalt, der Mann an die Arbeitsstätte', *VB*, 1 November 1933.
95.   In the last four months of 1933, when the loan scheme was operative, 141,559 loans were made; in 1934 the figure was 224,619. Only a very few of these can have been made without the wife's having to leave work. Figures from *St. J.*, 1936, p. 42.
96.   'Gesetz zur Änderung von Vorschriften auf dem Gebiet des allgemeinen Beamten-, des Besoldungs- und des Versorgungsrechts', *RGB*, 1933 I, 30 June 1933, pp. 434-5. This will be discussed in detail in Chapter 8, pp. 157-8.
97.   Report in *AfB*, March 1934, pp. 125-6; see also Mason, *op. cit.*, pp. 146 and 146A.
98.   *WuS, loc. cit.*
99.   'Arbeitszeitordnung', *RGB*, 1934 I, 26 July 1934, pp. 807-12.
100.   'Verordnung über den Schutz der jugendlichen Arbeiter und der Arbeiter-innen im Steinkohlenbergbau, in Walz- und Hammerwerken und in der Glas-industrie', *RGB*, 1935 I, 12 March 1935, p. 387.
101.   'The Law and Women's Work', ILO Studies and Reports, Series I, no. 4, p. 402.
102.   *WuS, loc. cit.*
103.   Michalke, *op. cit.*, pp. 439-42.
104.   Mason, *op. cit.*, pp. 590-6, 605, 642; H. R. Trevor-Roper, *The Last Days of Hitler*, London, 1972, pp. 53-4.

5   WOMEN'S EMPLOYMENT: ENCOURAGEMENT AND RESISTANCE

The Nazi Goverment's acceptance of the vital role of women in the German economy was formally demonstrated in July 1934, when a Women's Section was established in the German Labour Front, with Gertrud Scholtz-Klink, the National Women's Leader, at its head.[1] The Government thus acknowledged that the employment of millions of women was a permanent fixture, and that, therefore, attention would have to be paid to their special needs — in the national interest at least as much as for their own sake. Moreover, the creation of a Women's Section served the Nazi view that the sexes had separate needs and functions, and should therefore be segregated for most purposes. A similar process was taking place in 1934 in the professional organisations[2] which suggests that acceptance of women in employment of all kinds was reached at about the same time, and that the consolidation of Nazi power was sufficiently advanced to permit the regime to embark on its long term social policies by summer 1934.

The Women's Section of the Labour Front was responsible for the welfare and indoctrination of seven million women — all employed women apart from 'assisting family members' — and therefore required a large staff. By 1938 it had indeed built up a formidable network, with 291 women — fifty-two of them full-time — in Gau offices, 643 in Kreis offices, and 9,073 in Ortsgruppe units. These were the administrators; in addition, there were 47,870 representatives in factories and businesses, and 1,000 factory social workers, including 200 trainees; together, these last two figures constituted a four-fold increase over pre-1933 figures.[3] Thus employment was provided for a number of women in an area approved by the Government, and a degree of control and surveillance was maintained over the female work force.

The factory social workers fulfilled a variety of functions; they acted as advisers on employees' welfare to the management and the Council of Trustees; they were counsellors in disputes between workers and on personal problems; and they were to be consulted about the employment or dismissal of female employees. In particular, they were to supervise the maintenance of a high standard of hygiene in factories. To familiarise them with the position of working women, factory social workers had a spell of working on the shop floor; this was in addition to obtaining a qualification in social work, performing Labour Service, and attending a training camp run by the Women's Section. There was one further requirement: 'naturally', stressed the official literature on the subject, 'for such vital work a commitment to National Socialism ... is essential'. Any possibility of organised unrest among women workers was eliminated by the device of appointing this 'politically reliable' factory social worker – who was subordinate to the Women's Section and instructed to cooperate with management – to the post of shop steward, in which capacity she was supposed to act as sole representative of the female work force in any dealings with the management, the Trustees of Labour, and the Women's Section of the Labour Front.[4]

In addition to this vital function, in the Nazi view, of creating harmony between capital and labour – or, more accurately, a docile labour force – under the direction of the State, the Women's Section had four main tasks to fulfil. Frau Scholtz-Klink characterised these as social welfare for employed women, protection of their childbearing capacity at work, the evolving of more comprehensive labour legislation, and the provision of courses in practical housekeeping for women and girls who had worked since leaving school, to give them basic knowledge of and experience in the running of a home.[5] This last task was seen as particularly important, and working women were encouraged to take part in the domestic science and child care courses devised by the women's organisation. Although the fees for the course were waived for women who paid membership dues to the Labour Front, the women nevertheless had to attend the courses in their free time; it is therefore perhaps surprising that by 1937 as many as 600,000 working women were estimated to have attended a course.[6] Although this figure represented rather less than 10 per cent of working women, it seems reasonably successful, since there was no real incentive and no coercion, but only a barrage of propaganda in favour of attendance.

The three other major tasks of the Women's Section were broadly concerned with the health and welfare of the working woman. There was collaboration with the NSV to provide advice for pregnant women at work and to ensure that a woman's financial position was secure around the time of her confinement. Naturally, the interests of individual women were here purely incidental to the top priority of ensuring that working women would bear healthy children. This preoccupation was also at the root of other measures which undoubtedly brought benefit to individuals; for example, women were encouraged to avail themselves of the recreational facilities of the Labour Front's 'Strength through Joy' section.[7] Some women were afforded extra paid holidays because students, in vacation, and *NS-Frauenschaft* members who were not themselves employed volunteered for unpaid factory work for this purpose. In fact, between March 1935 and the end of 1938 6,001 women were replaced by 5,063 volunteers, who provided 86,072 extra days of paid leave.[8] These singularly unimpressive figures suggest that for once the Nazis were using the term 'voluntary' correctly. Nevertheless, official propaganda portrayed this venture as illustrative of the new community spirit that had developed in Germany since 1933, after the deep divisions of the 1920s; and it had the additional virtue of costing the Government nothing.

The Women's Section of the Labour Front claimed to be tackling the vexed problem of removing women from unsuitable, damaging work. Indeed, its representatives made reports about conditions at work, and sometimes proposed measures to remedy shortcomings.[9] But this tended to reflect local problems which were difficult to cope with in a rational way by a centralised organisation. The Government preferred to concentrate on working out broad measures which would have a beneficial effect throughout the country, and it produced a fairly creditable list of laws to deal with some of the worst problems. As early as July 1934 a law restricting the number of hours women might work, specifying the amount of overtime they might do under special circumstances, and completely banning nightwork for women in medium sized and large concerns after 10 p.m., was passed.[10] Women were banned from the most arduous kinds of work in a variety of industries, laws being passed in 1937, for example, restricting their employment in pottery and confectionery manufacture to light work which would not impose an unhealthy strain on them. And plans were afoot to try to ensure that women did not do potentially damaging work in home industry.[11] Further piecemeal legislation was enacted throughout the 1930s,[12] but it was all regarded as an interim solution only, until the Government could achieve its aim of drawing up a comprehensive Maternity Protection Law.[13] This was finally done in wartime, when the need to bring as many women as possible into industry was already vitiating the effectiveness of existing legislation.[14] The Maternity Protection Law, effective from 1 July 1942, in a modified form to meet the exigencies of war, was designed to protect not only pregnant women and nursing mothers, but all working women; the Government expected to amend and extend it substantially after the war.[15]

How much real influence the Women's Section of the Labour Front had is hard to judge. It would probably be fair to say that its effectiveness lay in the control it could exert over the female work force, chiefly in the negative sense of preventing industrial unrest. Its influence in policy making was, however, negligible. Indeed women benefited from protective legislation and from improved hygiene and welfare at work, but this happened because it was an integral part of the Government's population policy, not because of pressure by the Women's Section. Its ineffectiveness is illustrated by the failure to achieve a narrowing of wage differentials between the sexes,[16] although from 1935 it claimed to be campaigning for equal pay for equal work.[17] Such equalisation of wages as there was came about precisely to remove women from unsuitable employment.[18] With its desire to limit wage rises as far as possible, and with, in addition, the lower priority accorded to the consumer goods sector, in which women chiefly figured, the Government had no intention of restructuring wages.[19] It would, after all, be an expensive business, since not even a Nazi Government would have tried to lower men's wages to achieve equal pay, particularly in time of full employment, in the later 1930s. The only alternative was to raise women's wages, and the Government would not contemplate that.

When Hitler's Government actively began to prepare for the eventuality of war in the foreseeable future, in 1935-6, there was a rapid transition from a programme of job creation to attempts to tap every possible source of labour, for it quickly became clear that the most pressing problem would be a shortage of labour where there had so recently been mass unemployment. Therefore the reintroduction of conscription and the stepping up of rearmament openly and on a massive scale from March 1935 were supplemented by the National Service Law of May 1935. This provided that in time of war there should be conscription into the war industry and essential services of all men aged between fifteen and sixty-five who were not called up for military service, and of all women in the same age group who neither had children under fifteen to look after nor were pregnant. This as yet unpublished measure was to be the legal basis for ensuring that there would be sufficient armaments and food supplies once vast numbers of men had been transferred from their civilian occupations into the armed forces.[20]

The Government was well aware, however, that the National Service Law would by no means solve all the problems caused by massive conscription into the armed forces. A report made in February 1937 drew attention to how in the Great War all belligerent countries had experienced a drop in productivity, Germany's being about 20 per cent. This was primarily because men who were accustomed to certain jobs had had to be replaced by people — often women — who were unfamiliar with them, and often unsuited to them. With women only marginally represented during the 1930s in industries vital to the waging of war, it was likely that Germany would experience similar difficulties in a future war, unless action were taken at once. Investigations were already under way to ascertain which industries would provide employment possibilities for women once men had been withdrawn; this would be facilitated by the temporary lifting of restrictions on the employment of women in heavy industry, in cases where it seemed to be in the national interest. But the report also sounded a note of caution, pointing out that, as in the Great War, it would no doubt emerge that many of the women available for work had little experience of employment, and would be unlikely to make a valuable contribution to a war effort.[21] It was largely with this in mind that the Government was to try its utmost, particularly from 1938, to persuade as many women as possible to work, and particularly to find jobs in areas which had hitherto been exclusively or predominantly male preserves.

One useful indicator of the employment situation was the Government's attitude to the granting of marriage loans. The condition that the wife or fiancée must give up her job to be eligible for a loan had been applied strictly in time of high unemployment; but what would happen to this condition — claimed to be partly ideological — when there was full employment? Sure enough, the first slackening of the rule came shortly before the formulation of the Four Year Plan: at the end of July 1936 the Finance Minister was empowered to allow the wife in a loan aided marriage in exceptional cases to take a job even if her husband were not indigent.[22] Six months later, Reinhardt announced that the wives of students and of men performing Labour Service or military service should count as exceptions automatically under the previous ruling.

This move was welcomed by *Die Frau* as a clear restoration of women's freedom to work, in certain cases, regardless of their marriage loan.[24] Reinhardt's purpose was more pragmatic: in March 1936 wives of men in the Labour Service or the armed forces had been declared eligible for an allowance if they were unable to support themselves;[25] clearly, an anomaly existed whereby women in loan aided marriages might be unable to support themselves because of a legal restriction, and not necessarily because of family commitments. The Government might, then, be in the curious position of paying some women twice for not working, even if they were able and willing to work and, in 1936, at a time when there were job vacancies for them; Reinhardt's order thus saved the Government money, provided labour and removed the anomaly.

But the real change came in November 1937, in a law retroactive to 1 October 1937, which superseded all previous marriage loan legislation. It reaffirmed the proviso that the future wife must have held a job for at least nine months out of the two years preceding the application for the loan. But no mention was made of the wife's obligation to give up her job to be eligible for a loan.[26] The result was that it now became a condition of receiving a loan that the woman had worked for a substantial period since autumn 1935, when unemployment was well under control. This was a neat way of completely reversing the purpose of the marriage loan scheme at a time when labour was becoming scarce, for those seeking a loan would now have to arrange for a woman who was not already working to take a job for nine months. The scheme had apparently served its initial purpose well enough; by the end of 1937, 878,016 loans had been made,[27] so that at least three quarters of a million women must have given up work. But no doubt a substantial number of these would have married and left work — to start a family — even if there had not been a marriage loan scheme, so that its real effect is difficult to gauge.

Even with the shortage of labour creating anxiety by the end of 1937, the Government insisted that girls of fourteen or fifteen should not go straight from school into a factory, for 'biological' reasons.[28] Here, it seemed, the Nazis were not prepared to sacrifice a vital principle to growing necessity. There was, however, an ulterior motive. The municipal authorities in Hanover had already, in spring 1936, stipulated that in future girls would have to wait for a year after leaving school before being admitted to an apprenticeship in the area; further, preference would be given at the end of that year to girls who had in the interim engaged in work within the broad category of domestic science.[29] Now, in December 1937, the Labour Front followed this example, advising young girls throughout the country to spend a year between school and first employment in work of a domestic nature, to safeguard their physical development at the crucial age of puberty, and to ensure that they had some experience of the tasks they would encounter when they married.[30]

This still did not tell the whole story. The chief consideration was that the severe unemployment among domestic servants during the depression had now given way to a shortage which might be at least partially offset by encouraging young girls to spend a year in domestic service; if this became automatic, there would be a constant supply of labour in this area, even if the turnover were rather rapid. The problem had already been highlighted when Reinhardt announced that the tax relief granted in June 1933 to employers of domestic servants would be restricted to families with young children, who, for reasons of population policy, would continue to receive the rebate. But there was now no reason to provide incentives for the childless to employ a domestic servant.[31] The other area which was losing labour in an alarming manner was agriculture;[32] this, like the loss to domestic service, was a continuation of a trend already evident in the 1920s, but interrupted by the depression.[33] Already in May 1937 it had been announced that the employment exchange in Magdeburg would exercise strict control in future to stem the flow of women from work on the land, where they were urgently needed, into serving in the town's cafes.[34]

By contrast, women were increasingly choosing to work in industry in the later 1930s: while their share had dropped from 29.3 per cent of the industrial labour force in 1933 to 24.7 per cent in 1936, by

June 1939, at a time of full male employment, it had again risen to 27 per cent. In absolute terms, whereas both the 1925 and 1933 censuses had recorded almost 11.5 million women in employment, in mid-May 1939 the figure was 12.7 million; this meant that 37 per cent of the German labour force was female even before the outbreak of war.[35] Thus, the available reserve of women had been partially exhausted before men were conscripted into the armed forces in large numbers,[36] at a time when the total number of women of working age was falling because of the trend in the birth rate earlier in the century.

The increase in women's employment in 1939 was largely due to the appearance of women in work in which they had, on the whole, not formerly been found, since the areas which traditionally had a high proportion of women employees now had a low priority. In particular, women were being drawn into the transport services, whether as clerkesses or ticket collectors in the railways administration or as conductresses on trams.[37] And in June 1939 it was reported that in Bremen, among other cities, women were now being employed to deliver the post.[38] Somewhat sanctimoniously, the *Völkischer Beobachter* remarked on its pleasure at each manifestation of a changing attitude in those branches of employment where women had hitherto had to struggle against prejudice − prejudice, the paper failed to add, which it had formerly done its utmost to foster. The change in attitude, continued the homily, was noticeable in banking and insurance, where it was now realised that women could be employed in order to release men for occupations which only they could do; this doubtless meant active service.[39]

If it was relatively easy to justify the admission of women to work which they had not been accustomed to perform, and to explain the positive enthusiasm now officially accorded to employed women, given the obvious shortage of labour, the encouragement being given to married women to take a job was a more sensitive matter. *Der Angriff* adopted a characteristically direct approach, posing the question in January 1938: 'Why are married women working?' Its answer was equally frank, namely that the chief factor of economic significance was the glaring shortage of labour, so that the old campaign against the *Doppelverdiener* was now irrelevant.[40] The steep drop in the birth rate from the war years up to the *Machtübernahme* meant that there would soon be a severe drop in the number of workers available, so that women, both married and single, would have to be brought into employment in larger numbers than ever before.[41]

The *Völkischer Beobachter* went even further in October 1938, pointing out that the increase in women's employment had been so steep since 1936, and especially during 1938, that the only reserve of labour left, for further expansion of the economy, was among married women who were not already employed. The nation now needed the service of middle-class wives, who might have a grown-up family or be childless, and whose day was not fully occupied, especially if they employed a domestic servant. Women would have to take an increasing share in industrial work, but, of course this would be accompanied by increasing labour and maternity protection measures on grounds of population policy.[42]

Alice Rilke, of the Women's Section of the Labour Front, was less sanguine. She felt deep concern that married women, and especially mothers, were being drawn into industrial work in ever increasing numbers, and could see justification for it in the short term only, as a matter of urgent national necessity. It was not that she opposed the employment of women; rather, she believed that the long term needs of the nation, namely the health of future generations, necessitated a sensible division of labour between men and women, so that the 'hundreds of thousands of women' still involved in work that was too taxing physically could change places with the similar number of men who did relatively light work.[43] But this solution, too, was rather facile, particularly when it was envisaged that in wartime women would not merely augment but in large measure have to replace the male labour force.

So great was the desire to attract married women into work that, despite the misgivings of many employers, half-day shift work was recommended by the Government, for those women who were reluctant to commit themselves to full-time employment when they also had a family to look after. The first reports on this experiment, in spring 1939, were generally favourable. The benefit felt by the women themselves was stressed: now they had the strength for their two tasks, at home and at work, now those who had changed from full-time to part-time employment were no longer permanently harassed. In addition, there was higher productivity among women working a five hour day than among those reduced to exhaustion by the eight hour day.[44]

Seeing enormous possibilities in the half-day system, the Employment Minister ordered investigations in summer 1939 to consider where else it might be applied.[45] The clothing industry around Mönchen-Gladbach and Rheydt was one area in which it was claimed, in August 1939, that the experiment of a four and a half hour day had proved a happy one.[46] It was not only in wage earning occupations that married women were now found to be in demand; the authorities hoped to persuade married women with secretarial or clerical experience to return to work on at least a part-time basis, and were particularly anxious that those with training in welfare or social work should similarly respond.[47]

Piecemeal local restrictions and official exhortations were not, however, a satisfactory way of securing the labour required for an economy geared to the possibility of limited war. There would therefore have to be a concerted effort to mobilise every possible reserve of labour, either by persuading those who had chosen not to work to reconsider, or by imposing a degree of compulsion. It was perhaps characteristic of the Nazis that their policy should fall between these two possibilities — a mixture of considerable persuasion, limited coercion, and eventually threats of rigorous compulsion. The genuine reluctance of a dictatorial regime to try to force its subjects to bow to its will was based on apprehension, even fear, and not respect; but the result was still the failure to achieve its aim of an adequate supply of labour, even in the early years of the Second World War, while women stayed at home, unwilling to work.

One measure of compulsion which had been promised was that 'all young Germans of both sexes' would be required to perform six months' Labour Service.[48] Brüning's emergency measure had been nationalised in 1933, but its function was intended to be more ideological and educational than economic, although at first it proved useful in alleviating both the unemployment situation and the overcrowding of the universities.[49] While the **Labour Service became compulsory for** men from October 1935, however, the Women's Labour Service continued as a separate and still voluntary exercise, with some 12,000 girls at a time working in domestic service or agriculture.[50] Although administrative changes were made, and target numbers raised repeatedly — to 25,000 in 1937-8, to 30,000 by April 1939 and to 50,000 a year later — the Women's Labour Service remained a much smaller concern than the men's,[51] and was not made compulsory until 4 September 1939,[52] when the outbreak of war meant that girls would now have to replace men rather than provide additional labour. It was stressed that the purpose of the Labour Service for girls was above all to provide a pool of auxiliary workers for agriculture.[53] Thus, well before the outbreak of war the primacy of the 'educational' function of the Labour Service was overridden by the desperate need to find labour for agriculture, at a time when the aim was autarky.[54]

For the Government, the drawback about the Labour Service was that it cost money; girls, like boys, lived a communal life in a camp and wore a uniform, the funds for their subsistence and clothing coming from the Ministry of Finance. Krosigk was less than enthusiastic about the expansion of the Labour Service for this reason.[55] But Göring, as Plenipotentiary for the Four Year Plan, devised a less expensive tactic which could be applied to a larger number of girls than those in the Labour Service at any one time. On 15 February 1938 he announced that the Government reserved the right to require all unmarried girls under twenty-five to work for a year in domestic service or agriculture before entering employment, because of the severe shortage of labour in these areas.[56] There was no attempt to disguise the fact that this was a measure intended to fulfil the economic aims of State policy, although it was insisted that its deeper significance lay in the directing of girls into work which was particularly suitable for them in view of their future role as the wives and mothers of Germans.[57]

The Minister responsible for the Employment Exchanges made immediate use of Göring's enabling order: on 16 February he announced that it would apply to girls coming onto the labour market after 28 February 1938; those who had already worked were not to be included. In addition, the order was to apply in the first instance only to girls aiming to work in the textile, clothing or tobacco industries, or in an office, the occupations in which women had traditionally been best represented, but which were the least important in the Nazi scheme of things. But the applicability of the order was very restricted at this time, particularly since exemption was given to girls who had performed Labour Service or farm or domestic work for at least a year; this was extended to include work not classified as full employment for the purposes of the labour book, performed in the family, or with relatives, of the girl provided that there were four or more young children and that the girl was genuinely helping to look after them.[58] No doubt this provided a welcome loophole for some who dreaded being sent to work in a strange household.

To try to ensure that there was the minimum of evasion, it was also announced that all school leavers must present themselves at their local employment exchange within two weeks of leaving school. Failure to comply would result in the imposition of a substantial fine on the legal guardian of the defaulter.[59] It had been estimated that some 140,000 girls, or 30 per cent of those due to leave school in March 1938, had intimated that they had no desire to take a job or learn a trade, and would probably stay at home, at least at first.[60] No doubt the prospect of having to do the year of service before employment had confirmed this intention in many. But now they all had to register at an employment exchange, so that they would either have to provide badly needed labour in areas of paid employment where there was a shortage, or resign themselves to a year's work in agriculture or domestic service before taking a job in a less vital area of employment.

It soon became clear that most girls were opting for a job which exempted them from the obligation to perform the year of service. Further redirection of labour was to be achieved by a new order at the end of 1938 which stipulated that all girls aiming to enter manual or white collar occupations of any kind would be obliged to engage in the compulsory year, if they had not already performed a year of service voluntarily. There was a lengthy list of 'desirable' occupations which were exempted, including auxiliary nursing, welfare work and work with small children, and a provision that exceptions might also be made at the discretion of employment exchange officials.[61] But in summer 1939, when it was ordered that all girls under twenty-five were to engage in a year's service in domestic work or on the land,[62] the priority was clearly the provision of labour for these understaffed areas. Even so, only 188,695 girls performed their compulsory year in 1939-40, although the figure for those starting on their year in 1940 was more promising, at 335,972.[63] The permitting of a number of exempted categories[64] continued to ensure that recruitment for the compulsory year was much less effective than its outward paraphernalia of orders and propaganda suggested.

The result was to leave Germany still with insufficient labour in domestic service and agriculture, which testifies to the skill and ingenuity of girls and their parents in circumventing the new laws. In addition, three Nazi policies were in conflict here: the objectives of directing young unmarried girls into the Labour Service and the year of service, and of increasing the work force in industry, were matched by a preoccupation with encouraging early marriage. It is not inconceivable that the rise in the marriage rate towards the end of 1939 was partly occasioned by some girls' choosing to marry in haste rather than perform service. At any rate, in summer 1939 the employment exchanges were instructed to allow the employment of domestic servants in childless or small families only if demand had been met in large families; this was apparently necessitated by the turning down of vacancies in large families by the girls themselves because there were jobs available which were more to their liking.[65] On the land, too, the situation was so serious that Frau Scholtz-Klink appealed to girls and women who were not employed to give up a few afternoons, a weekend, or longer if possible, to help out at harvest time.[66]

In this increasingly serious situation Hitler's Government went to war, in September 1939; it at once announced that the girls' Labour Service was to be compulsory, and its numbers raised to 100,000; this level was to be achieved by Hierl's conscripting all single girls aged 17 to 25 who were neither in full-time education or employment nor 'assisting family members' working on the land.[67] In general, the central organisation of the expanded girls' Labour Service seems to have been singularly unintelligent. Discontent was perhaps at its highest in Bavaria, where it was complained that girls already working on the land, including some performing their compulsory year, were being conscripted into the Labour Service. Even worse, girls in the compulsory year scheme were volunteering for Labour Service in the hope of reducing the total time they would have to spend in service;[68] and farm workers were incensed when they realised that the Labour Service girls

worked a much shorter day than they.[69] As a matter of sheer inefficiency, the conscripting of girls familiar with office work of one kind
into office work of another, to replace enlisted men, was a source of
incredulity as well as discontent.[70] But the loudest complaints came
from rural areas, where the situation was such by 1941 that serious
doubts were being raised about the value of continuing to use the
Labour Service for work on the land.[71] Altogether, it is clear that
attempts to use compulsion to make girls work in areas designated by
the Government were largely unproductive; this was partly because of
the failure to implement conscription rigorously, but it was also the
result of the division of control among different agencies — Göring's
office, the Ministry of Employment, the Labour Service — which led
to duplication and contradiction instead of to coordination of the war
effort.

The creation of even a partial war economy, or *Blitzkrieg* economy,[72] in autumn 1939 necessitated the rapid transfer of women into
jobs vacated by men on their conscription into the armed forces, as
had long been anticipated. A law of July 1938, based on the unpublished National Service Law, provided for labour conscription for this
purpose.[73] Transfer was facilitated by a contraction in the consumer
goods industries in which women were chiefly employed,[74] so that
women who lost their job took over the new vacant places in the vital
war industries. It was believed that a short training course would be
sufficient to enable women already accustomed to the routine of
factory work to change from, for example, employment in a textile
factory to work in a munitions factory.[75] In addition, it was felt that
the change should be attractive for those women who were now given
the chance to undertake skilled and specialised work and, therefore, to
earn a higher wage than formerly.[76] The impression given was that the
entire nation was acting in unison, and that the redeployment of
labour into vital industries was going smoothly. As the *NS-Frauenschaft*'s magazine put it:

> 'Women have taken over at once and in all areas of employment the
> positions of the men who are fighting for Germany, with a natural
> readiness. There exists nowhere a gap, for as soon as a man with-
> draws a reliable and eager woman moves into his job.'[77]

It was natural that in time of war articles on the vital subject of
labour supply should be presented in a confident manner. But it was
soon apparent to the Government that the situation was far from satisfactory. As had been predicted, women brought into unfamiliar work
could not adequately replace men who had been used to it; as early as
October 1939, Himmler's agents were reporting that 'especially in
armaments factories, productivity has declined considerably, most of all

106

among the women'.[78] But unfamiliarity with the work was not the only reason for this; discontent at conditions of work soon became a major source of concern. As the National Service Law had provided, there was in September 1939 the suspension of at least some of the restrictions which had formerly protected women from having to work long and unsocial hours, so that in munitions factories they might be required to work for between 10½ and 13 hours per day, whether on day shift or night shift. This had dramatic results in a Kiel factory, where it was established that a series of explosions in October 1939 had been due not to sabotage attempts — as had at first been suspected — but to the exhaustion and consequent inefficiency of the women workers.

Only in a few places were eight hour shifts now in force, and women workers showed their discontent with the long hours by reporting sick or taking days off when their applications for holidays were refused, because the managers of war industries were not permitted to grant them.[79] The main complaints made by the women were that they did not have enough time to clean the house, wash clothes, go shopping or visit relatives, and that even an eight hour day was oppressive since many of them had to spend time travelling a long distance to work in addition. Mothers with children of school age found looking after them difficult enough; those with infants were faced with the problem that there were very few crèches.

The medical profession warned of the detrimental effect that long shifts on a long term basis might have on women's health and, especially, on their reproductive capacity, and suggestions were made that five hour shifts be introduced, carrying the earlier experiments with half-day working into war industry. This would be beneficial from several points of view: it would protect women from overwork; it would give them time to attend to their domestic duties; and, it was hoped, it would encourage more women to volunteer for work, since the long hours had so far acted as a considerable disincentive.[80] But the very fact that relatively few women were prepared to volunteer for work meant that those who were employed had to continue working long hours, and this led to mounting discontent which resulted early in 1940 in a decline in the number of women working.[81]

This was precisely the opposite of what the Government had hoped to achieve, but in many respects it had only itself to blame. In spite of its own enabling legislation, it had failed even to try to implement conscription of female labour. Thus, it had fallen back on propaganda to try to achieve its aim by attracting volunteers. But not only were hours and conditions of work sufficiently disadvantageous to discourage potential volunteers; wages, too, were thoroughly unattractive, and complaints were made continually about them. Some women asked what happened to the money firms saved by employing them instead of the men they had formerly had to pay at a higher rate; others were simply aggrieved because they had been transferred from their peacetime jobs to war industry where they earned substantially less, because they were unfamiliar and therefore slow with the work, and remuneration was on a piece work basis.[82] Managers of firms, as well as women workers, demanded a reform of the wage structure on the basis of equal pay for equal work regardless of sex,[83] but the Government stated that it had no intention of undertaking fundamental reforms of this nature in wartime,[84] although the need to attract women workers was becoming acute.

Even under these unsatisfactory conditions it might have been expected that many married women would have had no choice but to work, for purely financial reasons; husbands were now at the front, no longer providing for their families. The Government had itself, however, provided the solution for many women; in a law introduced in March 1936, and extended in July 1939, it had been decreed that an allowance would be provided for the families of men serving their country in the armed forces. In fact, it had been made abundantly clear in 1939 that each person entitled to this allowance was nevertheless required to work for a living unless youth, old age, ill health or taxing family commitments made this undesirable. The provisions applying specifically to women clearly allowed the exemption from this obligation of those who had the running of a household or the care of relatives to cope with, as well as of those whose employment would 'endanger the stable upbringing of children'.[85]

The intention here had been to avoid a situation where those who were unfit for work, and who had not had to work in peacetime, found that the source of their support had been removed and were now obliged, perhaps in distressing circumstances, to go out to work in order to survive. This was a laudable enough purpose. But the actual result was that, as employment exchanges reported in February 1940, a great number of married women who had previously been employed had given up work now that they were receiving their allowance as wives of enlisted men.[86] This, as Stuckart pointed out, was the case even with women who had worked before the war, out of necessity; now, their allowance obviated this need. The Government would therefore have to aim to arrest the resulting decline in the number of employed women.[87]

Meanwhile, reports of a continuation of this trend were still coming in, as more men were called up and more wives therefore became eligible for the allowance; in addition, working women who married serving soldiers were also entitled to it. The main reason for the rising number of retirements was that a substantial part of a woman's earnings was counted against her allowance, and an amount accordingly deducted.[88] Thus, in addition to the other considerable disadvantages attaching to employment, there was a positive financial disincentive to deter those eligible for the allowance from going out to work.

The failure to attract women into employment, and particularly into war industry, led to demands for coercion and even compulsion. The Mayor of Berlin complained in March 1940 that even childless wives of soldiers had given up work and were living on their allowance, and urged that the law be changed to prevent this.[89] Seldte, as Minister of Employment, was anxious to do so, and he and Stuckart collaborated in drafting a bill for the compulsory employment of women in the war effort. At the same time, discussions were taking place to frame legislation to compel women in receipt of the dependant's allowance to return to work if they did not fall into any of the exempted categories.[90] But the Government saw legislation as a last resort and hoped that a propaganda campaign would still produce the desired result.

The propaganda centred around the threat of introducing compulsion which, it was hoped, would persuade enough women that sooner or later they would be obliged to work, and that they might as well volunteer before they were conscripted. Not surprisingly, however, the threat had the opposite effect: the majority of women saw no point in volunteering at once if they were bound to be conscripted in any case.[91] Even Hitler's public references to the need to bring women into war work to back up the efforts of Germany's soldiers in the field[92] brought no response; no doubt Germany's very success in the war in 1940 and 1941, and the triumphant propaganda about it at home, helped to convince many that their contribution was not needed, and that the war would soon be brought to a victorious conclusion.

Not until 30 June 1941 was an order issued instructing the authorities who paid the dependant's allowance to examine each case with a view to giving women the choice of returning to work — if there seemed no genuine obstacle to this — or forfeiting their allowance. By late September 1941 over 80,000 cases has been examined, over 40 per cent of which had been judged justifiable. According to one source, only 17 per cent of the total had so far taken a job, but only 293 women had positively refused to do so; an immediate reduction in their allowance had led fifty-two of them to change their mind. There was caution about these figures, however, since they differed from those presented by the employment exchanges, which showed a higher number of those who had had their allowance reduced because of their refusal to work, and a lower number of those who returned to work.[93]

The poor results of this measure left the issue of labour conscription open, until at a meeting on 7 November 1941, Göring intimated that Hitler now felt that women who had so far refused to work would be workers of little value, and that in any case there were strong physiological grounds for objecting to women's doing strenuous work. The intention was therefore not now to try to increase women's employment by any means, but rather to reduce it when enough prisoners of war had been set to work.[94] This decision to abandon attempts to coerce women into war industry without actually imposing conscription came at a time when Hitler and his advisers still believed that Russia would be defeated by *Blitzkrieg* tactics and the partial war economy, although their confidence soon began to wane.[95]

The effects of the decision were, in fact, chiefly bad for Germany: industry desperately needed extra labour; and women already working were incensed by the unfairness, in their view, of their having been persuaded or even dragooned into work while those who had steadfastly refused to work in the face of strong pressure were now rewarded by being left alone. The circumstances of the working woman, which had caused so much discontent from the start of the war, had not been improved, and women with large families as well as a job were grossly overburdened while childless wives and single girls, who were making no contribution to the war effort, could, for example, shop for scarce commodities at leisure.[96] There was also the social divisiveness — at a time when national unity was the aim — of the fact that middle-class women and girls had been slow to volunteer in the first place, and had been ready with reasons or plausible excuses for resisting propaganda and pressure directed at persuading them to work.[97] Stuckart, for one, had argued that conscription would have the benefit of being seen by the population as a whole to apply to those who had so far chosen to be unproductive in time of national emergency, regardless of their station in life.[98] His voice went unheeded; whether the reasons Hitler gave in November 1941 were the real ones for abandoning the idea of compulsion, or whether the Government was anxious not to lose face if a conscription order were widely evaded, Germany was as a result desperately short of labour for war industry, and this was a major reason for her ultimate defeat.

At first sight, Nazi policy towards the employment of women appears to have experienced an ideological *volte-face*, with the crude, early demands for the return of women to the home being replaced by almost equally crude demands that women seek work to release men for the armed forces. But it is reasonably clear that the ultimate aim of Nazi policy towards women was to create a situation in which women could indeed return to the home once the German nation had achieved its 'rightful' place in the world. Even during the war, when the Government was still trying to break down the strong resistance on the part of many women towards going out to work, the debate continued about whether women should, in principle, be employed. While it was seen as

110

a bitter becessity that almost 12 million women should be working in 1940, the long term ideal was the creation of a situation where the German woman could be a full-time housewife.[99]

This was indeed a departure from the liberal view that each individual should be given the chance to find his or her *métier* in the way and at the pace he or she chose. But it was entirely consistent with the Nazi view that the interests of the State must have top priority. In wartime particularly, however, it quickly became clear that there was some disagreement and even confusion in the upper echelons of the Government and the Party as to what precisely were the interests of the State. Whereas in Britain there was no doubt that the top priority was the defeat of Nazi Germany, and that the compulsory direction of women between 18 and 50 into at least part-time work was essential for the war effort,[100] in Germany it was hoped by many, and even believed by some, that such an expedient would not be necessary.

The result was an absence of positive direction from the centre, so that local Labour Front representatives were to be found making 'official' utterances which were often not only different from each other but even positively contradictory.[101] This vagueness was partly the product of reluctance to antagonise the population by introducing unpopular policies. Perhaps even more fundamentally, it resulted from the division of opinion between the ideologues, who were determined to implement Party theory, even when it was totally impractical, and the men — like Seldte and Stuckart — who had to make the system work. In the case of trying to coerce women into war work, this combination of fear of popular discontent and ideological stubbornness led to the abandoning, until 1943, of attempts to force women to provide the labour Germany vitally needed. The arbitrary decision of the Führer, a man whose views were increasingly removed from reality, was sufficient to ensure that the long term Nazi obsession with protecting women 'biologically' took precedence over the essential immediate aim of ensuring the survival of the Third Reich.

NOTES

1.   BA, *Slg. Sch.*, 230, 'Einrichtung eines Frauenamtes in der DAF', order by Robert Ley, 12 July 1934.
2.   Details of this are given in Chapter 9, pp. 164-5.
3.   BA, *op. cit.*, 'Reichsfrauenführung Jahresbericht 1938', p. viii.
4.   *Ibid., Der Führerorden*, 'Die Aufgaben des Frauenamtes der DAF', 15.11.35.
5.   'Vier Jahre Einsatz für die schaffende deutsche Frau in Fabrik und Büro', *VB*, 14 May 1937.
6.   Alice Rilke, 'Frauenerwerbstätigkeit im neuen Deutschland', *FK*, January 1937, p. 11.

7.   BA, *loc. cit.*; 'Frauencongress am Nürnberg: Frau Scholtz-Klink über die Frau im Beruf', *FZ*, 15 September 1935.
8.   BA, *op. cit.*, 'Reichsfrauenführung Jahresbericht', p. viii.
9.   BA, R2/18554, letter from Marie Stoess to the Ministry of Finance, 27 September 1935.
10.   'Arbeitszeitordnung', *RGB*, 1934 I, 26 July 1934, pp. 807-12.
11.   BA, R22/2073, Generalakten des Justizministeriums, 'Neue Sozialgesetze in Vorbereitung', 3 June 1937.
12.   For example, 'Ausführungsverordnung zur Arbeitszeitordnung', *RGB*, 1938 I, 12 December 1938, pp. 1800-01; 'Glashüttenverordnung', *RGB*, 1938 I, 23 December 1938, pp. 1961-5; 'The Law and Women's Work', *op. cit.*, pp. 294-6, lists a number of measures.
13.   BA, *op. cit.*, letter from Wever at the Ministry of Finance to the Reich Ministers etc., 17 November 1938.
14.   'The Employment of Women Workers during the War', *ILR*, 1939, vol. 40, p. 802. Provision had been made in advance for the suspension of labour protection measures for women in the event of war, IfZ, MA 468, frame 5723, 'Arbeitseinsatz im Kriege', 2 February 1937.
15.   BA, *op. cit.*, 'Entwurf: Gesetz zum Schutze der arbeitenden Mutter (Mutterschutzgesetz)', 1940 (exact date not given). A second draft was produced on 23 February 1941, and the law finally passed on 17 May 1942; Martha Moers, *Der Fraueneinsatz in der Industrie*, Berlin, 1943, p. 144.
16.   Bry, *op. cit.*, pp. 100-01, 247, shows that throughout the Nazi period wage differentials remained very much what they had been in the Weimar period. For these, see Chapter 4, pp. 75 and 79. 'Indexziffern der Arbeitsverdienste', *WuS*, 1940, no. 18, p. 433, and *St. J.*, 1941-2, p. 390, give illustrative figures.
17.   'Das Frauenamt der DAF', *Deutsches Frauenschaffen*, 1938, p. 50.
18.   See Chapter 4, p. 89.
19.   'Die Frauenlohn im Kriege', *FZ*, 20 March 1940.
20.   IfZ, *op. cit.*, frame 5719, *op. cit.*
21.   *Ibid.*, frames 5719-23.
22.   'Sechste Durchführungsverordnung über die Gewährung von Ehestandsdarlehen', *RGB*, 1936 I, 28 July 1936, p. 576.
23.   'Wiederbeschäftigung von Empfängerinnen von Ehestandsdarlehen', *RAB*, 1937 I, no. 4, 19 January 1937, p. 24.
24.   'Frauenarbeit trotz Ehestandsdarlehen', *Die Frau*, May 1937, p. 463.
25.   'Familienunterstützungsgesetz', *RGB*, 1936 I, 30 March 1936, p. 327.
26.   'Drittes Gesetz zur Änderung des Gesetzes über die Förderung der Eheschliessungen', *RGB*, 1937 I, 3 November 1937, pp. 1158-9.
27.   Calculated from figures in *St. J.*: 1936, p. 42; 1937, p. 44; 1938, p. 48.
28.   Mädel am Arbeitsplatz', *VB*, 25 December 1937.
29.   'Lehrstellen für Mädchen erst ein Jahr nach Schulentlassung', *FZ*, 6 May 1936.
30.   *VB, loc. cit.*
31.   'Beschränkung der Steuerermässigung für Hausangestellte', *FZ*, 9 October 1937.
32.   Mason, *op. cit.*, discusses this; see particularly pp. 651-4.
33.   Michalke, *op. cit.*, p. 437. See Chapter 4, p. 86.
34.   'Weibliche Arbeitskräfte vom Lande (Magdeburg)', *FZ*, 22 May 1937.
35.   Figures from *St. J.*: 1933, p. 19; 1939-40, p. 386. And from *Statistisches Jahrbuch für die Bundesrepublik Deutschland*, 1959, p. 9.
36.   Dietmar Petzina, 'Die Mobilisierung deutscher Arbeitskräfte vor und während des Zweiten Weltkrieges', *VjhZ*, 1970, p. 449, comments on this.
37.   'Die Reichsbahn stellt die Frau ein', *FZ*, 7 April 1939; reports in *FZ*,

18 June 1939 and 2 July 1939.
38.   Report in *FZ*, 18 June 1939.
39.   'Einsatzmöglichkeiten für die Frau', *VB*, 19 July 1939.
40.   'Von uns notiert . . . : Warum arbeitet die verheiratete Frau?', *Der Angriff*, 26 January 1938.
41.   Walter Stothfang, 'Verstärkung der Frauenarbeit', *Der Angriff*, 26 August 1938.
42.   'Die Frauenarbeit in der Gesamtwirtschaft', *VB*, 22 October 1938.
43.   BA, NSD30/1836, *Informationsdienst* . . . , August 1939, Alice Rilke, 'Die Frauenberufs- und Erwerbstätigkeit in der Betrachtung des medizinisch-bevölkerungspolitischen Schrifttums', p. 190 (first published in January 1939).
44.   BA, *op. cit.*, Ilse Buresch-Riebe, 'Erfahrungen bei der Beschäftigung von Frauen in Halbtagsschicht', p. 190 (first published in April 1939).
45.   'Die Halbtagsarbeit für verheiratete Frauen', *FZ*, 9 July 1939.
46.   'Die Beschäftigung verheirateter Frauen', *FZ*, 4 August 1939.
47.   Report in *Die Frau*, June 1939, p. 499.
48.   'Reichsarbeitsdienstgesetz', *RGB*, 1935 I, 26 June 1935, pp. 769-71.
49.   Benz, *op. cit.*, pp. 333-7; c.f. the propagandist picture in Freising, *op. cit.*, pp. 42-3. More is said about the last point in Chapter 7, pp. 134 and 140-41.
50.   BA, *Slg. Sch.*, 262, Karl Pollmann, 'Die Reichsanstalt für Arbeitsvermittlung und Arbeitslosenversicherung und der Deutsche Frauenarbeitsdienst', *Deutscher Arbeitsdienst*, Sonderausgabe: 'Der Deutsche Frauenarbeitsdienst', ? summer 1935, p. 3.
51.   See orders in *RGB*: 1936 I, 15 August 1936, p. 633; 1936 I, 26 September 1936, p. 747; 1937 I, 24 November 1937, p. 1298; 1938 I, 7 September 1938, p. 1157.
52.   'Verordnung über die Durchführung der Reichsarbeitsdienstpflicht für die weibliche Jugend', *RGB*, 1939 I, 4 September 1939, p. 1693.
53.   'Arbeitsdienstpflicht der weiblichen Jugend und Hilfe in der Landwirtschaft', *VB*, 2 July 1936.
54.   On the limitations on autarky, see Berenice A. Carroll, *Design for Total War*, The Hague, 1968, p. 103; Chapter VII is devoted to a discussion of the Four Year Plan; see also Dieter Petzina, *Autarkiepolitik im Dritten Reich*, Stuttgart, 1968, pp. 197-8.
55.   *RGB, loc. cit.*; BA, R2/4525, letter from Krosigk to Frick, 14 October 1938.
56.   'Anordnung zur Durchführung des Vierjahresplans über den verstärkten Einsatz von weiblichen Arbeitskräften in der Land- und Hauswirtschaft', 15 February 1938, *Deutscher Reichsanzeiger*, no. 43, 21 February 1938.
57.   Max Timm, 'Das Pflichtjahr für Mädchen', *RAB*, 1938 II, no. 7, 5 March 1938, p. 75. I am most grateful to Dr T. W. Mason for generously sending me a copy of this article.
58.   'Durchführungsanordnung zur Anordnung über den verstärkten Einsatz von weiblichen Arbeitskräften in der Land- und Hauswirtschaft', 16 February 1938, *Deutscher Reichsanzeiger, op. cit.*
59.   'Anordnung über die Meldung Schulentlassener', 1 March 1938, *Deutscher Reichsanzeiger*, no. 51, 2 March 1938.
60.   'Warum immer neue Forderungen an die Mädel?', *VB*, 10 March 1938.
61.   'Durchführungsverordnung zur Anordnung über den verstärkten Einsatz von weiblichen Arbeitskräften in der Land- und Hauswirtschaft', 23 December 1938, *Deutscher Reichsanzeiger*, no. 305, 31 December 1938.
62.   'Weibliches Pflichtjahr für alle', *Westdeutscher Beobachter*, 12 June 1939.
63.   Figures from *St. J.*, 1941-2, p. 420.
64.   E.g., 'Anrechnung hauswirtschaftlicher Ausbildungen in staatlich aner-

kannten Lehranstalten auf das Pflichtjahr für Mädchen', *RAB*, 1940 I, 15 March 1940, p. 102, and 'Pflichtjahr für Mädchen; hier: Befreiung durch Besuch der Berufsfachschule für Hotel- und Gaststättengehilfinnen in Heidelberg', *RAB*, 1940 I, 25 April 1940, p. 184.

65. BA, NSD30/vorl. 1836, *Informationsdienst* . . . , August 1939, 'Hausgehilfinnen und Kinderreiche Familien', p. 189.

66. 'Alle Kräfte werden gebraucht', *Westdeutscher Beobachter*, 24 June 1939.

67. 'Verordnung über die Durchführung des Reichsarbeitsdienstpflicht für die weibliche Jugend', *RGB*, 1939 I, 4 September 1939, p. 1693.

68. BA, *Slg. Sch.*, 262, letters from the Bavarian Minister of the Interior to the Bavarian NSDAP Gau leadership, and from the Bavarian office of the Reichsnährstand to the Bavarian Minister of the Interior, both dated 30 October 1939.

69. IfZ, MA 441/6, frames 2-757123-26, *MadR*, 13 July 1942.

70. IfZ, MA 441/5, frame 2-755206, *MadR*, 10 November 1941.

71. *Ibid.*, frames 2-755478-79, *MadR*, 15 December 1941.

72. Alan Milward, *The German Economy at War*, London, 1965, pp. 7-10, explains this term.

73. 'Gesetz über Leistungen für Wehrzwecke', *RGB*, 1938 I, 13 July 1938, pp. 888-9.

74. Mason, *op. cit.*, pp. 601-2, argues that home consumption was not restricted and no factories producing consumer goods had been closed by early 1940. The reports of Himmler's agents, however, suggest that capacity was run down from September 1939.

75. 'Der Fraueneinsatz in der Kriegswirtschaft', *NS-Frauenwarte*, May 1940, inside of front cover and p. 417.

76. Walter Stothfang, *Der Arbeitseinsatz im Kriege*, Berlin, 1940, pp. 23-5.

77. 'Frauenhände packen zu', *NS-Frauenwarte*, October 1939, p. 210; Ilse Buresch-Riebe, *Frauenleistung im Kriege*, Berlin, 1942, paints a very rosy picture of women's response here, especially pp. 29-38, 45-111.

78. IfZ, MA 441/1, frame 2-750111, *BziL*, 20 October 1939.

79. *Ibid.*, frames 2-750094-95, *BziL*, 16 October 1939.

80. *Ibid.*, frames 2-750490-91, *MadR*, 18 December 1939.

81. BA, R18/3282, letter from Stuckart to Suren, 15 February 1940; IfZ, *op. cit.*, frames 2-750862-63, *MadR*, 19 February 1940.

82. *Ibid.*, frames 2-750440-41, *MadR*, 11 December 1939.

83. *Ibid.*, frame 2-750865, *MadR*, 19 February 1940.

84. 'Die Frauenlohn im Kriege', *FZ*, 20 March 1940.

85. 'Familienunterstützungsgesetz', *RGB*, 1936 I, 30 March 1936, p. 327; 'Verordnung zur Ergänzung und Durchführung des Familienunterstützungsgesetzes', *RGB*, 1939 I, 11 July 1939, pp. 1225-32.

86. BA, R18/3282, letter from Beisiegel, at the Ministry of Employment, to Frick, 15 February 1940.

87. *Ibid.*, letter from Stuckart to Suren, 15 February 1940.

88. IfZ, MA 441/1, frame 2-750864, *MadR*, 19 February 1940.

89. BA, *op. cit.*, letter from the Mayor of Berlin to Krug von Nidda at the Ministry of the Interior, 26 March 1940.

90. *Ibid.*, 'Verordnung zur Durchführung der Verordnung über den Verstärkten Einsatz von Frauen für Aufgaben der Reichsverteidigung', May 1940 (exact date not given); *ibid.*, letter from Stuckart to the Ministerial Council for the Defence of the Nation, 9 May 1940.

91. 'Der Fraueneinsatz in der Kriegswirtschaft', *NS-Frauenwarte*, May 1940, p. 417; Boberach, *op. cit.*, no. 189, 26 May 1941, pp. 146-8. Boberach states that all the talk about and plans for the conscription of female labour were purely for propaganda purposes, to encourage volunteers (p. 147n.). The document

cited suggests, however, that this tactic had precisely the opposite effect.

92.   Domarus, *op. cit.*, quotes two major speeches in which Hitler appealed to German women in these terms, on 16 March 1941 (p. 1674), and on 4 May 1941 (p. 1707-8).

93.   BA, *op. cit.*, letter from Sicha at the National Statistical Office to Krug von Nidda, 27 September 1941.

94.   *Ibid.*, letter from Jacobi to Suren (both at the Ministry of the Interior), 17 November 1941. The number of prisoners of war working in Germany was 294,393 in February 1940; by December 1940 it had risen to 1,178,668. Figures from *St. J.*, 1941-2, p. 424. POWs could clearly provide a substantial reserve of labour.

95.   Milward, *op. cit.*, p. 45; Carroll, *op. cit.*, pp. 229-30.

96.   IfZ, MA 441/6, frames 7412-4, *MadR*, 17 August 1942.

97.   IfZ, MA 441/1, frame 2-750862, *MadR*, 19 February 1940; Boberach, *op. cit.*, p. 148.

98.   BA, *op. cit.*, letter from Stuckart to the Ministerial Council for the Defence of the Nation, 9 May 1940.

99.   Wiener Library Dossier, 'Frauenarbeit', *FZ*, 9 June 1940.

100.   Alva Myrdal and Viola Klein, *Women's Two Roles*, London, 1968, pp. 51-3, gives a brief account of this.

101.   IfZ, MA 441/6, frames 7414-16, *MadR*, 17 August 1942.

6   GIRLS' SENIOR SCHOOLING IN THE 1930s

As a result of the progress made in opening the universities to women before the Great War and providing senior schooling to prepare girls for higher education, the 1920s saw an improvement in educational and professional opportunities for women. This was not, however, universally welcomed. The Nazis were to benefit from the mounting hostility to girl students and professional women in the depression as they attacked the 'Jewish-intellectual' concept of the highly educated woman and the 'liberal-democratic-Marxist' practice of encouraging women to achieve the same aims as men, when their natures were different and complementary.[1] Girls, they said, appeared inferior because they were being judged by the same criteria as boys, criteria irrelevant to the female disposition.[2] Here, as elsewhere, there was some truth in the Nazis' claims: great stress had, after all, been laid on giving girls access to the kind of academic education available to boys, although only a very small — if increasing — minority of schoolgirls was likely to benefit from it. Consistent with Hitler's dictum that 'future motherhood is to be the definite aim of female education',[3] the Nazis promised that in the Third Reich they would free women from the 'masculine elements of education, the intellectual ones, to which they were not suited'.[4]

The Nazis' attitudes were a conglomeration and extension of conservative ideas prevalent at the end of the nineteenth century when women were trying to gain admission to the universities, still apparent after the Great War, and increasingly popular by 1930. The assertion that girls should be educated differently from boys because the sexes were essentially different mentally as well as physically was only a restatement of a view current around 1900.[5] Similarly old fashioned was the idea that women were subjective whereas men were objective, women were emotional and sentimental whereas men were creative and rational; for these reasons women were considered basically unsuited to academic study.[6] The emphasis on the formal and abstract, to the neglect of the actual and practical, had led, the Nazis claimed, to a corruption of girls' education during the Weimar Republic, with girls who valued their essential womanliness treated as exceptions and the 'natural calling' of woman, as housewife and mother, devalued.[7] It was true that in spite of official recognition of the vital place of women 'in the family, in a vocation, or in some other place in the interests of general welfare',[8] the academic senior schools had given no homecraft

116

lessons apart from a little needlework. Domestic science classes were provided only for girls who were not pursuing an academic curriculum, and the *Frauenschule* (Women's School), which conducted them, had been treated as inferior to the other types of girls' senior school.[9]

The Nazis had always criticised the overvaluing of academic study, and their strong anti-intellectualism[10] was complemented by an insistence on the merits of practical occupations. One of the demands of Point 20 of the Party Programme was that teaching curricula be brought into line with the needs of daily life.[11] *Mein Kampf's* version was that priority should be given to physical training, with spiritual nourishment taking second place and academic study a poor third. In this respect, at least, girls' education was to be governed by the same principles as boys'.[12] But the Nazis' basic belief in the need for the 'separate development' of the sexes invested the Party's view of girls' education, and immediately made coeducation anathema.[13] This was another issue on which the Nazis attacked the Weimar 'system'; in the late 1920s, with economic recession, coeducation became more widespread, since small senior classes, and even schools, for girls could be disbanded, and expenditure on salaries and buildings saved. In some Länder, coeducation increased so much that girls formed a very significant proportion of pupils at schools primarily intended for boys. In Thuringia, an extreme case, there were in 1933 more girls attending boys' schools than girls' schools, while in the ten smaller North German states 25 per cent of all girls receiving senior schooling were at boys' schools.[14] Throughout Germany, however, the proportion was smaller, with 35,600 girls at boys' schools in 1931-2, constituting 6.7 per cent of the pupils there; this was a slight increase over the 1926-7 figures of 28,800 and 5.2 per cent.[15]

This development did not signify official acceptance of the principle of coeducation; its merits were vigorously debated throughout the Weimar period, with socialists its chief advocates and the Roman Catholic Church its strongest opponent. It had been accepted as a necessary but temporary measure before 1914 in areas where the only girls' senior school was the *Höhere Töchterschule*, but those who opposed it in principle grew anxious as its incidence increased rather than diminished in the 1920s. Even the relatively enlightened Prussian Education Ministry admitted to being 'seriously opposed to coeducation for reasons based on developmental psychology and educational sociology . . . coeducation, or rather coinstruction, as a makeshift is in a rather different position'.[16] In Bavaria, the power of the Catholic Church and the Bavarian People's Party meant that coeducation was barely a live issue, while in general the Centre Party was able to block attempts to desegregate the sexes. A radical feminist regretted that 'tentative experiments' with coeducation had not succeeded in converting its opponents, and remarked that in village schools, where small numbers made coeducation a necessity, boys and girls sat at opposite sides of the classroom.[17]

Because the Nazis aimed to relate education more to the needs of practical living, girls would, they said, be educated separately from boys, to correspond with the different roles they were destined to play. But while training for the future wives and mothers of Germans was to be provided the need, it was felt, was less for mechanical instruction in housekeeping and child care — although these would definitely figure — than for education to an awareness of the girls' responsibility to the community and to the future generation of Germans.[18] Individualism (a regular Nazi bogey) was to be discouraged, and service — in the family, in the community, at work, even in public life — was to be the motive of education. Announcing this, Hedwig Förster, an official in the Prussian Education Ministry, added that there would be a sharp reduction in the academic content of girls' curricula and a corresponding increase in subjects which would guide girls into occupations of a practical or an artistic nature, particularly into social welfare.[19] The emphasis would be on German history and culture, and on health, family life, and physical exercise. Girls were to be prepared for occupations to which their maternal instincts were relevant, including medicine, social work and teaching in girls' and elementary schools; it was therefore conceded that academic study would have a place in the education of some girls, and that the universities would not be closed to them.[20]

But, above all, the emphasis was to be shifted from the Weimar practice of giving domestic science instruction only to girls who were clearly not academically talented to a system where all girls were given a grounding in the tasks involved in running a home, and where the academically inclined were treated as the exceptions they undoubtedly were. As Hedwig Forster said:

'Only a very small proportion of our girls is ever really suited to purely academic study in a university . . . Immeasurably greater is the number of those who later as wives and mothers, and also as career women, must and want to play a leading part in the special areas of women's work and women's culture.'[21]

With few facilities for domestic science available in the senior schools, the Nazis decided that the easiest way to provide them on the scale they desired was to increase the number of *Frauenschulen*, which were devoted to intensive domestic science education, and to integrate them into the senior school system; this would enhance their status and facilitate a degree of uniformity which had been lacking because of the differences in the development of the *Frauenschule* in the separate

Länder.[22]

From 1933, much was done to upgrade the standard and status of the *Frauenschule*. One-year courses were provided to give a general education to girls who were leaving senior school before taking the *Abitur* (university qualifying examination), while three-year courses were designed to train girls for a variety of occupations deemed particularly suitable for women and not requiring a university degree; these included teaching in primary, technical, art and music schools, youth leadership, and the obvious careers directly connected with domestic science. From Easter 1935 the three-year courses included, besides theoretical and practical training in domestic science, instruction in Nazi ideology: racial 'science', nordic culture, the history of the German peasantry and the development of National Socialism were compulsory for all.[23] The rationalisation of the *Frauenschule* courses was, however, only an interim measure; the final aim was to incorporate them fully into the girls' senior school system. This was finally achieved in the reform of January 1938.

Given the Nazis' outspoken opposition to the educational system of the post-war years, it might have been expected that they would introduce reforms to suit their purposes as quickly as possible after taking power; if the consolidation of political power, the alleviating of economic problems and rearmament were the top priorities, the education of the young was nevertheless a vital area for a regime which would not tolerate dissidence. From 1933-7, however, the Government contented itself with a number of piecemeal measures designed to modify the existing system immediately, until their comprehensive reform was drawn up. Several of the interim measures reflected the Nazi view that education should prepare German girls for their role as wives and mothers. For example, among the qualifications girls required for admission to a Prussian teacher-training college, announced in January 1935, was evidence of proficiency in domestic science, needlework, sport and music.[24] For the senior schools, it was decreed at Easter 1935 that the timetable for each class must include two hours of needlework every week. This would be at the expense of one hour each of English and mathematics, or French, if mathematics had already been reduced by one hour to accommodate biology.[25] With the Nazis' obsession with all matters of race and heredity, it is hardly surprising that biology became compulsory for all school children. As Friederike Matthias, the national spokeswoman on girls' senior schooling, said: 'There is an obvious need for a basic knowledge of biology in girls' senior schools, for the cultivation, development and preservation of our race.'

Fräulein Matthias also believed that the need to include more gymnastics, biology, needlework and German in the girls' curriculum would mean a corresponding reduction in the time given to science, mathematics and foreign languages.[26] But by October 1935 Rust, the Reich Minister of Education, obviously felt that such a development — however desirable — was not practicable, since he announced that the increased demands of academic work in the higher grades of girls' senior schools meant that in future there would be no room for homecraft in their timetable. It was, he added, still nevertheless essential that no girl leave a senior school without knowledge of, and proficiency in, basic domestic science. Therefore a girl's family, especially her mother, should — as he claimed had been the case in former times — educate the daughter systematically in all important household tasks. This was the only apparent alternative to keeping girls at school for an extra year devoted to domestic science, which would be contrary to the Nazi desire to encourage early marriage and motherhood. Rust claimed that academically gifted pupils should have no difficulty in coping with household instruction in addition to their normal school work, and that any problems which might arise could be solved by cooperation between parents and school. To ensure compliance, he ordered that from Easter 1937 girls should be admitted to the upper classes of senior schools only if they could provide evidence of familiarity with the simplest household tasks.[27]

From the start, the Nazi Government had felt that the precondition of effective reform was the elimination from the senior schools of those they considered unsuited to an academic education. Already before 1933 there had been talk of limiting entry to both senior schools and universities,[28] and the Nazis included the senior schools in their law of 25 April 1933, to reduce student numbers.[29] As they succeeded in reducing university student numbers — further than they wished, in the event — so they also achieved a reduction in the number of senior school pupils. The low wartime birth rate affected senior school numbers until 1937, and was a major factor in the drop in the senior school population by 100,000 in the years 1931-4, out of a total of over three quarters of a million in 1931, of whom 283,000 were girls. The failure of the post-war birth rate to match pre-war figures compounded this.

At first, however, the losses were sustained equally by both sexes, so that girls' share remained around 37 per cent in the first half of the decade. Then the girls sustained a slight loss percentually, to leave them with a share of 34.5 per cent in 1938.[30] The reason was the campaign launched by the Nazis against private schools, particularly the Roman Catholic schools of Bavaria, which challenged the Government's authority in the vital area of educating the young.[31] The boys' private schools suffered, too, but the numbers involved were much less significant since there had always been far more private schools for girls. In the State

120

senior schools girls' representation returned to its high level of 1931 and 1932 in 1938 after a slight fluctuation in the middle of the decade, while their absolute numbers, also, were higher than they had been since 1932.[32]

The more favourable position of girls in State senior schools in 1938 was the result of an order issued late in 1936 which shortened boys' senior schooling by one year, because of 'the operation of the Four Year Plan as well as the recruitment needs of the army'.[33] The withdrawal of some 20,000 boys at the end of their twelfth school year, instead of at the end of the thirteenth, in 1937 and 1938 had a small, but noticeable, effect on girls' share in the senior schools,[34] and created an anomalous situation where for almost two years girls were receiving more education, of a kind designated unsuitable for them, than were boys. Rust was aware of the implicit contradiction here, and insisted that this measure was a temporary expedient until the promised reform of the senior schools was prepared.[35] To reinforce this, Trude Bürkner, national leader of the BdM, announced in February 1937 that a reform of the school system was imminent which would relieve girls of the obligation to undergo the kind of education to which they were not suited. This did not mean, she emphasised, that girls' education would be reduced to the notorious '3 K's', as foreigners claimed; the Government was well aware that that would be totally insufficient. The schools should rather prepare girls to be fitting comrades for their future husbands, by giving them instruction in politics, economics and culture;[36] the most important element in girls' schooling, as in boys', then, was to be instruction in the National Socialist view of significant issues, and, indeed, of life as a whole.

At last, on 29 January 1938, Rust published his *Neuordnung des höheren Schulwesens*, the reform of the senior schools. In it, the first point of substance was: 'For important reasons of population policy I have shortened the nine-year period of senior schooling to eight years.' This formalised the provision already made for reducing boys' schooling, and at last brought girls into line with it, although they did not have military service to perform. A substitute was, however, quickly produced, in the form of Göring's proposed year of compulsory service on the land or in domestic work for girls seeking employment for the first time, from March 1938. The Government's order of priorities was thus made perfectly clear: while the desire to encourage early marriage, to promote population growth, was rivalled by the urgent need for cheap labour on the land and in domestic service, these two aims could be largely reconciled by relegating education to third place. Naturally, it was denied that this would happen: Rust insisted that the shortening of schooling must not result in a lowering of standards, and that the *Abitur*, in its traditional form, would remain the goal of senior schooling. He also warned that those unable or unwilling to meet the new requirements would be removed from the senior schools. The new provisions were not, he said, really harsh, since in the Nazi State, school was only one branch of the educational system;[37] for girls, the other branches were the BdM and the Labour Service. These agencies could work in harmony, since they were all ultimately under the same leadership, all working in complementary ways towards the same goals.

In the new plan for the senior schools, every pupil would continue to be scrutinised closely, with a view to eliminating those who had not the ability to make a success of the full course. It was stressed that in structure and aims, schools for boys and schools for girls would be the same.[38] But the plans for the curricula for the senior schools, which accompanied the new order, showed that in content the education given to the two sexes was to differ considerably, chiefly with the effect of weakening the academic constitution of the girls' timetables. This was only what had been promised, particularly since girls' education, as Rust stressed, was not to be merely a poor imitation of boys', which was what post-war developments had made it. The Nazi view was that

> 'the natural difference between the sexes makes itself apparent even in childhood . . . so that the schooling of girls to an awareness of their responsibility to the nation and the State must develop from its own special roots.'

The result was that the cumbersome multiform system of schooling, with its variations in the separate Länder, was dismantled, and a national senior school structure established in which there was a basic type of girls' school which was markedly different from the corresponding basic type of boys' school.

After four years at the *Volkschule* (elementary school) — or three for talented pupils, to achieve a further shortening of schooling if possible — boys proceeded to the first five years of the senior school, which were the same for all; they then had the choice of languages or science as their speciality for the last three years, which meant that there was more time for concentration on the chosen field, but still some instruction in the other. Biology was not included in the scientific option since it was already compulsory. There was, naturally, a strong emphasis also on German and history, but it remained possible for boys to study the classics in an institution which continued to be called the *Gymnasium*. True to their antipathy to the influence of a foreign culture, the Nazis made it plain that this form of senior school was to cater only for a very small minority of boys.

The girls followed the same pattern as the boys, with three or four *Volkschule* years followed by five general senior school years, before specialisation in one of two courses. In the general years, the girls' schooling was substantially the same as the boys', with one significant exception: four hours of Latin each week in the third, fourth and fifth years of the boys' schools were matched by compulsory needlework and a little extra music for the girls. With Latin still a requirement for some university courses, its absence from the girls' curriculum could work to their disadvantage at the higher levels of education. The decisive difference between boys' and girls' schooling came, however, in the last three years. The two options open to the girls were the language stream and the homecraft stream; in the former no domestic science, besides needlework, was taught, while in the latter there was compulsory English for two hours a week, but no chance to learn another foreign language. More positively, the language course allowed girls to choose two foreign languages – one of which might be Latin – in addition to compulsory English, while the domestic science course gave instruction in nursing, social work, work with young children, and household tasks. Both streams included science and mathematics to an extent greater than that provided for boys in the language stream, but significantly smaller than that for boys specialising in science.[39] Thus, no provision was made in the girls' schools for those wishing to specialise in science and mathematics, again putting girls at an immediate disadvantage in the universities. This had doubtless been attractive at a time – when reform of senior schooling was first projected – when there was graduate unemployment; but by the time it was promulgated, even before it became effective, it was out-of-date and potentially disastrous.

The homecraft course was hailed as an educational form unique in the world. It was claimed that it was not intended for 'less gifted' pupils who were unable to cope with the academic course, since its scope was very wide and would make considerable demands on the participants. Not only were the girls to receive instruction in the theoretical aspects of everything that 'the State must expect from the National Socialist woman in the family and in the community'; there was also to be a strong element of practical work performed outside the school, in crèches and kindergartens, on farms and in families. With this stream an integral part of the girls' senior school system, the separate *Frauenschule* became redundant, and its name was adopted for the new course. The wide choice of occupations for which it would qualify girls was emphasised, the only ones not included being those for which a further period of study in a university or college was required.[40]

Even if the new curricula contained features disadvantageous to girls aiming for higher education, the formalising of the structure of the girls' schools signified official recognition of the need to provide courses with a high academic content for a considerable number of girls, and not just for a minority of unusual cases. This was precisely what the hard liners in the Party had hoped to eliminate, on ideological grounds, but which had proved necessary in the light of the country's need for skilled personnel in all branches of administration, welfare and the professions.

As usual, the new measure was accompanied by explanations and justifications in the press. The *Völkischer Beobachter* reported in March 1938 that many people were asking, 'Why prepare girls for a career which they will just give up when they marry?'. Although the Party had done much to encourage this old fashioned idea, its official newspaper now remarked that neither parents nor children seemed to have given any thought to the possibility that some girls would not marry. Naturally, girls should be sure to prepare themselves for the tasks they would face if they became wives and mothers; but now the old bourgeois days were past when girls were expected to sit at home waiting for a husband. The need was for girls who, whether they were to marry or not, were prepared to play their part in the service of their country by training for an occupation, especially in areas where the growing shortage of labour was most acute.[41] Similar propaganda appeared in girls' and women's magazines, but it was obviously felt that exhortation would not be sufficient to prevent a number of girls from choosing to remain idle when they left school instead of training for an occupation: for this reason, the year of service introduced by Göring in February 1938 was at first restricted to girls who had never been employed, while signing on at an Employment Exchange became compulsory for all school leavers.[42] But girls proceeding to courses in higher education were exempt from these provisions, since intending students were obliged to perform Labour Service before commencing their studies, and were not, in any case, proposing to remain idle.

One of the points made firmly in the *Neuordnung des höheren Schulwesens* was that 'coeducation contradicts the National Socialist conception of education'.[43] With attempts at progress towards a co-educational system of senior schooling consistently frustrated before 1933, it must have been expected that an unequivocal policy of segregation would be enforced thereafter, given the strength of the Nazis' opposition to coeducation. Certainly, some Länder showed willingness in this respect: Saxony passed a law on 9 October 1933 stating that, other than in exceptional cases, girls must attend only girls' schools.[44] The Prussian Ministry of Education followed suit on 12 February 1934, with an order that 'as a matter of principle girls are not to be admitted to boys' schools if there is in the district a middle school or a girls' senior school at which girls can receive an education more suited to their nature'. Exceptions to this harsh ruling, which implied that middle schooling was adequate for female needs, required the Minister's permission; but it was conceded that girls already attending boys' schools should be allowed to complete their education there.[45] It should, however, have been an easy matter for a totalitarian Government to prevent girls from being admitted to boys' schools in the future.

On the contrary, however, coeducation continued throughout the 1930s. The 35,628 girls at boys' senior schools in Germany in 1931 constituted 6.3 per cent of the pupils there. Although absolute numbers declined to 31,102 in 1935, girls' percentual share rose fractionally, to 6.4 per cent; and in 1937, an increased number of 33,752 gave them a share of 6.8 per cent, which, if only a marginal rise, was a rise nevertheless.[46] Therefore it is clear that attendance by girls at boys' senior schools was not being phased out in the way envisaged by the Government, and that, contrary to Rust's orders, girls were continuing to be admitted to these schools.

In the 1938 Act, then, the Government was reiterating opposition to coeducation which had already been expressed on several occasions, but which had not been backed up by effective action. It was, however, conceded that there might still occasionally be special circumstances in which girls could be admitted to boys' schools, although on no account were boys to attend girls' senior schools.[47] The number of boys likely to be affected by this ruling was, in fact, minimal: in 1931 there were 849, constituting the tiny fraction of 0.3 per cent of the total number of pupils in girls' senior schools; by 1937, the numbers had risen to 1,313 and the proportion to 0.6 per cent, but remained insignificant.[48] The new law stressed that the differences between the sexes necessitated forms of schooling with different emphases, and added that where girls did attend boys' schools provision should be made for their 'special needs'.[49] These were described in a subsequent order as separate toilet facilities and a needlework room for girls in boys' schools where there was consistently a large number of girls.[50] This was a clear admission that coeducation had not been, and was not being, stamped out, although in theory it was anathema. An order of 18 January 1939 even urged that if there were a large enough number of girls at a boys' school, a domestic science class should be formed, so that they would not be deprived of some elements of a 'womanly' education.[51]

One reason for girls, or their parents, flouting Government policy was undoubtedly a growing fear before 1938 that even talented girls would be handicapped by attending girls' schools in which, it had been predicted, the academic content would be reduced in favour of domestic science. The 1938 reform made it clear that girls would have a better chance of reaching university standards in the boys' schools, which provided more teaching of science and Latin than the girls' schools. To try to block one loophole, it was ordered in August 1938 that girls in the lower grades of boys' schools should not receive Latin lessons, to match the absence of Latin in the first five years at girls' schools. Girls hoping to proceed to the higher grades of boys' schools would therefore have to make up the Latin lessons they had missed by private tuition.[52] But the exigencies of war rendered special teaching for girls at boys' schools impracticable, and the announcement abolishing this in January 1940 also stated that girls would be allowed to study Latin on the same terms as boys, and to be educated with boys in all subjects except sport.[53]

Thus although segregation of the sexes was a firm tenet of Nazi policy and although the Nazis were indisputably in control of the Government of Germany from 1933, a measure of coeducation continued throughout the 1930s, to be finally accepted as necessary in wartime. There can be little doubt that the wartime expedients were envisaged as temporary, but it is still amazing that coeducation had not been stamped out long before the war. After all, the Nazis did not have to face the problems of the 1920s, when the political parties were deeply split on this issue, and when there was no Reich Ministry of Education. In addition, large scale dismissals of teachers and administrators for political reasons removed at the start potential opposition to Nazi policies at the local level. Therefore it appears that the Nazis themselves failed to enforce their policy in an effective way. The result was a continuation of the stalemate of the 1920s, which prevented progress towards a system in which schools were open to boys and girls equally. Thus, if a number of girls attended boys' senior schools, these nevertheless remained schools which were primarily intended for boys, while there were other institutions intended specifically for girls.

The *Neuordnung des höheren Schulwesens* was scheduled to take effect from autumn 1938, although a short transition period was envisaged. In the first year some allowances, and the provision of extra tuition in some subjects, if necessary, would be made for the senior pupils most affected by the change-over.[54] But already during this first year, even before the war, it was clear that the new system would present difficulties. The propagation of the homecraft stream in girls' schools was at odds with the need — apparent even before 1938 — to encourage more girls to aim for university study. In consequence, as early as January 1939 Rust ordered that girls obtaining the certificate of the homecraft stream and wishing to proceed to university must sit a further examination in history, mathematics, physics and two languages to be eligible for admission.[55]

This topsy-turvy arrangement was the outcome of the stubborn insistence of the Minister of Education and Party ideologues, who did not have to operate practical policies, that girls should be guided into a 'womanly' education instead of an academic one, even when events were proving them wrong. The final contortion came in August 1939, with the order that from Easter 1941 the certificate of the homecraft course would entitle girls to enter university in the same way as the certificate of the language course, although the former's academic content was significantly weaker.[56] Given the Government's contradictory and capricious attitude to girls' education, and also, by implication, to university standards, it is hardly surprising that there were complaints in 1942 about the irresponsible behaviour of many girl students, since the new entrance requirements meant that many would be ill equipped to cope with courses designed for students from the academic stream in the senior schools. This was indeed a serious state of affairs at a time when girls formed a high proportion of the student body.[57]

This, then, was the Nazi answer to the 'mistaken development' of education during the Weimar years. Their stated aim at the start had been 'to reduce the number of senior pupils and students to the extent that basic education is afforded and the needs of the professions are satisfied'.[58] It was probably a combination of ideological absurdity, given the Party's basic anti-intellectualism, and the administrative inefficiency, given the mediocrity of its leading figures, that led to this policy's being pushed far beyond the desirable limit until it was realised that the process would have to be not only halted but reversed. As for girls' education, it was indeed desirable that more attention be paid to domestic science, which was too often despised in intellectual circles and given no place in the academic schools. But the switch from overemphasising academic talents to overemphasising 'womanly' education and the virtues of motherhood was a grotesque distortion and bore no relation to the needs of the German economy as the 1930s wore on: there was to be a consistent shortage of qualified personnel to the end of the decade and, to the nation's disadvantage, during the war. This was still true after the *volte-face* in autumn 1936, when official pronouncements began to stress the importance of encouraging academically talented girls to go to university, because even at this time the school system was being altered to divert girls from academic study.

Even so, Hitler must have been greatly removed from reality to be able to say, in 1942, that 'girls . . . have received education in accordance with the principles of National Socialism'.[59] Certainly, girls had been constantly bombarded with Nazi propaganda about the role of women in society. But this could not change the situation that the Nazis themselves created. For, in the end, it was their own policies, the expansionist ones which were inevitably given precedence over the enforcement of the Party's educational and social policies with regard to women, which rendered impossible the already difficult task of implementing points of doctrine once considered immutable.

NOTES

1.   Hitler's speech to the *NS-Frauenschaft* at the 1934 Party Rally, found in Domarus, *op. cit.*, p. 451; Rudolf Hess, 'Die Aufgaben der deutschen Frau', *VB*, 27 May 1936.
2.   H.-J. von Schumann, *Die nationalsozialistische Erziehung im Rahmen amtlicher Bestimmungen*, Langensalza, n.d. (? 1934), pp. 39-40; F. Hiller, 'Mädchenerziehung', F. Hiller (ed.), *Deutsche Erziehung im neuen Staat*, Langensalza, 1934, p. 350.
3.   Hitler, *op. cit.*, pp. 459-60.
4.   Hiller, *loc. cit.*
5.   Arthur Kirchhoff (ed.), *Die Akademische Frau*, Berlin, 1897, p. xi; J. E. Russell, *German Higher Schools*, New York, 1907, pp. 131, 420.
6.   Schumann, *loc. cit.*; Marie Schorn, 'Frauenstudium in der Zukunft', A. Reber-Gruber (ed.), *Weibliche Erziehung im NSLB*, Leipzig and Berlin, 1934, p. 16.
7.   'Die Geschlechter im Dritten Reich', *Fränkische Tageszeitung*, 17 April 1934; Mayer, *op. cit.*, pp. 30-2.
8.   I. L. Kandel and T. Alexander (trans.), *The Reorganisation of Education in Prussia*, New York, 1927, p. 541.
9.   T. Alexander and B. Parker, *The New Education in the German Republic*, London, 1930, pp. 256-7, 275-6.
10.   Hitler's speech at the first congress of the German Labour Front, 10 May 1933, found in Domarus, *op. cit.*, p. 268; Bernhard Rust, 'Das Preussische Kultusministerium seit der nationale Erhebung', Hiller, *op. cit.*, pp. 39-40.
11.   Found in W. Hofer, *Der Nationalsozialismus*, Frankfurt a.M., 1957, p. 30.
12.   Hitler, *loc. cit.*
13.   Johannes Büttner (ed.), *Der Weg zum Nationalsozialistischen Reich*, Berlin, 1943, p. 858.
14.   Ludwig Wülker, 'Die öffentliche höhere Mädchenschulen der norddeutschen Länder im Philologenjahrbuch von 1933', *Deutsche Mädchenbildung (D. Mäd.)*, April 1934, pp. 84-6.
15.   *St. D. R., op. cit.*, p. 31.
16.   Kandel and Alexander, *op. cit.*, pp. 102-3.
17.   Mathilde Drees, 'Das Mädchenbildungswesen', Zentralinstitut für Erziehung und Unterricht (ed.), *Die Reichsschulkonferenz in ihren Ergebnissen*, Leipzig, 1921, pp. 69-73; Rühle-Gerstel, *op. cit.*, pp. 49-50.
18.   Hiller, *op. cit.*, p. 351.
19.   Hedwig Förster, 'Die künftige Gestaltung des Mädchenschulwesens', *FZ*, 8 July 1933.
20.   BA, R43 II/427, letter from Frick to Reich Ministers and Land Governments, 5 October 1933; Siber, *op. cit.*, p. 30.
21.   Hedwig Förster, 'Die Frauenschulen', *D. Mäd.*, 1934, no. 7, p. 317.
22.   Homeyer, *op. cit.*, p. A16; 'Bekanntmachung von 3.7.35', *Amtsblatt des Bayerischen Staatsministerium für Unterricht und Kultus*, no. IX 27 409, p. 211.
23.   'Ziel und Aufgaben der 3-jährigen Frauenschule', *D. Mäd.*, 1934, no. 8, p. 337.
24.   'Bessere Berufsaussichten für Volksschullehrer', *VB*, 4 January 1935
25.   'Nadelarbeitsunterricht in Lyzeen', *Deutsche Wissenschaft, Erziehung und*

Volksbildung (DWEuV), 1935, no. 198, 3 April 1935, p. 143.
26.   Friederike Matthias, 'Grundsätzliches zur Reform der höheren Mädchenschule', Reber-Gruber, *op. cit.*, p. 30.
27.   'Aufnahme in die wissenschaftlichen Oberstufen der höheren Mädchenanstalten', *DWEuV*, 1935, no. 582, 11 October 1935, p. 478.
28.   Christoph Führ, *op. cit.*, pp. 28-9.
29.   'Gesetz gegen die Überfülling deutscher Schulen und Hochschulen', *RGB*, 1933 I, 25 April 1933, p. 225.
30.   Conclusions drawn from figures in *Deutsche Schulerziehung*, 1940, p. 117.
31.   A brief account of this campaign is to be found in Rolf Eilers, *Die Nationalsozialistische Schulpolitik*, Cologne and Opladen, 1963. pp. 85-97.
32.   *Deutsche Schulerziehung, loc. cit.*
33.   IfZ, MA 387, frame 725473, letter from Hess to the SS leadership, 12 December 1936.
34.   *Deutsche Schulerziehung, loc. cit.*
35.   BA, R43 II/938b, report from *Deutsches Nachrichtenbüro (DNB)*, no. 474, 19 April 1937.
36.   'Die Erziehung der Mädchen im BDM', *FZ*, 20 February 1937.
37.   'Neuordnung des höheren Schulwesens', *DWEuV* 1938, 29 January 1938, pp. 46, 48.
38.   Grete Brenner, 'Fragen der höheren Mädchenbildung in Deutschland', *FK*, April 1939, p. 6.
39.   *DWEuV, op. cit.*, pp. 51, 54-6.
40.   Grete Brenner, *op. cit.*, pp. 6-7.
41.   'Warum immer neue Forderungen an die Mädel?', *VB*, 10 March 1938.
42.   'Einführung des weiblichen Pflichtjahrs', *VB*, 22 February 1938. See above Chapter 5, pp. 103-05.
43.   *DWEuV, op. cit.*, p. 46.
44.   'Aufhebung der Gesetze über die Gemeinschaftserziehung an höheren Schulen (usw)', *Sächsisches Gesetzblatt*, 1933, order of 9 October 1933, pp. 175-6.
45.   'Erlass des Ministers für Wissenschaft, Kunst und Volksbildung vom 12.2.1934', *D. Mäd.*, 15 May 1934, p. 144.
46.   *Deutsche Schulerziehung, loc. cit.*
47.   *DWEuV, loc. cit.*
48.   *Deutsche Schulerziehung, loc. cit.*
49.   *DWEuV, loc. cit.*
50.   'Mädchen an Jungenschulen', *DWEuV* 1938, 27 August 1938, no. 477, pp. 429-30.
51.   'Mädchen an Jungenschulen', *DWEuV* 1939, 18 January 1939, no. 46, pp. 56-7.
52.   *DWEuV* 1938, *loc. cit.*
53.   'Sonderunterricht für Mädchen, die Oberschulen für Jungen besuchen', *DWEuV* 1940, 12 January 1940, no. 53, p. 76.
54.   'Neuordnung des höheren Schulwesens', *DWEuV* 1938, 29 January 1938, p. 47.
55.   'Berechtigung der Reifezeugnisse der Oberschule für Mädchen, hauswirtschaftliche Form', *DWEuV* 1939, 24 January 1939, no. 77, p. 80.
56.   'Berechtigung der Reifezeugnisse der Oberschule für Mädchen, hauswirtschaftliche Form', *DWEuV* 1939, 23 August 1939, no. 467, p. 463.
57.   IfZ, MA 441/6, frame 2-757141, *op. cit.*
58.   'Rechtsentwicklung', *Jahrbuch des Deutschen Rechts*, 1934, p. 24.
59.   *Hitler's Table Talk 1941-44*, London, 1953, no. 223, 20 May 1942 (Midday), p. 491.

7   NAZI POLICY TOWARDS GIRL STUDENTS [1]

As the Nazis tried to guide schoolgirls into a 'womanly' education, so their propaganda suggested that they would also deny girls the chance of studying in universities, in a coeducational situation. Pronouncements to this effect have often been taken at face value, with the result that it has been generally assumed that girls were severely discriminated against in universities and colleges in the Third Reich.[2] But many of the early educational policies attributed to the Nazi Government were prefigured in measures conceived by the last Weimar Governments in an attempt to solve the problems of the economic depression. The policies initiated by the Nazis were similarly moulded by necessity, with the result that dogma which was conveniently relevant in 1933 had to be abandoned in the later 1930s as it proved increasingly unrealistic in the changed circumstances of the employment market. In addition, attitudes considered reactionary and philistine were by no means the prerogative of the NSDAP alone. Even among the better educated, there was the feeling that far from too little progress having been made in making higher education available to a wider range of people, there had been too much change, especially in the provision of opportunities for women.

The most pressing problem in higher education in 1930 was that as student numbers continued to rise, professional job opportunities were rapidly contracting, in the shrunken market of the depression years. There was widespread concern about the emergence of an 'academic proletariat' of jobless graduates. *Das Deutsche Studentenwerk*, which administered the payment of grants to able but needy students, criticised the recent indiscriminate flood of young people into higher education,[3] and discussions were held from 1930 onwards at the Reich Ministry of the Interior − since there was no Reich Ministry of Education − to examine ways of reducing pressure on senior schools and the universities. The inescapable conclusion drawn was that there would have to be a rigorous selection process for applicants for higher education, and it was suggested that the Labour Service be particularly recommended to school leavers, since in view of the saturation of the professional market many more of them would have to find jobs of a practical nature.[4]

With prospects for students deteriorating, women's representation was at this time stronger than it had ever been: in summer 1931, 19,394 girls formed 18.7 per cent of the record total of 103,912 students, and in the following semester they increased their share to 18.9 per cent, the strongest point of their representation before the Second World War.[5] This trend was by no means universally welcomed: many were unconvinced that women either benefited from academic study or were an asset to the universities.[6] Male students, particularly, claimed that not only were academic standards falling because of the rising number of girl students, but, in addition, the long standing tradition of 'student comradeship' was being destroyed. A radical feminist retorted that women were indeed performing a service if they were destroying the exclusive, beer swilling male corporations, and claimed that some men were launching an attack on women at university to divert attention from their own inadequacies.[7] Certainly, the reaction against the overcrowding of the universities, aimed at students in general, not at girls alone, caused alarm among the men, to the extent that a male students' magazine proposed that girls be denied full rights of matriculation and confine themselves to 'their characteristic occupations'.[8] It was abundantly clear that this meant running a home and bearing children.

This point of view is strikingly similar to official opinion repeatedly expressed after the Nazi takeover and exemplified in the following passage:

'It is clear that study cannot offer women a suitable general education. Women will in future be employed much less in occupations requiring a period of study . . . Therefore senior schools will not need to prepare girls for university.'[9]

Those who felt that this judgement was somewhat harsh contended that women might perform adequately, and even well, in many academic subjects, but still denied that girls might study mathematics and the deductive sciences successfully, since women were intuitive by nature rather than rational.[10] The once reasonably favourable position of women in university mathematics and science departments began to deteriorate after 1935, as a result of deliberate policy by which men were given preference in jobs requiring scientific or mathematical training, as a matter of principle. Poor employment prospects acted as a disincentive to girls who might have studied these subjects, although they were not barred from such study.[13]

The Nazi view of the role of women, which was constantly reiterated, certainly gave the impression that the Government was unequivocally on the side of the men, and that if there were too many students women would be the first to be excluded. This encouraged the launching of open attacks on the admission of women to university. In 1935, one male student leader stated categorically that universities should be largely a male preserve, with women admitted as guests in instances where the 'special womanly occupations' necessitated a measure of academic study. He conceded that the surplus of women in the population might mean that some would have to do men's jobs, but denied that a place should be made for them in academic occupations.[12] This view was hotly contested by a girl student who argued that male and female students ought to be able to serve the *Volk* together, not in conflict with each other. But her spirited defence of women's right to study was somewhat different from the uninhibited retaliation of women in response to male attacks before 1933: it was necessarily accompanied by pious affirmations of loyalty to Hitler, of motherhood as woman's natural calling, and of opposition to the liberal idea of 'emancipation'.[13] It is clear, however, that the conflict between men and women over the right of women to study in universities was not the result of Nazi policies, but was generated by the prospect, in the early 1930s, of a limitation of student numbers in the face of graduate unemployment.

The Nazi Government wasted little time in tackling the immediate problem in education, that of sheer numbers. But Kälin, director of the Employment Exchanges, was simply continuing his previous function in surveying the prospects for graduates. He predicted in February 1933 that within four or five years there would be a crisis in the professional labour market as a result, he said, of the trebling of student numbers since 1914. He repeated the conclusion drawn by the committee which had been looking at the problem since 1930, that in future many school leavers would have to find their niche in positions which did not require academic study, even if they were qualified for university entrance.[14] Two days later, it was announced that each applicant for higher education was to be vetted by an examination board, and those regarded as least suitable advised against further education. Those rejecting such advice were to be observed closely during their first three semesters to assess their progress.[15] As yet, then, there was no coercion, nor were girls treated differently from boys. It emerged, however, that selection was designed to serve a purpose additional to that of reducing numbers: 'suitability' was to be gauged partly by a character reference, so that pressure could be exerted on the politically or socially 'undesirable' to prevent them from entering the universities.[16]

Apart from this discrimination, the policy followed here was largely that envisaged under the Weimar governments; but at last action was being taken, action which had been lacking because of the absence both of a central agency to direct education and of stable government. German universities were administered by the government of their Land, so a unified policy had been difficult to achieve.[17] But Frick, the new Reich Minister of the Interior, who assumed responsibility for education at the national level, achieved agreement on united action for the selection of university entrants by the Land Education Ministers, in February 1933.[18] Exhortation and counsel, however, failed to reduce student numbers sufficiently, and eventually it was found necessary to resort to compulsion: on 25 April 1933, a national law 'to combat the surplus in German schools and colleges' ordered that, apart from the statutory minimum attendance requirements, the number of pupils and students was to be so regulated as to safeguard basic educational standards and provide sufficient candidates for the professions. The governments of the Länder were empowered to decide the numbers their senior schools and colleges could accommodate. But it was insisted that non-'Aryans' were to enjoy no higher representation than they did in the total population.[19] This was the first statutory discrimination in education against a specific group, and while it cannot be condoned, it is hardly surprising, given the Nazis' fantastic and fanatical racial beliefs.

When this law equally failed to have the desired effect, Frick ordered a much more explicit restriction on 28 December 1933. This fixed the total number of new students to be admitted to universities and colleges each year at 15,000. Each Land was allotted a specific number which it might not exceed, and the choice of students was to be based on the mental and physical maturity, the strength of character, and the political reliability of the candidates. For the first time, a particular restriction was placed on girls' numbers, which were in no case to exceed 10 per cent of the quota for each Land. School leavers who were refused admission were advised to engage in work of a practical nature,[20] in line with Nazi theory. For girls, this invariably meant domestic service or work on a farm.

These restrictions on entry to higher education are generally characterised as typical of the philistinism and evil mindedness of the Nazis. Certainly, discriminations against non-'Aryans' and political opponents are to be viewed in this way. But, otherwise, the quota system was a logical response to the effects of the depression on the employability of graduates. It was also a more effective continuation of the policy envisaged before 1933 which had found support among people of various political persuasions. If the 10 per cent restriction on the intake of girls seemed to reflect the Nazi view of women's role, it was also bound to be popular with many. In any case, it was not rigorously enforced, with a figure for 1934 of 12.5 per cent. This was appreciably lower than the 1933 figure, 16.7 per cent,[21] but was nevertheless noticeably above the decreed level.

The number of new entrants to higher education had begun to drop even before the restrictions, after the abnormally high figure of over 30,000 in 1931; in 1933, there were fewer than 21,000 new students.

With the restrictions in force, the 1934 intake was in fact below the quota, at less than 14,000.[22] Clearly, the cure had been too effective, for as early as February 1935 Rust, the new Reich Minister of Education, rescinded this 'temporary measure'.[23] But it had not been the only reason for the reduction by one third of the total number of students in three and a half years; in addition, the smaller numbers of children born during the Great War were now reaching university age. Further, matriculation had generally been delayed, rather than averted, by the introduction of compulsory Labour Service for all school leavers aiming for higher education; thus, potential new students for the summer semester of 1934 did not matriculate until winter 1934-5.[24] The reintroduction of conscription in March 1935 also affected student numbers: the withdrawal of young men to perform military service was an important factor in the decline to 57,000 in the number of students in summer 1935; this was the lowest figure since 1916, in wartime. That this was largely due to a reduction in the number of male students is evidenced by the increase in the proportion of girls in the student body in 1935 to almost 17 per cent.[25]

While the Technical Universities, which specialised in the applied sciences and engineering, and in which the number of girl students was always very small, followed a pattern roughly similar to that of the conventional universities, the teacher-training colleges showed a different trend. In 1935 these *Hochschule für Lehrerbildung*[26] had a record number of students; but the lowest ever percentage of girls among them, at 12 per cent; this was in contrast with a share of over 30 per cent only two and a half years earlier.[27] But a reduction of these dimensions was not, apparently, considered sufficient, since in April 1936 Rust placed a firm restriction on the number of girls to be admitted to the colleges. He explained that there were already more than enough women senior school teachers, and, in addition, a large number of students preparing for this career. To arrest the flow of girls into teaching, therefore, none would be admitted to a Prussian college in the winter semester of 1936-7. And to avoid circumvention of the order, no girl aiming to teach was to be admitted directly to a university; she must first spend two semesters at a teacher-training college. Rust conceded that this restriction might be lifted for the summer semester of 1937, but only to an extent compatible with the demands of the labour market. Girls having to wait for a year before acceptance were advised to perform Labour Service and, if possible, also to engage in some form of domestic service or work on a farm.[28]

It would be misleading to suggest that this was designed to prevent girls from receiving higher education and preparing themselves for a career outside the home. The Nazis always hoped, of course, that all girls would have experience of household tasks before they married,

134

and that all young people training for non-manual careers would have experience of physical work; these aims could well be fulfilled in this enforced period of waiting between school and college, necessitated by the surplus of teachers over available teaching positions. The limitation in this case did, however, apply only to girls, which was in line with Nazi Party policy that men should have preference in career opportunities to enable them to marry and support a family as early as possible. But the admission of girls was to be delayed, not prevented, since teaching was one of the occupations the Nazis considered suitable for women.

Rust's restriction of April 1936 was, in fact, singularly ineffective: in the winter semester of 1936-7 there was actually an increase in the number of girls attending teacher-training colleges, so that there were almost twice as many as there had been even in the peak year of 1931. Over one third of these 1,500 girls attended the two-year-old college in Hanover, which was exclusively for girl students, while another 188 were at the new all-female college at Schneidemühl.[29] Particularly since both these colleges were in Prussia, it is clear that, for some reason, the Minister's order was not being enforced. This does not seem to have reflected a change in policy, since in April 1937 Rust decreed that in future there would be one intake each year into the colleges, instead of the traditional two. He also made it clear that while 1937 school leavers might apply for a place in 1937, preference would be given to those who had left school in earlier years; and if places were available for 1937 school leavers, preference would be given to members of the *Bund deutscher Mädel* (League of German Girls).[30] This order applied in a corresponding way to intending male students, whereas the 1936 decree had applied only to girls; it is thus quite clear that in this branch of higher education the Nazi Government did not relentlessly discriminate against girls.

Anxiety about the number of college applicants took a different form from 1937. Rust himself opened a new college in Koblenz, exclusively for girl students, stressing 'the special mission of women teachers', in November.[31] The changed circumstances of the employment market had led to a change of attitude, although — in spite of attempts to prevent this — the number of students at teacher-training colleges had continued to rise sharply. Even before the war withdrew men into the armed forces, it was apparent that there would soon be a shortage of teachers. Here, as elsewhere, the only reserve of labour was among women. To encourage recruitment to the profession, therefore, it was announced at the end of 1939 that the number of special courses designed to prepare girls with only an elementary school education for teacher-training college would be doubled, from 80 to 160.[32] Involvement in the Second World War made the shortage of trained teachers, already a source of concern, even more serious.

The Nazis' wholesale departure from their earlier policy of trying to restrict the entry of girls into teaching resulted in girls' constituting 12 per cent of the colleges' student population in summer 1939, still in peacetime. But even this unprecedentedly high share was more than doubled in wartime, so that in summer 1940 the figure was 88 per cent. And, unlike the universities, the colleges had not suffered a severe drop in absolute numbers: the 1940 figure was significantly larger than that of the peak year of 1933.[33] The Government had really only continued the policies of the later Weimar period in imposing — or trying to impose — a limit on entry to over-full occupations and to the courses preparatory to them. Practical considerations equally led to positive encouragement to girls to prepare themselves for a teaching career, given the increasing shortage of male candidates.

But doctrine was not to be abandoned altogether, especially when it could be reconciled with necessity; thus, retreat from one point of earlier Nazi policy was matched by adherence to another. In January 1937 compulsory domestic science and needlework, to the extent of four hours each week in the first four semesters, were prescribed for all girl teacher-training students aiming to work in senior schools. This was absolutely consistent with the Nazi aim of ensuring that all girls received a 'womanly' education. But it should not be seen as an attempt to guide girls towards housekeeping rather than a profession. That it was an integral part of the Nazis' anti-intellectualism and their emphasis on the virtues of practical skills is shown by another clause in the same order which decreed compulsory technical instruction for male students at the hours when the girls had their homecraft classes.[34] This does, however, underline the Nazis' insistence on the separate functions of the sexes. But there was only a degree of actual segregation in the colleges, in spite of the Nazis' opposition to coeducation. Of the twenty-eight colleges, half were for students of both sexes, while eleven admitted only men, and three were exclusively for women.[35]

The change in official policy, exemplified by the new attitude to trainee teachers, became increasingly apparent and urgent from 1936. Early in 1937, Rust announced that school leavers must be encouraged to enter universities in greater numbers, particularly in order to study scientific and technical subjects. The Four Year Plan, announced in September 1936, required many more chemists and engineers, and the general expansion involved would mean a demand also for experts in other disciplines.[36] It quickly emerged that the new policies were not to be restricted to men. A few days before the Four Year Plan was announced, the Thursday women's section of the *Völkischer Beobachter* was devoted to a justification of both an academic education and professional employment for women, insofar, it was emphasised, as these would benefit the community. Parents were urged to make sacrifices, if necessary, to enable a talented daughter to study so that the nation might benefit from her abilities; studying for one's own satisfaction was obviously still regarded as egotistic and decadent. The final judgement was: 'It is wrong if today a gifted and capable girl takes the attitude that there is no point in studying because she will not find employment.'[37] Trude Bürkner, leader of the BdM, echoed this view, insisting that girls of ability aiming for a professional career ought to attend a university, since antagonism to the universities was 'not in accordance with the attitude of the *BDM*'.[38]

But in spite of official exhortations, student numbers continued to decline in the mid- to late-1930s, and the proportion of girls in the student body also declined, until the outbreak of the Second World War. From a share of over 18 per cent in the summer semester of 1933, girls' representation in the universities dropped to less than 15 per cent in the winter semester of 1937-8, but revived to its highest point yet in autumn 1939, at 20 per cent.[39] This was, of course, at a time when the total number of students was greatly reduced by the removal of men who, it was felt, could better serve their country in the armed forces in wartime. In the following terms[40] student numbers rose again slightly, and the now favourable position of women improved even further, so that in the third term of 1940 they comprised almost 30 per cent of all students in German universities.[41]

Girls were traditionally best represented in Arts faculties, where from 1931 they occupied more than one third of all places. In absolute terms, however, the number of girls studying medicine overtook that in Arts, although their share of places remained around one fifth. This trend rendered groundless early fears that the Nazis would ban, or at least strongly discourage, the admission of women to medical faculties. The other subject with a consistently high percentage of girl students was pharmacy, where they constituted between 20 per cent and 30 per cent of the total number of students throughout the 1930s, reaching the uniquely high figure of 52 per cent in 1940: in no other subject did girls enjoy anything approaching this share at this time.

In contrast with the consistently strong position of women in Arts, medicine and pharmacy, their favourable representation in the sciences in the early 1930s was not maintained. From 25 per cent in physics and mathematics in 1931, their share plummeted to 7 per cent in winter 1937-8; in absolute terms, this meant a drop from almost 2,800 to a mere 99. There had always been fewer girls studying chemistry than maths and physics; at the beginning of the 1930s, their numbers were consistently around 500, or between 15 per cent and 17 per cent of the total. A less spectacular, but still significant, drop in their numbers brought their share in 1937-8 to 8 per cent, representing 208 girls.[42]

This development was, of course, the result of deliberate Government policy in the early years of Nazi rule. But by the time it was fully effective, its consequences were causing anxiety, in view of the pressing need in the later 1930s for skilled scientific and technical personnel. In November 1937 a writer in a women's magazine observed that the number of girl students in scientific subjects had 'fallen alarmingly'. She urged that girls who had the ability turn to these subjects, since their contribution 'to the serious and important work of scientific investigation is essential today'.[43]

As the decline in the number of girls in science faculties had been the result of Government policy, so reversal of that policy led to a revival of girls' fortunes. The position reached in 1937-8 was their nadir, and the improvement thereafter was given added impetus by the outbreak of war in September 1939. By 1940, girl chemistry students once more numbered over 500, with a share of 14 per cent. At the same time, the number of girls studying maths and physics rose to only 138, but these constituted 17 per cent of all students there, a high proportion for subjects once pronounced unsuitable for girls.[14] As a writer in the *Frankfurter Zeitung* observed:

> 'The technical and scientific occupations, which were long regarded as a male preserve, are now once again open to women as chemists, physicists, engineers, biologists, on account of the shortage of male candidates.'[45]

Girl students in both law and economics fared similarly to female science students. In law, their numbers declined steadily and sharply from over 1,000 in 1932 until in winter 1937-8 they reached a mere 59.[46] Hitler's pronouncement in 1936 that women should no longer be employed as judges and barristers[47] doubtless ensured that the downward trend in girls' numbers continued. In economics, the decline was less sharp but equally steady, from over 1,000 girl students in summer 1931, to only 194 in 1937-8.[48] Again, the Nazis might have congratulated themselves on the effectiveness of their initial policy by the end of 1937, had circumstances not changed. Now, however, the value of women economists was pointed out in the various publications directed at women,[49] and the number of girls in economics departments began to revive.[50]

In 1937, too, there was growing concern about the decline in the number of girl law students. Dr Eben-Servaes, the legal expert in the National Women's Leadership and leader of the Nazi Association of Women Lawyers, in August 1937 asked her representatives to report how many girl law students there were in each Gau and how far advanced their studies were, with a view to encouraging recruitment to law faculties. She explained that although Hitler's ban on women lawyers' being admitted to practice in the courts had closed this avenue to female graduates, there were many other areas in which their participation would be increasingly necessary.[51] Girls' numbers in law faculties did revive from about this time,[52] but not, apparently, enough; a male legal expert urged in August 1939 that 'each girl with university entrance qualifications ought to consider whether she is suited to a legal career, rather than just medicine or teaching'.[53] This was even before the outbreak of war; in autumn 1939, with young men called up for active service, the shortage of law graduates became acute.[54]

If the reasons for encouraging girls to take up academic study in fields once pronounced unsuitable for them were purely practical, similar considerations lay behind the continuing discouragement of students from studying dentistry. The Ministry of the Interior announced on 3 August 1936 that, until further notice, new students would not be admitted because of the large surplus of dentists. This decision was slightly mitigated after an agreement between the Ministers of Education and the Interior, by which there would be a quota agreed between Frick and the leader of the dentists' organisation instead of a total ban on new entrants. But Pfundtner still found it necessary to give an additional warning that prospects in the profession remained poor and precarious.[55] This concern about entry to dental faculties and to the profession itself was directed at men and women alike, without differentiation between them.

Women had always formed a tiny minority in the Technical Universities, with a figure just above 900 between 1931 and 1933; this dropped to 213 by winter 1937-8, while the number of male students declined less dramatically. Although these institutions prepared students for occupations deemed vital to the partial war economy, it was not until after war broke out that the number of girl students revived significantly, passing the 800 mark at the end of 1940.[56] This figure gave them a share of 9 per cent, twice as high as the peak of their representation in the early 1930s. Even allowing for the withdrawal of a substantial number of men for war service, it is evident that women were responding to the encouragement given to them to study scientific and technical subjects.

It was in fact only the increased attendance of women that kept student numbers from falling to negligible proportions during the war. Young men continued to study when on leave from their units, but in summer 1942 it was reported that the return of many of them to the army was followed by an actual rise in numbers at some universities, because of the large intake of girls. In Berlin at this time, girls' numbers had increased by 20 per cent, compared with the winter semester of 1941-2, and for the first time they constituted a majority of the students in three faculties there. At Freiburg, there were altogether more women than men at this time. Medicine and Arts subjects continued to be the fields most favoured, but the sciences also benefited, so that at Freiburg, Göttingen, Halle, Berlin and Würzburg there were more women than men studying science. This general development was considered desirable, since the exodus of men from the professions and academic study had left a great shortage of recruits in these fields, which would have to be made good by admitting women.[57]

Even if there had been no Four Year Plan and no Second World War, women students and graduates would have been essential to the Nazi order; a system based on elitism requires a corps of leaders. Rust acknowledged this when he expressed the desire to found universities in Germany on the model of Oxford and Cambridge, which provided the leading element in British public life.[58] The network of organisations which the Nazis built up to some extent before, and much more intensively after, the *Machtübernahme* needed leaders who were intelligent and educated, as well as devoted Party hacks. And this applied to women as well as men, given the Nazis' view that the functions of the sexes should be kept separate. The initial experience in 1933 of having a man in direct charge of the women's organisations was a singularly unhappy one, and after this the day-to-day running of them was left to women themselves, even if ultimate authority rested with the Party's male leadership.[59] Thus, trained personnel was required for the *Frauenwerk*, the Women's Section of the Labour Front, the BdM, the Women's Labour Service and the NSV. There was even a place for women in research institutes;[60] for example, Hildegard Behr received her doctorate in February 1937 and then became a research worker in a genealogical records office.[61] The leader of the Nazi student organisation, Dr Scheel, boasted that the new Germany had provided employment prospects for women in a wide variety of fields requiring an academic education, without departing from the Nazi principle of guiding women into jobs suited to the female nature.[62] There was some justification for this claim, although it became increasingly clear in the 1930s that the concept of work suitable for women was rather elastic.

The Nazis were well aware that the existence of an academic elite whose members were destined to occupy the leading positions might lead to the formation of a compact group within the community which would be an obstacle to national unity and to complete control by the Party. Male students were brought into contact with contemporaries from all walks of life once military service was introduced in 1935. In addition, from 1933 the Labour Service, which had formerly been voluntary, became compulsory for male students.[63] Then in March 1934 it was decreed that all school leavers of both sexes seeking admission to higher education must first perform six months' Labour

Service.[64] This requirement fulfilled three important functions. In the first place, it was an effective way of reducing student numbers immediately, in 1934, when this was a top priority. In addition, intellectually gifted young people were to be educated to respect the value of manual work, and therefore to respect their fellow citizens who performed it. Finally, a cheap reserve of labour was automatically permanently available for jobs — particularly on the land — which were regarded as vital but which were unattractive as permanent occupations. If the nature of the work performed by boys and girls tended to differ, the general principles behind the student Labour Service applied to both equally; thus, it could not be claimed that girls were being discriminated against by being excluded, nor that they were being privileged by being admitted to study straight from school. The urgent desire to increase student numbers in the later 1930s was clearly in conflict with the equally urgent desire to maintain a reserve of cheap labour for agriculture, and eventually, in 1940 the period of service was tailored — reduced from twenty-six weeks to twenty-two — to allow intending students to fit it in between leaving school in spring and entering university at the beginning of the autumn term.[65] The Government thus endeavoured to have the best of both worlds, namely a substantial period of Labour Service from each aspiring student and as many recruits as possible for university study.

Fear of academic elitism, one of the motives behind the student Labour Service, did not prevent the continued existence, and indeed the growth of student organisations, since these were now designed rather to involve the students as a group in the life of the community than to be exclusive. Matriculation automatically made each student a member of the *Deutsche Studentenschaft* (National Union of Students), in which the Nazis had had a majority since 1931.[66] The various associations and clubs, which had been exclusively, and often unattractively, male bastions were obliged to dissolve by 1935,[67] to be replaced by a single body, the Nazi Students' Association (NSDStB), whose local branches were responsible for the 'political education' — that is, indoctrination — of students.[68] Party membership was a condition of entry to the NSDStB,[69] and from 1936 NSDStB members had also to belong to one of the Party's special organisations. For girls, this meant joining either the BdM or the *NS-Frauenschaft*.[70]

In keeping with the Nazi desire to separate the sexes for most purposes, a special section for girls, the *Arbeitsgemeinschaft der nationalsozialistischen Studentinnen* (ANSt), had been created in 1927 within the NSDStB.[71] Its aim, according to Scheel, was 'to involve the girl student in the work of the university in a manner compatible with her womanliness'.[72] Membership of the ANSt was theoretically voluntary, but the conclusion of an agreement between it and the BdM, to the

141

effect that all students in the BdM must join the ANSt, achieved a large membership. At a time when student numbers were being restricted, a girl who joined the BdM had a better chance of being admitted, and so a large number of students automatically became members of the ANSt. It was estimated that in 1936 65 per cent of all girl students were members, and that the figure rose to 75 per cent in the following year. This meant that most girl students had to participate in their first three semesters in group discussions for the purpose of 'education to comradeship', another euphemism for political indoctrination.[73]

The ANSt was only a small part of the organised activity available to – and to some extent compulsory for – girl students. Like the men, they were obliged to engage in sporting activities in their first three semesters, in keeping with Hitler's demand in *Mein Kampf*.[74] The *Frauendienst* (Women's Service), too, was compulsory, for the first six semesters. This involved training in air-raid protection, first aid and signals – areas with ominously martial connotations.[75] Then it was recommended that in their spare time –if, one might add, they had any left – girl students should help out in the welfare and charitable organisations, the NSV and the *Winterhilfswerk* (Winter Relief Scheme), thus performing useful community service, and at the same time associating with women and girls from all walks of life. To demonstrate even further their consciousness of belonging to a national community which superseded all divisions of class or occupation, the girls were encouraged to perform 'voluntary' stints of work in factories or on the land, in vacation, to allow women workers an extra paid holiday, and a small minority of idealistic girls responded enthusiastically.[76] This was not the end of their extramural activities: they were urged to interest themselves in the work of the Nazi women's organisation, to maintain contact with German students abroad, and to attend meetings to which women without a university education were invited, to show them what girl students did in their work and in their organisations.[77]

The creation of a great variety of activities and organisations for girl students confirms that what the Nazis opposed was not the existence of universities and the presence of women in them – as had perhaps seemed to be the case in 1933 – but rather academic freedom and independent minded intellectuals. The overriding Nazi aim was to stamp out the last vestiges of 'liberal' and 'internationalist' culture, and to replace it with a German, National Socialist approach to learning. As Scheel proclaimed at the 1937 Party Congress: 'We do not want a scholarly National Socialism, but a National Socialist scholarship.'[78] Scheel was clearly oblivious to the fact that this was bound to be a contradiction in terms.

As far as girls were concerned, the ANSt leader in 1935, Lieselotte

Machwirth, explained that there had never been hostility in Nazi ranks to the girl student *per se*. The Party had indeed deplored the attendance at university of girls from wealthy backgrounds, who were attracted by student social life, not by academic study; equally abhorrent to the Party was the feminist bluestocking, whose *raison d'être* was to outshine her male colleagues by any means.[79] It was these 'undesirables', along with those disqualified for racial or political reasons, who had had to be removed from the universities; once this was achieved, there was a warm welcome for the girl student who worked alongside her male counterpart as 'the comrade . . . in the common task of achieving a National Socialist reconstruction of the university'.[80]

This welcome was emphasised when in 1938 the thirtieth anniversary of the admission of women to Prussian universities was made an occasion for celebration. Tribute was paid to the tenacity of those, particularly Luise Otto and Helene Lange, who had fought for this aim, without, it was stressed, sacrificing their humanity and womanliness. Ironically, these were the very women who had founded and built up the Women's Movement which the Nazis had attacked so often both before and after 1933. To try to resolve the implicit contradiction, the Nazis claimed that the Women's Movement, worthy in its initial phase, had fallen under the influence of 'Jewish women's rights' advocates' and a 'liberal-individualistic leadership' during the Weimar Republic. Fortunately, the story continued, the situation had been saved by the Nazis, and the consequent reorientation of the universities had been towards the 'only valid standpoint: the good of the community'. The result was that the girl student now found support instead of hostility among the female population as a whole, and played a valuable part in the cultural life of the nation.[81] The emphasis placed on these last points was doubtless aimed at reassuring girls and their parents that university study was not only acceptable but actually highly desirable for girls with academic ability; this reassurance was essential if the desired increase in student numbers in the later 1930s was to be achieved, after the doubts sown by the Government itself in earlier years about the validity of intellectual pursuits.

From the very start, then, considerable interest was taken in girl students by the Nazi Party. The first objectives with regard to them applied equally to male students, however; these were the elimination from higher education of those unacceptable to the Party for any reason, and the reduction of student numbers at a time when they were inflated out of all proportion to the employment opportunities available to graduates. Other restrictions necessitated by this situation generally applied to students of both sexes in equal measure, although there were some exceptions. But the fundamental point is that girls continued to be admitted to higher education in relatively large numbers. Given this, the Nazis' chief aim was to ensure that those admitted were made aware of the responsibility they owed the nation. Then, while girl students were to be the comrades of their male colleagues, they were also to be closely involved in activities in which German women from all sections of society took part, to remind them that what distinguished them above all else was not their intellect but their gender — or, as the Nazis preferred to say, their 'womanliness'. As the unemployment situation eased and the shortage of skilled personnel became apparent and then acute, the idea which had found currency in earlier Nazi theory — that high intelligence and womanliness were incompatible — was categorically denied.

NOTES

1.   An earlier and more detailed draft of this chapter was published as 'Girls' Higher Education in Germany in the 1930s', *Journal of Contemporary History*, January 1975, pp. 41-69.
2.   Examples of this are: Otto B. Roegele, 'Student im Dritten Reich', Otto B. Roegele (ed.), *Die Deutsche Universität im Dritten Reich*, Munich, 1966, pp. 161-2; Eilers, *op. cit.*, pp. 18-21; Karl Bracher, 'Die Ideologische Gleichschaltung', K. D. Bracher, W. Sauer, G. Schulz, *Die nationalsozialistische Machtergreifung*, Cologne and Opladen, 1960, p. 322; Grunberger, *op. cit.*, pp. 260-61, 285-6.
3.   E. W. Eschmann (ed.), *Wo findet die deutsche Jugend neuen Lebensraum?*, Berlin and Leipzig, 1932, p. v.
4.   Christoph Führ, *op. cit.*, pp. 28-9.
5.   Calculated from figures in *St. J.*, 1932, pp. 426-7.
6.   For detailed examples, see Michael Kater, *op. cit.*, pp. 219-29.
7.   E. Knowles, 'Ketzerische Gedanken über die Invasion der studierenden Frau', *FiS*, April 1930, p. 9.
8.   'Die Lage der Frau in den geistigen Berufen', *BF*, July/August 1932, p. 2.
9.   J. W. Mannhardt, *Hochschulrevolution*, Hamburg, 1933, p. 72.
10.   *Fränkische Tageszeitung, op. cit.*
11.   Luise Raulf, 'Frau und Naturwissenschaft', *FK*, November 1937, p. 13.
12.   Otto Schuster in *Wissen und Dienst*, 1935, no. 1, p. 13.
13.   Edith Runge in *Wissen und Dienst*, 1935, no. 2, pp. 39-40.
14.   BA, R36/1929, 'Gesichtspunkte für die Berufsberatung der Abiturienten in der Krise', letter of 16 February 1933.
15.   BA, R43 II/936, 'Ein Sieb für das Studium', cutting from *Vossische Zeitung*, 18 February 1933.
16.   Joachim Haupt, *Neuordnung im Schulwesen und Hochschulwesen*, Berlin, 1933, p. 9.
17.   *Deutscher Akademischer Austauschdienst* publication, *German Universities – a Manual for Foreign Scholars and Students*, Berlin, 1932, p. 7.
18.   BA, *loc. cit.*
19.   'Gesetz gegen die Überfüllung deutscher Schulen und Hochschulen', *RGB*, 1933 I, 25 April 1933, p. 225.
20.   BA, R43 II/936, 'Zahlenmässige Begrenzung des Zuganges zu den Hochschulen', *Wolff's Telegraphisches Büro*, 28 December 1933.
21.   *Deutsche Hochschulstatistik*, Berlin, 1934-5, pp. *4-*5.

22.	Conclusion drawn from figures given in *St. J.*: 1932, pp. 426-7; 1933, pp. 522-3; 1934, pp. 534-5; 1935, pp. 520-21.
23.	Report in *WuS*, 1935, vol. 15, no. 9, p. 334.
24.	BA, *op. cit.*, 'Das Diensthalbjahr der Studenten', cutting from *Vossische Zeitung*, 9 March 1934.
25.	Calculated from figures in *St. J.*, 1936, pp. 544-5.
26.	The Prussian Education Minister, Rust, issued orders on 20 April and 6 May 1933, by which the classically derived name *Pädagogische Akademie* was replaced by the truly Germanic *Hochschule für Lehrerbildung* (Schumann, *op. cit.*, p. 21, and Haupt, *op. cit.*, pp. 22-3).
27.	Calculated from figures given in *St. J.*: 1936, pp. 547-8; 1933, pp. 526-7.
28.	'Studium der Abiturientinnen, die Studienrätinnen oder Volksschullehrerinnen werden wollen', *DWEuV*, 1936, no. 288, 8 April 1936, p. 209.
29.	Conclusions drawn from figures given in *St. J.*, 1937, p. 582.
30.	'Aufnahme an den preussischen Hochschulen für Lehrerbildung, Herbst 1937', *DWEuV*, 1937, no. 255, 21 April 1937, pp. 241-2.
31.	BA, R 43 II/938b, 'Rust eröffnet Hochschule für Lehrerinnenbildung, Koblenz, *DNB*, no. 1532, 10 November 1937.
32.	'Aufbaulehrgänge für Mädchen von der Volksschule zur Akademie für Lehrerbildung', *Die Frau*, December 1939, p. 84.
33.	Calculated from figures given in *St. J.*: 1939-40, p. 620; 1941-2, p. 645.
34.	IfZ, MA 1163, frame 95585, 'Entwurf einer Reichsregelung der Ausbildung für das Lehramt an höheren Schulen', 16 January 1937.
35.	Homeyer, *op. cit.*, p. K4.
36.	BA, *op. cit.*, 'Die Inflation auf den Hochschulen beendet', *DNB*, no. 74, 18 January 1937.
37.	'Die Akademikerin von heute', and 'Was Zahlen lehren', *VB*, 4 September 1936.
38.	Report in *Die Frau*, April 1937, p. 402.
39.	Calculated from figures given in *St. J.*: 1934, pp. 534-5; 1938, p. 602; 1939-40, p. 615.
40.	The *Semester* (or *Halbjahr*, which the Nazis preferred) was replaced in autumn 1939 by the *Trimester* for flexibility in wartime (Hans Huber, *Erziehung und Wissenschaft im Kriege*, Berlin, 1940, pp. 18-20). The *Semester* was reinstated, however, in 1941 (IfZ, MA 441/6, frame 2-757139, *op. cit.*).
41.	Calculated from figures given in *St. J.*, 1941-2, p. 640.
42.	Calculations made from figures given in *St. J.*: 1932, pp. 426-7; 1933, pp. 522-3; 1934, pp. 534-5; 1935, pp. 520-21; 1936, pp. 544-5; 1937, pp. 580-81; 1941-2, p. 644.
43.	Luise Raulf, *loc. cit.*
44.	Calculated from figures given in *St. J.*, 1941-2, p. 643.
45.	Margaret Esch, 'Die Aussichten des Frauenstudiums', *FZ*, 19 March 1939.
46.	Calculations made from figures given in *St. J.*: 1932, pp. 426-7; 1933, pp. 522-3; 1941-2, p. 643.
47.	BA, R43 II/427, letter from Bormann to Frank, 24 August 1936. This is discussed in Chapter 9, pp. 170-71.
48.	Calculations made from figures given in *St. J., loc. cit.*
49.	See, e.g., 'Was Zahlen lehren', in 'Die deutsche Frau', *VB*, 4 September 1936; Marilese Cremer, 'Mitarbeit der Frau in der Wirtschaftswissenschaft', *FK*, November 1937, p. 11.
50.	Conclusion drawn from figures given in *St. J.*, 1941-2, p. 643.
51.	HA, Reel 13, folder 253, 'Rundschreiben Nr. FW 76/37', from Ilse Eben-Servaes to her Gau representatives, 12 August 1937.
52.	Conclusion drawn from figures given in *St. J., loc. cit.*

53. IfZ, MA 205, NSDAP/HA-Wissenschaft, Dr W. Donke, 'Der Rechtswahrer', cutting from *Deutsche Allgemeine Zeitung (DAZ)*, 11 August 1939.
54. IfZ, MA 441/1, frames 2-750072/4, *BziL*, 13 October and 10 November 1939.
55. 'Aufhebung der Sperre des Neuzugangs zum zahnärztlichen Studium und zum Dentistenberuf', *DWEuV* 1937, no. 200, 22 March 1937, p. 187.
56. Calculated from figures given in *St. J.*: 1932, p. 429; 1933, p. 525. 1938, p. 602; 1941-2, p. 641.
57. IfZ, MA 441/6, frames 2-757139-41, *op. cit.*
58. 'Rede des Preussischen Kultusministers Rust bei der Einweihung der land-gebundenen Hochschule für Lehrerbildung in Lauenberg, 24 Juni 1933', Hiller, *op. cit.*, p. 43.
59. Stephenson, *op. cit.*, Chapter 6, pp. 354-73.
60. Gustav Adolf Scheel, 'Aufgaben und Erziehungsform des deutschen Studententums', *Deutscher Hochschulführer*, 1938, p. 12.
61. BDC, Hildegard Behr, 'Lebenslauf, 27. November 1937'.
62. Gustav Adolf Scheel, *loc. cit.*
63. Otto B. Roegele, *op. cit.*, p. 153.
64. BA, R43 II/936, 'Das Diensthalbjahr der Studenten', cutting from *Vossische Zeitung*, 9 March 1934.
65. IfZ, MA 205, NSDAP/HA-Wissenschaft, 'Der Arbeitsdienst der Studierenden', cutting from *DAZ*, 23 February 1940; Homeyer, *op. cit.*, p. E9.
66. Report in *Deutscher Hochschulführer*, 1939, p. 87.
67. BA, R43 II/938, 'Gemeinschaft studentischer Verbände', *DNB*, no. 157, 29 January 1935, and 'Auflösung studentischer Verbände', *DNB*, no. 1599, 21 October 1935.
68. BA. *Slg. Sch.*, 279-1, letter from Lammers to Derischsweiler, 1 July 1935.
69. *Ibid.*, 'Die Neuorganisation des NSDStB', n.d. (? late 1932).
70. *Ibid.*, letter from the Reich Student Leader to all offices of the NSDStB, 22 April 1936.
71. Anna Kottenhoff, 'Aufgaben und Ziele der Studentinnenarbeit', *Deutsches Frauenschaffen*, 1938, p. 81.
72. Gustav Adolf Scheel, *Die Reichsstudentenführung*, Berlin, 1938, p. 28.
73. Anna Kottenhoff, *op. cit.*, p. 83.
74. 'Hochschulsportordnung', *DWEuV* 1935, 30 October 1934, no. 4, pp. 6-10.
75. Mathilde Betz, 'Einsatz der Studentinnen im Frauendienst', *Deutsches Frauenschaffen*, 1939, p. 103. Gisela Rothe, 'Die Studentin im Frauendienst', *VB*, 18 October 1934.
76. Lieselotte Machwirth, 'Politische Erziehung durch die ANSt', *VB*, 11 December 1935.
77. 'Zur Zusammenarbeit der nationalsozialistischen Studentinnen', *Die Frau*, April 1935, pp. 437-8; 'Was eine Studentin erzählt', *VB*, 4 September 1936. Inge Wolff, 'Hochschulgemeinschaft deutscher Frauen', *FK*, November 1937, inside front cover.
78. Quoted in Otto B. Roegele, *op. cit.*, p. 146.
79. Lieselotte Machwirth, *op. cit.*
80. Lili Michaelis, 'Studentinnen an der Arbeit', *Der Deutsche Student*, July 1936, p. 326, used these words; others expressed similar sentiments, e.g., Scheel, *loc. cit.*; Anna Kottenhoff, 'Das Studium als völkischer Einsatz', *Deutsches Frauenschaffen*, 1939, pp. 97-103.
81. Else Boger-Eichler, 'Rückblick auf die Entwicklung des Frauenstudiums in Deutschland', *FK*, July 1938, p. 3.

8 PROGRESS, PREJUDICE AND PURGE IN THE PROFESSIONS[1]

No area has proved a more sensitive indicator of a society's attitude to the status of women than the professions — that is, those occupations for which a degree or a diploma is required. With the availability of higher education the first prerequisite for admission to the professions, prospects for women in the professions in Germany after the Great War should have been bright, with girls admitted to every German university before the war and the rapid expansion of girl students' numbers in the 1920s. But, at the same time, women had been admitted to full membership of the civil service and the legal and medical professions, as well as to university lectureships, only after the war; and married women had then been admitted to professional positions for the first time. The tradition of male dominance in the professions and prejudice against women achieving positions of responsibility and influence persisted throughout the 1920s into the 1930s, while the straitened economic situation restricted the room for manoeuvre of those prepared to promote the interests of the extremely small minority of women who aspired to a professional career. The depression also gave the National Socialists the excuse to try to put theory into practice by circumscribing the activities of professional women, as of employed women as a whole. But, again similar to the situation in the employment market generally, this soon proved impractical, and the policies which had priority in the Nazi State necessitated warm encouragement to women to enter professional occupations.

Some progress was, however, made in the 1920s, including the achievement of equal pay for women in the public service — whether as teachers, lawyers, doctors, lecturers or civil servants — as a result of Article 128 of the Weimar Constitution. This was in line with practice after the war in the majority of European countries;[2] but the obstacles to full acceptance of women in the professions remained formidable. Speaking of the Federal Republic in the early 1960s, one campaigner of the 1920s could still complain of prejudice against the employment of women on university staffs and as senior civil servants.[3] And an official report published in 1961 admitted that 'in spite of the legally embedded equality of rights, women in professional employment have in no way the same chances as men'.[4] These words well describe the situation in Weimar Germany and the disillusionment felt by those who had imagined that legal equality would revolutionise professional

147

opportunities for women.

There were two main strands in the development of women's position in the professions after the Great War. The first concerned the female sex as a whole, and was conditioned by the relatively recent admission of women to the universities, the losses sustained by men during the war, and general attitudes to the equality of opportunity for women written into the Weimar Constitution. The other element was more specific, concerning the employment of married women, which became a contentious issue across the occupational spectrum after the war, but nowhere more than in the professions. Those who had opposed the admission of women to the professions on the grounds that they were neither intellectually nor physically suited to such demanding and responsible work,[5] were reluctantly prepared in the 1920s to accept the appointment of a select number of dedicated career women — who were by definition unmarried — to meet the demands of the feminist lobby. But there remained many men and women who were opposed in principle to the employment of married women in professional positions, not least because of the decline in the birth rate after the war. Studies of the birth rate among married women graduates which appeared during the 1920s provided little consolation for those who supported unconditionally a woman's right to work: on average, the families of women in professional positions were marginally larger than those of men in similar jobs, but both these groups had a lower birth rate than any other section of the community.[6] The declining birth rate, therefore, continued to be used as ammunition against the professional *Doppelverdiener*.

While the campaign against the professional married woman gathered momentum, it seemed as if the position of women generally in the professions was becoming more secure. The early governments of the Republic, and Hermann Müller's government in 1928-30, were generally well-disposed towards women's advancement, although those of the more economically stable middle years, when the Social Democrats were out of office and the Centre Party dominant, were not inclined to accelerate the progress initially made. Still, if there was no woman Cabinet Minister in Germany during the 1920s and 1930s, the same was true of other European countries, with the exceptions of Britain and the Soviet Union. And women were appointed to senior administrative positions at both the national and Land level.[7] These were, of course, outstanding exceptions, and while a number of other women were appointed to minor official positions, there was only ever a tiny handful at the top. Nevertheless, given the barriers of prejudice which women had to face, the steady progress achieved in the 1920s, particularly in teaching and medicine, was considered reasonable by moderate feminists, even if it was deemed derisory by radical feminists and excessive by conservatives.

With their admission to all areas of the medical profession after 1918 women increased their numbers so that by the end of 1930 there were 2,648 women doctors, 5.6 per cent of the total.[8] In teaching, their share rose to 25 per cent in 1927 in the elementary schools, compared with the pre-war figure of 21 per cent; in the middle schools the rise was from 32 per cent to 50 per cent; and in the girls' senior schools their share remained around 75 per cent.[9] Women were also admitted to university lectureships, and in summer 1927 thirty-one women lecturers formed the tiny proportion of 0.6 per cent of the total number.[10] Probably the biggest breakthrough came in October 1922, when three women were admitted as junior barristers to a Berlin court, thus entering one of the most sacrosanct of male preserves. But although their numbers had increased to twenty-five by September 1930, women made little progress beyond the lower levels of the legal profession.[11]

Like their male colleagues, professional women joined together in organisations. Some became members of groups which had male members, but the large number of professional organisations exclusively for women testifies to an alignment chiefly by sex, following the precedent set by the feminists who had campaigned before the war for the unconditional admission of women to the professions. This was reinforced by the association of the women's professional organisations with the other women's clubs — whether of a vocational, social or a charitable nature — in the annual Women's Congress.[12]

The strongest and most senior women's professional group was the *Allgemeiner Deutscher Lehrerinnenverein* (General Union of German Women Teachers), founded by Helene Lange in 1890. By 1930, it had more than 40,000 members, from a variety of localities, denominations and types of school.[13] As many of the women's organisations became corporate members of the BDF, so the organisations of women doctors, teachers, civil servants, lecturers and students had their own federation, the *Deutscher Akademikerinnenbund*.[14] There were also groups which remained outside this combine, chiefly the denominational teaching associations like the *Verein Deutscher Evangelischer Lehrerinnen*,[15] and the *Verein katholischer Lehrerinnen*.[16] The identity of the women's professional organisations was often asserted in the publication of an independent journal; for example, the magazine of the women doctors, *Die Ärztin*, paralleled the men's *Der Arzt*.[17] A latecomer to the field of women's professional groups was the *Vereinigung Deutscher Hochschuldozentinnen*, founded in 1927 by Professor Rhoda Erdmann, for the small but growing number of women lecturers in universities and colleges.[18]

The governments of the Reich and Länder found themselves faced with two conflicting demands: Article 128 of the 1919 Constitution demanded the abolition of all discriminations against women in the civil service; but there was a desperate need to cut public spending and, therefore, to reduce the number of professional people in the public service. This could be most easily achieved, it was thought, by persuading married women to resign, and as an emergency measure — which later served as a useful precedent — the Reich Minister of Finance announced that married women civil servants in the postal and transport services would receive a lump sum if they resigned during the chaotic financial year 1922-3.[19] But if the Minister had agonised over this decision, some of the Länder had no compunction in blatantly ignoring the provisions of Article 128; it was left to the courts to reverse measures enacted to discriminate against married women teachers in both Bavaria and Württemberg.[20]

Opposition to employed married women concentrated on those in professional jobs for two reasons: firstly, it was regretted but recognised that many working-class women were forced to bring a second wage into the home to support the family; secondly, it was conceded that many married women, particularly in agriculture, the textile trade and some clerical jobs, were doing work seldom done by men; but it was claimed that professional women could easily be replaced by men, and might well be preventing a suitably qualified man from finding a post. In some cases, complaints were made about the employment of married women by single women who felt that they should have priority. In June 1923, the Union of German Evangelical Women Teachers asked the Minister of Finance to provide severance pay to encourage married women to retire from the profession since, said its President, many would do so if they could afford to, and would thus leave vacancies for jobless single women teachers.[21] This was no isolated instance: in March 1923, Christine Teusch, a Centre Party deputy, had asked the Minister of Finance to authorise payment to married women who retired from a professional post; but the Minister had regretfully refused because, he said, the money was not available.[22]

Even in difficult times, the goodwill of the more liberal Reich Governments was not in doubt. In 1920, draft regulations were framed to define the status of married women in the public service, to bring the Civil Code into line with the Constitution.[23] By 1929, however, this had still not been achieved,[24] and, although he regarded the matter as urgent, Severing — as Reich Minister of the Interior — had to admit in September 1929 that the majority necessary for legislation could not be constructed. Instead, he planned to incorporate it into his projected comprehensive civil service law.[25] But Müller's Government had demonstrated its good faith by instructing Hilferding — the Reich Minister of Finance — to make provision for increasing the number of places for women administrators in the Reich Ministries in his 1929 budget. The aim was to open an avenue to promotion for women clerical workers who had obtained a qualification which made them eligible for the higher civil service.[26] This measure was accepted by the Reichstag as part of the 1929 budget.[27]

But this was when the economic situation was worsening, and with it prospects in the professions. In autumn 1929 the Reich Ministers were again seeking ways of saving money by reducing staff and were increasingly convinced that the most convenient solution was to offer severance pay to married women if they resigned voluntarily.[28] In teaching the situation was grim, with 29,000 qualified teachers jobless in Prussia alone,[29] and by the end of 1929 there was a large surplus of applicants for professional positions of every kind.[30] The situation only deteriorated in 1930 and 1931, while the number of students — who would soon join the queue for professional jobs — rose to record proportions.[31] It was claimed that women were suffering even more than men,[32] and certainly while there were 15,000 male candidates waiting for vacancies among 13,600 male teachers with permanent jobs in Prussia in 1931, 7,500 qualified women teachers waited for vacancies among the mere 1,900 permanent female members of school staffs.[33]

The deepening of the economic crisis led to increasing attacks on the *Doppelverdiener*, especially in the professions. In response, a Government Commission, appointed in 1931 to investigate ways of mitigating the unemployment problem, particularly recommended the offering of 'compensation' to professional married women who retired. Reporting this, a radical feminist observed that 'There does not yet exist a law which entitles or obliges the State or a private employer to dismiss female civil servants or clerical workers just because they are married'. But, she predicted pessimistically, it seemed likely that such a measure would figure in the law being contemplated on the basis of the Commission's report.[34]

The feminists were convinced that the Government's attitude towards employed women, and particularly women in the professions, was at best negative, and probably hostile.[35] But the Brüning Government was extremely unwilling to discriminate against any group, including married women; reluctantly, at the end of 1931, it sounded out the Reichstag to find if support could be secured for a bill to permit the dismissal of married women civil servants. The response was positive.[36] As the Government prepared its bill, feminists of all colours began a campaign to oppose it. Indeed, they had a degree of reason on their side: the figures that were bandied about — based on the 1925 census — showed that the furore concerned at most 7,000 out of a total of 3,700,000 employed married women; thus the retirement of even all married women civil servants would make a negligible contribution to solving the unemployment problem, even if it provided jobs for a few more male graduates.[37]

If the feminists were alarmed by this development, they were even more concerned by the way the campaign against the *Doppelverdiener* seemed to be broadening into an attack on the general position of women in employment, particularly in responsible, well-paid positions. One example of this was a proposal made in the Prussian Landtag by the Centre Party – with the support of leading Catholic women – that employed single women as well as married women should be replaced by men.[38] Further, the increasing strength of the National Socialists, evidenced in the Reichstag elections of 1930 and 1932, gave rise to fears that the situation could become very much worse. Lida Gustava Heymann warned that in the Third Reich women would be forced to revert to their role in Imperial days, which she characterised as that of childbearing machine and maidservant of men, with all political rights revoked.[39] A more prosaic, but equally grim picture was painted by a DVP supporter, who predicted that under the Nazis women would lose not only their political rights but also the right to work in the public service. She was able to support her gloomy forecast with references to *Mein Kampf*, the Nazi Party Programme, and speeches by Nazis, including Alfred Rosenberg and Hermann Esser.[40]

Nazi propaganda indeed justified fears of this nature, but, as was to become increasingly apparent, Nazi propaganda did not always represent the Party's ideas faithfully. In fact, the Nazis recognised that many women were obliged to earn a living, often against their will.[41] These, at least – including perhaps some of the 128,000 professional women[42] – could be lured back into the home by family allowances and the marriage loan scheme. But it would be much more difficult to persuade women in the professions who looked on their job as an absorbing career that their vocation lay exclusively within the sphere of home and family. They would therefore have to be coerced into accepting their 'natural calling', in which they would find true happiness. So ran the theory.[43] It was recognised, however, that not all women would marry, and so those who did not would have to find employment in occupations concerned with women, children and domestic matters. In this way, they would at least be able to fulfil their maternal instincts at second hand.[44] The nation would benefit, too, from the best use of their womanly talents: 'Helfen, Heilen, Erziehen' (helping, healing, training) were women's natural functions.[45] The Nazis, therefore, perhaps unintentionally, implicitly recognised the need for women in the medical and teaching professions and also in skilled social work.[46]

To this extent, there was to be little for the Nazis to change. The census of May 1933 showed that half of all professional women were engaged in teaching at various levels, with another 10 per cent involved in occupations connected with health and welfare. The other most significant employer of women in the professional grade was the Ministry of Posts, with almost 34,000, or more than a quarter of all women in this category. This group might well be a target for Nazi discriminatory measures; and there could be little doubt that the Nazis would view with greatest disfavour the 10,000 women employed as officials at the national and local level. In both absolute and relative terms, the number of married women in this group was small: a mere 4,000 professional married women in 1933 constituted less than 4 per cent of the total category; by contrast, more than one third of all employed women were married, with the result that almost one third of all married women were employed.[47] Thus, any campaign against this section of working women could, even at its most effective, have only negligible results for the labour market as a whole.

Some of the Nazis' work was, however, done for them before they came to power, as the reduction in the number of married women in the professions from 7,000 in 1925 to 4,000 in 1933 — the census coming before Nazi legislation in this matter — shows. In May 1932, Groener, as Reich Minister of the Interior, introduced a measure which provided that married women employed in responsible positions by the State would not only always, understandably, be permitted to resign at their own request, but might also be dismissed without such a request, if 'their financial maintenance seemed from the size of the income in their family to be guaranteed in the long term'. Three months' notice had to be given, and reasonable compensation paid; but this severance payment cancelled all existing pension rights. Provision was made for the possible re-employment of a woman who left her job as a result of this measure, if there were a dramatic change for the worse in her financial situation.[48] But this promise could not disguise the stark fact that the Constitution was, in the context of equal rights for women in the public service, a dead letter.

The law clearly found favour in some quarters; on 7 June 1932, the Minister of Posts issued his own version of it. This included the more positive approach of asking all married women officials in the postal service whether they wished to resign. Those who did not were required to declare the income of their family as a whole and the occupation of their husband, so that an arbitration committee could decide if they really needed their income; if not, they were to be dismissed, although the order of dismissal would be revoked if their financial position ceased to be secure.[49] The Minister of the Interior approved of these regulations to the extent of recommending their adoption by the other Reich agencies, to achieve national uniformity.[50]

The feminists' reaction was, naturally, one of opposition, but they were by no means united. A stinging attack on the law of 30 May came from a radical feminist, Dr Kläre Schoedon. In an article entitled 'Sic transit gloria . . .' she claimed that Article 128 of the Constitution had been torn to shreds and that a married woman had lost any right to independence. Pouring burning scorn on the clauses designed to mitigate the measure, she condemned those who had passed it into law in the Reichstag. The Centre Party had been the bill's sponsor, and its view of the place of married women was faithfully reflected in the measure, wrote Kläre Schoedon; the views of the Nationalist Party were sufficiently similar to the Centre's to guarantee the bill its support. Only the Communists were prepared to vote against it, insisting in debate that it amounted to an outright denial of equal rights for women; such a suggestion did not deter the Social Democrats from voting for the bill, as — not surprisingly — did the Nazis.[51]

Apart from the Communists, only one party did not support the bill; members of the tiny Staatspartei, the former DDP, including Gertrud Bäumer — who ought to have been leading a parliamentary campaign against the bill — abstained. Indeed, Gertrud Bäumer spoke against the measure in debate, prophetically calling it 'a dangerous precedent', but it was her docility, and that of the other women deputies, in the name of Party solidarity, which most disgusted Kläre Schoedon, particularly the way in which Helene Weber of the Centre Party — herself a high ranking civil servant in the Prussian Ministry of Welfare[52] — had spoken in favour of the measure. The other source of deep concern to Kläre Schoedon was that the dismissal of the relevant eight or nine hundred women would do more to damage women's rights than to benefit the unemployment situation, the purpose it was supposed to serve.[53]

But there were clearly enough women, both in and outside the Reichstag, who were prepared to accept this measure to ensure that there would be no concerted opposition from the ranks even of interested women. Marie-Elisabeth Lüders, a Staatspartei deputy at the time, has since written that a hard campaign was fought in the Reichstag against the law, but that some of the women's professional organisations approved of this 'arbitrary measure'.[54] Certainly, the attitude of those affiliated to the Churches seemed to justify Kläre Schoedon's fear that the measure would succeed in setting the unmarried against the married woman civil servant.[55] The law did, however, have one redeeming feature. As a result of a campaign waged by the Union of Women Post and Telegraph Officials, a married woman who had to retire because of 'secure' financial circumstances was to be re-employed 'if at all possible' if her husband ceased to be able to provide for her. This was an improvement on the situation which had obtained for a year, in which married women were the last to be considered for a job, regardless of their circumstances. But the law was generally regarded by feminists as a clear attack on women's rights, and it was as such that both the BDF and the Union of Civil Servants condemned it.[56]

If the situation was depressing for those in favour of equality of opportunity for women in 1932, the appointment of Adolf Hitler as Chancellor on 30 January 1933 added the new dimension that many had feared. The Nazis accused intellectual men and women of a selfish individualism which was antithetical to the Party's principle of 'Gemeinnutz vor Eigennutz', the subordination of self-interest to the general good,[57] and were quick to exert tight control over the professions.[58] The new Government moved with breathtaking speed: within a month of the *Machtübernahme*, Gertrud Bäumer lost the job she had held in the Ministry of the Interior for almost fourteen years, and other women in the higher civil service were quickly dismissed as well.[59] Since there was as yet no legislation to provide for such action, the message Gertrud Bäumer received, without warning, on 27 February 1933, was that she was being granted 'leave of absence until further notice' by the new Minister, Wilhelm Frick. After asking the reason, she was told that her policies in respect of both youth and women's affairs 'are contrary to the attitude of the Minister and make collaboration impossible'. Gertrud Bäumer wryly commented that Frick's knowledge of her policies was restricted to the distorted way in which they were described in his own Party's propaganda.[60] Along with a number of other officials, she was finally given notice of dismissal on 12 April, as a result of a law of 7 April;[61] paragraph four of this permitted the dismissal from the public service of those whom the Nazis felt to be 'politically unreliable'.[62] To add insult to injury, Gertrud Bäumer's pension was made as small as possible, with her pre-war service as a school teacher left out of the reckoning.[63] She did, however, derive grim humour from the information that not one but two men had been brought in to replace her at the Ministry 'since no-one has a grasp of all the business involved'.[64]

Gertrud Bäumer was convinced that the dismissal on political grounds of herself and other women in responsible positions was a deliberate act of discrimination against 'women as such'.[65] But among school teachers it is clear that members of both sexes were being affected in a similar way by the provisions of the law of 7 April, although proportionately women tended to fare worse. In Prussia in 1933, twenty-two of the 261 headmasters of girls' senior schools and twenty-three of the sixty-eight headmistresses were dismissed. But, in most cases, these men and women were re-employed as senior teachers. Of the teachers themselves, 1 per cent of the men and 4.5 per cent of the women in established positions were dismissed; it was estimated that at least two-thirds of the women were non-'Aryan'. And almost all of the seventy-nine probationary women teachers who were dismissed were found to be non-'Aryan', too. It was, no doubt, convenient to have categories of women teachers who could be dismissed on unconventional, if now legal, grounds, since there was still the problem of a surplus of candidates for their jobs. During 1933 — probably largely as a result of the dismissals — the situation improved so far that of the 1,320 candidates available at the start of the year, only one third were still without a position twelve months later.[65]

There were protests against the dismissal of both men and women as a result of provisions in the law of 7 April, but often these led to the dismissal of the protester. Professor Anna Siemsen of the University of Jena suffered because she courageously criticised the dismissal of a valued male colleague.[67] No doubt her membership of the SPD — she was an SPD Reichstag deputy from 1928 to 1930 — set the seal on her own dismissal, after which she emigrated to Switzerland.[68] There could be little surprise that the Berlin lawyer, Hilde Benjamin, was banned from the practice of law; in addition to having been one of the defence team in the trial of the murderer of the Nazi hero, Horst Wessel, she was a card carrying Communist; now she joined in the work of the Communist underground.[69]

Other women immediately found disfavour with the Government because of their outspoken pacifism and internationalism during the 1920s, and lost their jobs, often under a clause of the law of 7 April. Women like Alice Salomon — immediately unacceptable, as a Jewess — who had had a distinguished career in social and educational work,[70] and Minna Specht, a teacher who had turned her attention to radical, experimental education after the war,[71] had acquired an international reputation, but now saw no alternative to emigration. Marie-Elisabeth Lüders, distinguished as a politician as well as in her professional activity in social work and education, stayed on in Germany, like Gertrud Bäumer, in relative obscurity, deprived of her job and eventually forbidden to publish her writings.[72] But these women suffered because of their politics, in the broadest sense, rather than because of their sex; the large number of women who continued to hold professional posts, and to be newly appointed to them, in and after 1933 confirms that the reasons the Nazis gave for the dismissals were the true ones.

However, since a substantial number of the women who had been admitted to the professions and found a position in public life under the Weimar Republic had also been at least moderate feminists, and often belonged to a liberal or socialist political party, the proportion of women who lost their positions for 'political' reasons was high in relation to their representation. The resulting depletion of women's numbers was regretted not only by feminists and progressives: misgivings, and even protests, were voiced also by women from among the ranks of the Nazis' own supporters. Sophie Rogge-Börner, a sympathiser but not a Party member, wrote a heartfelt plea to Hitler in February 1933 for the inclusion of the best people in the leadership of the country, regardless of sex. She claimed, in the light of the previous couple of years' experience, that the State and various official bodies were working to deny women their rightful place in the professions. Her outspokenness brought her into trouble with the Gestapo in 1934, and in May 1937 her magazine, *Die Deutsche Kämpferin*, was banned on the grounds that her articles were so criticial of the regime that they were considered abroad to be examples of opposition to National Socialism within Germany.[73]

Less impulsive than Sophie Rogge-Börner, the conservative *Ring Nationaler Frauen* was anxious to demonstrate its approval of the elimination of dissidents from prominent positions. But, in a letter written to Hitler in April 1933, the leadership of the *Ring* expressed concern that those women who were deservedly being dismissed for 'political unreliability' were too often being replaced not by suitable women but by men.[74] Such protests were no surprise to Gertrud Bäumer, who firmly believed that the women in the Party, also, would have to take up the struggle for women's rights, particularly in the teaching profession.[75] She based her hopes largely on Gertrud Baumgart's book *Frauenbewegung Gestern und Heute*, a moderately feminist tract demanding equality of opportunity for women in the professions,[76] written by a woman who had joined the NSDAP in 1932.[77] But Gertrud Bäumer underestimated the ruthlessness with which the Nazis would subdue any 'women's rights' campaign in their own ranks.

As she had feared, the law of 30 May 1932 proved a convenient precedent. Section three of a law of 30 June 1933 consisted of amendments to the 1932 Act, all of which further eroded the position of married women civil servants. Firstly, dismissal was to be unconditional for women whose husbands were also employed by the State, since it was assumed that their financial position was therefore secure. In another modification the period between notice of dismissal and the termination of employment was reduced from three months to one month; at the same time, the maximum possible severance pay for long service was reduced, although the amounts for shorter periods of service were not changed. The paragraph permitting the re-employment of women dismissed remained, surprisingly, intact, but since the 1932 law had specified that this would occur 'if at all possible', it would be easy for a Government to ignore the provision *de facto*. And now dismissal and — in theory, at least — reinstatement were to be at the discretion of the Government alone, instead of being in the hands of the

157

committee of arbitration set up under the 1932 Act.

One of the saving graces of the 1932 Act had been that it applied only to women employed by Reich agencies, thus exempting school teachers. In June 1933, however, the Government made the new provisions applicable to any married woman employed in the public service at Land and local level also. Exceptions to the rule of dismissal on the grounds of financial security were still to be permitted in individual cases, if the Minister of the Interior approved; but the general tone of the law suggested that such exceptions would be rare. Then a small sub-paragraph of major importance was inserted: it provided for the possibility of 'departure from the provisions of Article 128, paragraph 2, of the Constitution', and thus allowed, once again, for women in the public service to the remunerated at a different — in fact, a lower — rate from men. And finally, it was decreed that women could not be appointed to public service positions on a permanent basis until they reached the age of thirty-five.[78]

Most of the provisions in the law of 30 June applied specifically to married women but the clauses affecting remuneration and appointment on a permanent basis caused considerable apprehension, especially among female civil servants and teachers, that there was to be a systematic campaign to drive women out of professional positions altogether. The new measures certainly reinforced Nazi propaganda about the Party's view of the role of women. Frick now found himself having to allay the fears which his own Party had consciously generated by publicly announcing that a number of authorities had proceeded with far more vigour than was necessary in the matter of dismissing or demoting women, in the belief that this was in accordance with National Socialist policy. The zealous officials of Hamburg, for example, dismissed 103 permanent and sixty-eight probationary married women teachers only a month after the passage of the law.[79] Frick emphasised that the law did not provide for a general campaign against women in the public service, whether as civil servants or teachers; rather, the law of 7 April applied to men as well as women. As for the law of 30 June, he said, it seemed that he had to repeat that its section covering the dismissal of married women should be applied only to married women, and that their financial security must by guaranteed 'in the long term'; he had received a number of complaints that this law was being applied more freely than was legally permitted, which he regretted. But Frick did mention that, in his view, if a man and a woman of equal ability were candidates for a post, the man should be given preference, although he also felt that women ought to be appointed to positions to which they were specially suited, particularly those connected with youth welfare and some areas of education.[80]

Although Frick demonstrated moderation here, it became apparent that much of the damage had already been done. Women had not been well represented in the higher grades of the professions before 1933, but now those who had been employed at this level were no longer to be found there; this was very largely, of course, the result of the law of 7 April. But the women dismissed from high level positions were not, on the whole, replaced by other women. The dismissal of women who had been employed as higher officials in ministries of the Reich, Prussian and Saxon governments before 1933, as advisers in matters of female and child labour, positions which came within the scope of the welfare activities deemed suitable for women, was not followed by the appointment of more women. However, of the four women who had been senior industrial welfare superintendents before 1933, three were retained in office, along with a number of their more junior colleagues.[81]

In teaching, it was claimed that women were being driven out of their jobs — particularly in the senior schools — in favour of men. Hamburg was regarded as a particular offender, since in addition to dismissing its married women teachers it was also forcing unmarried women into premature retirement at the age of fifty-two.[82] On a larger scale, Rust announced in April 1934 that the ratio of male to female teachers in Prussian girls' schools of 3:5.3 should be adjusted to 3:2 by filling vacancies with men. Male teachers wounded in the Great War were to be given priority, except in biology and gymnastics, which should continue to be taught only by women.[83] Two Nazi principles were obviously in conflict here: the Party emphatically rejected any kind of coeducation and insisted on the separate functions of the sexes, which would logically mean that girls should be taught exclusively by women; but it also asserted that men should be given preference in job opportunities, particularly in the professions. In this instance, the practical advantage attaching to the second of these in time of unemployment was regarded as the overriding consideration.

Effective protests on a corporate basis against discrimination were hardly possible, since the Nazis promptly took the astute step of 'reforming' the professional organisations. In April 1933 Gertrud Bäumer wrote to Emmy Beckmann, President of the *Allgemeiner Deutscher Lehrerinnenverein*, advising that the organisation join the *NS-Lehrerbund* (Nazi Teachers' League), without protest and if necessary under different leadership, in order at least to continue in existence.[84] But a month later she was asking Emmy Beckmann to write an article about the ADLV for *Die Frau*, as an epitaph.[85] Official pressure had led its leadership to dissolve the organisation early in May 1933; its last act was to recommend its members to join the Nazi Teachers' League, an organisation for men and women teachers alike.[86] The control of the Party over the teaching profession seemed undisputed when in January 1934 Hans Schemm, Bavarian Minister of Education and leader of the League, announced that 90 per cent of all German teachers were members of it. Women teachers lost not only their organisation but also their magazine, which was first taken over by a Nazi teacher, Hedwig Förster, and then replaced by a new publication under the editorship of Auguste Reber-Gruber, an official of the Nazi Teachers' League.[87]

A few groups did manage to survive, at least for a time, while the *Gleichschaltung* (coordination) of the professional organisations proceeded apace. But these were special cases; for example, the Union of Catholic Women Teachers (VkdL) was protected by the Concordat of 20 July 1933 between the Nazi Government and the Vatican.[88] But, even so, its days were numbered: it was finally dissolved in October 1937,[89] when relations between the Catholic Church and the Nazi regime were becoming increasingly strained. The *Deutscher Akademikerinnenbund* was allowed to continue in existence largely because it had sacrificed its leader, Mari-Elisabeth Lüders,[90] and shown complete willingness to cooperate with the new order.[91] But, as always, the Nazis could not tolerate for long the survival of any group which was not of their own creation, and in December 1935 the *Deutscher Akademikerinnenbund* was dissolved to allow the Nazis' own *Reichsbund deutscher Akademikerinnen* a monopoly.[92]

The old multiplicity of organisations within each profession was superseded by monolithic bodies under Party control. In addition to the *NS-Lehrerbund* (NSLB) for teachers there was the *NSD-Dozentenbund* for university lecturers, Hans Frank's *Bund Nationalsozialistischer Deutscher Juristen* for lawyers,[93] the *Reichsbund der Deutschen Beamten* (RDB) for administrators[94] and the *Reichsärztekammer* (Reich Chamber of Doctors) for the medical profession.[95] The lines were now firmly drawn between the individual professions, with men and women belonging to the same associations. This contrasted noticeably with previous practice, and was hardly in line with the Nazis' policy of keeping the sexes in separate groups. But it was completely consistent with the Nazi view that political leadership was the concern of men alone (these new professional groupings were primarily political formations), and it was also in keeping with the Nazi idea of the 'community', whether that of the nation as a whole or that of a section of it.[96] However, since women were in a minority in all professions, and in a small minority in administrative posts and the legal profession, their chances of influencing the running of these organisations — insofar as this was possible in the Nazi State — were minimal.

NOTES

1.   An earlier and less detailed draft of this chapter and Chapter 9 together was published as: Jill McIntyre, 'Women and the Professions in Germany, 1930-1940', Anthony Nicholls and Erich Matthias (ed.), *German Democracy and the Triumph of Hitler*, London, 1971, pp. 175-213.
2.   Vera Douie (ed.), *The Professional Position of Women: a World Survey immediately preceding World War II*, London, 1947, pp. 20-38.
3.   Marie-Elisabeth Lüders, 'Aus der Frauenarbeit des Reichstags 1919-33', Ernst Deuerlein (ed.), *Der Reichstag. Aufsätze, Protokolle und Darstellungen zur Geschichte der parlamentarischen Vertretung des deutschen Volkes, 1871-1933*, Bonn, 1963, p. 113.
4.   'The Position of Women', *Germany Reports* (Bundesrepublik publication), Bonn, 1961, p. 679.
5.   Kirchhoff, *loc. cit.*; Russell, *loc. cit.*; report by Maximilian Harden in *Die Zukunft*, 24 August 1918, pp. 224-32.
6.   Agnes Martens-Edelmann, 'Frauenstudium, Ehe und Mutterschaft', *Die Frau*, November 1936, pp. 84-9.
7.   The detail of this is given in Chapter 1, p. 24.
8.   Mathilde Kelchner, *Die Frau und der weibliche Arzt*, Leipzig, 1934, p. 14; *St. J.*: 1928, p. 486; 1931, p. 406.
9.   *Ibid.*: 1914, pp. 322-4; 1924-5, pp. 355-7.
10.   *Ibid.*, 1928, p. 512.
11.   '10 Jahre weibliche Richter', *Die Frau*, January 1933, p. 249.
12.   BA, *Nachlass* Katharina von Kardorff, no. 28, p. 9, 'Der XI. Frauencongress in Berlin, 17.-22.6.1929: Ehrenbeirat der Verbände'.
13.   Puckett, *op. cit.*, p. 178.
14.   Kirkpatrick, *op. cit.*, p. 50.
15.   BA, R2/1291, letter from the committee of the VDEL to the Reich Minister of Finance, 7 June 1923.
16.   Eilers, *op. cit.*, p. 76n.
17.   Report in *FiS*, May 1929, p. 4.
18.   'Die deutsche Frau in Lehre und Forschung', *FK*, February 1938, p. 3.
19.   BA, *op. cit.*, letter from the Württemberg Minister of Finance to the Reich Minister of Finance, 31 March 1923.
20.   Auguste Steiner, 'Zur Berufsarbeit der verheirateten Frau', *BF*, February 1933, p. 6.
21.   BA, *op. cit.*, letter of 7 June 1923, *op. cit.*
22.   *Ibid.*, letter from the Reich Minister of Finance to Frau Teusch, May 1923 (exact date not given).
23.   *Ibid.*, letter from the Reich Minister of the Interior to the State Secretary in the Chancellery, 10 July 1923.
24.   *Ibid.*, letter from Severing to Reich Ministers *et al.*, 12 July 1929.
25.   *Ibid.*, letter from Severing to Reich Ministers *et al.*, 21 September 1929.
26.   *Ibid.*, letter from Hilferding to the State Secretary in the Chancellery, 19 November 1928.
27.   *Ibid.*, notice issued by section IB of the Reich Ministry of Finance, undated (? end of March 1929).
28.   *Ibid.*, letter from the Minister of Transport, Dr Rocholl, to the German Railways Corporation, 5 October 1929.
29.   Christoph Führ, *op. cit.*, p. 29.
30.   Georg Gothein, 'Die wirtschaftlichen Aussichten für Industrie und Mittelstand', *Deutsche Handels-warte*, 1929, no. 4, p. 90, found in BA, *Nachlass* Gothein, no. 79.

31. See above, Chapter 7, pp. 130-31.
32. Report in *BF*, July/August 1932, p. 2.
33. Report in *BF*, February 1932, p. 6.
34. Grete Stoffel, 'Die Arbeitslosigkeit und die Frauenarbeit', *FiS*, August/September 1931, p. 5.
35. 'Die Lage der Frau in den geistigen Berufen', *BF*, July/August 1932, p. 2.
36. BA, R45 II/64, Lotte Garnich, 'Krise und Frauenberufsarbeit', *Frauenrundschau*, 4 February 1932, pp. 1115-7.
37. *Ibid.*; Grete Stoffel, *loc. cit.*; Maria Hellersberg, 'Die Berufsarbeit der Frau', *BF*, February 1932, pp. 1-2.
38. Grete Stoffel, *loc. cit.*
39. Lida Gustava Heymann, 'Nachkriegspsychose', *FiS*, March 1931, pp. 1-2.
40. BA, *op. cit.*, Elisabeth Schwarzhaupt, 'Die Stellung des Nationalsozialismus zur Frau', *Frauenrundschau*, 6 April 1932, p. 1169.
41. Alice Rilke, 'Die erwerbstätige Frau im Dritten Reich', *NS-Frauenbuch*, Munich, 1934, p. 65; Angela Meister, 'Die deutsche Industriearbeiterin', Munich University dissertation, 1938, pp. 26-7.
42. *St. D. R.*, vol. 451, section 3, p. 49.
43. 'Die Geschlechter im Dritten Reich', *Fränkische Tageszeitung*, 17 April 1934.
44. Siber, *op. cit.*, pp. 26-7; Lydia Gottschewski, *Männerbund und Frauenfrage*, Munich, 1934, p. 71. An account of the role played by Paula Siber and Lydia Gottschewski in the Nazi women's organisation is given in Stephenson, *op. cit.*, pp. 352-64.
45. Report in *VB*, 17 March 1934.
46. Vogel, *op. cit.*, p. 6; Elfriede Eggener, *op. cit.*, pp. 37 and 47.
47. *St. D. R.*, *op. cit.*, pp. 37, 76.
48. 'Gesetz über die Rechtsstellung der weiblichen Beamten', *RGB*, 1932 I, 30 May 1932, pp. 245-6.
49. BA, R43 II/427, 'Ausführungsanweisungen der DRP', 7 June 1932.
50. *Ibid.*, letter from Freiherr von Gayl to the Reich Ministers and authorities, 15 June 1932.
51. Kläre Schoedon, 'Sic transit gloria . . .', *FiS*, July 1932, pp. 5-7.
52. Horkenbach, *op. cit.*, p. 766.
53. Kläre Schoedon, *op. cit.*, pp. 6-7.
54. Marie-Elisabeth Lüders, *op. cit.*, p. 122.
55. Kläre Schoedon, *op. cit.*, p. 6.
56. Auguste Steiner, *op. cit.*, pp. 4-6.
57. Point 24 of the Nazi Party Programme, found in Hofer, *op. cit.*, pp. 30-31.
58. Taylor Cole, 'The Evolution of the German Labour Front', *Political Science Quarterly*, 1937, pp. 540-41; *Organisationsbuch der NSDAP*, Munich, 1938, p. 154; Wolfgang Schäfer, *NSDAP. Entwicklung und Struktur der Staatspartei des Dritten Reiches*, Hanover, 1956, p. 57.
59. Beckmann, *op. cit.*, letter to Emmy Beckmann, 13 April 1933, p. 50.
60. BA, *Kl. Erw.*, no. 296-(1), letter from Gertrud Bäumer to Dorothee von Velsen, 7 March 1933.
61. Beckmann, *loc. cit.*
62. 'Gesetz zur Wiederherstellung des Berufsbeamtentums', *RGB*, 1933 I, 7 April 1933, pp. 175-7.
63. Beckmann, *op. cit.*, letter to Emmy Beckmann, 30 June 1933, p. 53.
64. *Ibid.*, letter to Emmy Beckmann, 13 April 1933, p. 50.
65. *Ibid.*, pp. 50-51.
66. Ludwig Wülker, *op. cit.*, pp. 83-5.
67. Kurt Grossmann, 'Der Fall Anna Siemsen', *FiS*, March 1933, pp. 7-8.

68. Wilhelm Kosch, *Biographisches Staatshandbuch*, 1963, vol. 2, p. 1110.
69. Stockhorst, *op. cit.*, p. 51.
70. Kosch, *op. cit.*, p. 1060.
71. *Internationales Jahrbuch für Geschichtsunterricht*, 1961/2, p. 3.
72. Kosch, *op. cit.*, p. 792.
73. BDC, no. 280, report in *Ahnenerbe*, 18 August 1938; Sophie Rogge-Börner, 'Deutsche Frauen an Adolf Hitler', Irmgard Reichnau (ed.), *Deutsche Frauen an Adolf Hitler*, Leipzig, 1934, p. 8.
74. BA, R43 II/427, letter from the committee of the *Ring Nationaler Frauen* to Hitler, April 1933 (exact date not given).
75. Beckmann, *loc. cit.*
76. Gertrud Baumgart, *Frauenbewegung Gestern und Heute*, Heidelberg, 1933, pp. 17 and 31.
77. BDC, Gertrud Baumgart's Party Membership Card.
78. 'Gesetz zur Änderung von Vorschriften auf dem Gebiet des allgemeinen Beamten-, des Besoldungs- und des Versorgungsrechts', *RGB*, 1933 I, 30 June 1933, Section III, 'Rechtstellung der weiblichen Beamten', pp. 434-5.
79. Report in *FZ*, 4 August 1933.
80. BA, R43 II/427, letter from Frick to the Reich Ministers, Land governments and *Reichsstatthalter*, 5 October 1933; 'Die Beschäftigung weiblicher Beamten und Lehrer: Eine grundsätzliche Stellungnahme des Reichsinnenministers', *VB*, 13 October 1933.
81. Else Lüders, 'Weibliche Aufsicht in Fabriken', *Die Deutsche Kämpferin*, August 1935, pp. 182-3.
82. 'Mädchenbildungs- und Lehrerinnenfragen in der Pädagogischen Presse', *Die Frau*, June 1934, p. 571.
83. Report in *FZ*, 9 April 1934.
84. Beckmann, *op. cit.*, letter to Emmy Beckmann, 13 April 1933, p. 50.
85. *Ibid.*, letter to Emmy Beckmann, 11 May 1933, p. 52.
86. Gertrud Bäumer, 'Das Haus ist zerfallen', *Die Frau*, June 1933, p. 513.
87. *Die Frau*, June 1934, *op. cit.*, pp. 570-71.
88. Report in *DMäd*, 15 February 1934, p. 48.
89. Report in *FZ*, 20 October 1937.
90. Kirkpatrick, *op. cit.*, pp. 50 and 55.
91. BA, *Kl. Erw.*, 296-(1), letter from Gertrud Baumer to Dorothee von Velsen, 15 November 1934.
92. 'Fünf Jahre Reichsfrauenführung', *FK*, February 1939, p. 4.
93. This changed its name to the more Germanic *NS-Rechtswahrerbund (NSRB)* in April 1936 (*Meyers Lexikon*, vol. 8, Leipzig, 1940, col. 150).
94. Hermann Neef, *Das Beamtenorganisationswesen im nationalsozialistischen Staat*, Berlin, 1935, pp. 4-5, 11-12.
95. 'Reichsärzteordnung', *RGB*, 1935 I, 13 December 1935, pp. 1433-44.
96. Auguste Reber-Gruber, 'Die Stellung der Frau im NSLB', Reber-Gruber, *op. cit.*, p. 4, explains and justifies the new order in the NSLB to women teachers.

9 COORDINATION AND CONSOLIDATION IN THE PROFESSIONS

The early Nazi policy of purging the professions revealed that the Government's aim here, as elsewhere, was to eliminate those it found undesirable on grounds of race or politics, not to remove women as a group from professional positions. On the contrary, recognition was quickly given to the fact that there were within each profession areas of particular concern to women. Early in 1934, the NSLB, the professional organisation in which women were best represented, appointed women 'advisers' for the areas in which women were chiefly involved. Thus, Auguste Reber-Gruber became the representative of women teachers within the NSLB, while Hedwig Förster was appointed leader of the section for girls' schooling in the NSLB.[1] Both were teachers, and both had joined the NSDAP before 1933.[2] Dr Reber-Gruber's position developed into one of considerable scope, with her responsibilities divided into seven sub-sections each of which was led by a reliable woman Party member; for example, Elise Lenz supervised the affairs of women teachers in the elementary schools, while Friederike Matthias was responsible for the interests of women teachers in the girls' senior schools.[3] In addition women 'advisers' were appointed in each Gau and Kreis, to represent women teachers' interests in the NSLB as a whole, and to keep Auguste Reber-Gruber in touch with the affairs of women teachers at the local level.[4]

The *Reichsbund der Deutschen Beamten*, in similar fashion, established a Women's Section. The leader of this section, Dora Hein, a civil servant and long standing Party member, took up her duties on 1 October 1934.[5] In addition, it was recommended that, where necessary 'a suitable female Party member' should be appointed as an assistant responsible for women's affairs in the local branches of the RDB.[6] The legal profession, too, had its woman representative: Ilse Eben-Servaes, a solicitor who had joined the Party soon after the *Machtübernahme*, became the delegate in charge of legal matters of special interest to the women in the Nazi lawyers' organisation. Her appointment to positions in the Party leadership and the National Women's Leadership[7] ensured that there would be close contact between the women in the profession and the mass of German women as represented by the women's organisations.

The appointment of these women to positions in the professional organisations signified the acceptance by the Nazis of women in professional occupations. It was made clear that women in the professions were, however, to regard themselves primarily as women, who just happened to be civil servants or doctors or teachers. To emphasise this, separate groups of women in each profession were eventually created, which were affiliated to the DFW as corporate members as well as being an integral part of the national professional organisations. More than merely tolerating the presence of women in these occupations, the Nazi leadership even appointed married women — Auguste Reber-Gruber and Ilse Eben-Servaes, for example — to their representative positions, in direct contrast with their earlier opposition to the professional *Doppelverdiener*. There was even for a time a National Association of Married Women Teachers affiliated to the DFW.[8] The Nazis' fundamental objection was indeed to 'politically unreliable' women, while sound Party members were not to be denied advancement because they were women. This applied to the Party's organisations, but to neither the higher echelons of the Party itself nor the Government, since it remained policy that women should play no part in 'political' affairs. Consistent with treating the sexes as separate groups, women could hold key positions only in the women's section of a national organisation which was firmly under male leadership, or in special cases (like Ilse Eben-Servaes) as isolated female representatives in such an organisation.

Throughout 1934 teachers continued to be dismissed or demoted as a result of the law of 7 April 1933. Both men and women suffered in this process of 'purification' of the profession. But there were cases of women being promoted to responsible positions: Hedwig Förster was certainly 'reliable' enough to become headmistress of a senior school, and no doubt the others who were similarly favoured were considered equally suitable on political grounds. Here, at least, were examples of dismissed women being replaced by other women.[9] Also in 1934, Frick expressed concern that the number of qualified women welfare workers was declining. Naturally, he said,

'this profession, too, must be purged of those elements whose character prevents their performing service to the national State. But it is not the intention of the National Socialist State to remove all female civil servants and employees from the service of the State on account of their sex, as a matter of principle ... Often the decrease in the number of women welfare workers is the result of a false application of the principles concerning the *Doppelverdiener*.'[10]

Moves were made, also, to allay the fears which had arisen about the prospects for women doctors. It was reported early in 1934 that there were persistent rumours that women were to be barred from panel practice and probably also from studying medicine at university. To dispel these, the leader of the doctors' organisation, Dr Wagner, had announced that it was intended to admit to panel practice doctors of either sex in the lower income bracket; this meant, he said, that there would be no special regulations for women, but since the incomes of the doctor and his or her spouse were to be assessed together, more men than women were bound to be eligible. Preference was to be given to the married, in particular those with families, without reference to sex. Thus, concluded Dr Wagner, 'there can be no talk of any plan to throw women out of the medical profession'.[11] This statement clarified a situation which had been in doubt largely as a result of his own earlier threats to ban women from panel practice and to restrict their activity within the profession.[12]

The number of women doctors, and their share of places in the profession, increased steadily throughout the 1930s, from 2,455 (5 per cent) at the beginning of 1930 to 2,814 (6 per cent) at the beginning of 1934, and to 3,650 (7.6 per cent) at the beginning of 1939.[13] By 1936, almost half of all employed women doctors were engaged in panel practice. In addition, 42 per cent of all women doctors were married, and of these 70 per cent were mothers.[14] At least in the medical profession, Nazi fears that women would 'selfishly' sacrifice motherhood for a career were proved groundless. Women doctors assumed great importance in the network of organisations built up by the Party to try to involve women and girls directly in the life of the community. The women's Labour Service, the BdM, and educational and welfare services were among the areas in which expert medical advice was required,[15] and the desire to keep the sexes separate in their organisational acitivities meant that this advice, and treatment, would have to be provided by women.[16]

In teaching, the continuing surplus of candidates led to attempts to arrest the steady flow of girls into courses to prepare them for it, even as late as 1936. But in the following year this policy was reversed, and increasing encouragement was given to girls to train as teachers.[17] Given this degree of policy change, and the removal of a number of women from teaching on political or racial grounds, it is perhaps surprising that the proportion of women in the profession remained fairly stable throughout the 1930s. It was understandable that their numbers increased, if only marginally, on the staffs of the elementary schools, since the Government particularly recommended women to work with young children. In the middle schools, for children from ten to sixteen years of age, women's share among the teachers fell during the decade by about 5 per cent. But in the senior schools their proportion declined by about 2 per cent between 1931 and 1939 which was remarkable in view of the setting of the 3:2 ratio in favour of male teachers for the girls' senior schools in Prussia in 1934. As it was, women remained very much in the majority on the staffs of German girls' senior schools, with a share of 68 per cent in 1939.[18]

The Nazis were well aware of teachers' influential position *vis-à-vis* young people, and were therefore determined to involve teachers in the work of the Party and its organisations, to ensure that their influence was exerted to propagate the National Socialist *Weltanschauung*. Auguste Reber-Gruber pointed out that the proportion of women teachers among holders of the Party's Gold Badge was high, and expressed the opinion that all women teachers ought to be members of the *NS-Frauenschaft*. Many women teachers were, she claimed, already heavily involved in the work of the women's organisations, in the Labour Service, and in the provision of evening classes. Equally, women teachers should accept and welcome the work of the *Bund deutscher Mädel*, which had great educational value in the realm of character development. Dr Reber-Gruber issued a warning in this connection, saying that 'Whoever opposes the work of Adolf Hitler's young people . . . has absolutely no right to be a teacher in the Third Reich'.[19]

Lip service in this context was not sufficient. A Party official in Trier reported in 1935 that one woman teacher in the area

> 'has been a member of the *NS-Frauenschaft* since 1 July 1934. She does not buy our newspapers and has a very close association with the clergy. As it was reported to me in confidence, she is anything but a National Socialist. Her entire attitude to us at present can only be considered a façade in order to maintain her position.'[20]

On the other hand, zealous Party workers were praised and sometimes rewarded. For example, Friederike Matthias, an official of the NSLB, was given a senior post in the Kiel education authority in 1935 because she had dissolved a teachers' organisation in autumn 1935 and enrolled its members in the NSLB; in addition, she had won for the *Reichsbund deutscher Akademikerinnen* a respected position in the international association of professional women, without departing from National Socialist principles.[23]

The favourable position of women in the teaching and medical professions was not maintained in the academic life, although, as Gertrud Bäumer — hardly an apologist for the Nazi regime — pointed out in 1939, a number of women were appointed to university staffs after 1933.[22] Women had never constituted more than about one per cent of university staff members, a level reached in winter 1930-1; after the purge of 1933, their numbers dropped in winter 1934-5 to twenty-eight (0.5 per cent) from an unprecedentedly high figure of seventy-four in 1932-3. New appointments did, however, bring their numbers up to forty-six (0.8 per cent) by 1936. In the technical universities, where there were very few women lecturers, the same pattern emerged, so that in winter 1935-6 eight women lecturers constituted 0.5 per cent of the total number. The teacher-training colleges experienced a different trend, with a continuous drop in the female share of their staffs from 20 per cent in 1931 to below 4 per cent in 1934-5, and to less than 2 per cent in 1935-6.[23] The heavy losses sustained by female academics after 1933 were largely attributed in the Nazi press — and by Gertrud Bäumer, too — to the purges sanctioned by the law of 7 April 1933. The losses included the two women who in 1930 had been full professors in universities; one of these, Margarete von Wrangell, a botanist, had died in 1932, while Mathilde Vaerting had been dismissed from the University of Jena 'on political grounds'.[24] But in spite of the Nazi view that some subjects were much less suitable for women to study and teach than others — the 'rational' ones, particularly mathematics and the sciences being deemed the least suitable — women continued to be represented, albeit in very small numbers, in a wide variety of disciplines; in 1936 they were actually better represented in the medical and science faculties than in Arts.[25]

The professional occupations to which women were most suited were, in the Nazi view, those which had a direct practical application. This was what justified the large numbers of women in the teaching profession, and also those in medicine. In 1935, a contributor to the official magazine of the NS-Frauenschaft, NS-Frauenwarte, claimed that architecture was a practical subject, because the design of buildings was something which very greatly impinged on one's daily life. Thus, she continued, women's role in the home and her appreciation of the practical merits and limitations of a house made her particularly suited to be an architect.[26] It was to be another three years before an official spokesman would suggest that engineering was another practical occupation which was eminently suitable for women.[27] The changes in the economic situation and the professional market in these crucial years, and the course of German foreign policy by 1938, made such a suggestion acceptable in a way that it was not in 1935 or even 1936.

When they referred to the practical occupations to which women were most suited, the Nazis invariably meant social work of any kind. This was largely because it was absolutely compatible with their theories about the nature and abilities of women. But it was a view that was increasingly justified by the growing need within the organisations, particularly those involving women and children, for the advice and practical assistance which only a trained social worker could give.[28] The operation of the women's section of the Labour Front, for example, required a considerable number of factory social workers and inspectors, as well as experts in its numerous advisory centres throughout the country.[29] Social workers were also required in the Party's welfare organisation, the NSV, in the women's Labour Service, as medical social workers, in youth welfare, and, above all, among families, both in urban areas and on the land.[30] With the outbreak of war in 1939 priority was given to the recruitment of factory welfare workers, even, if necessary, from among women in other branches of welfare work, since the growing shortage of social workers in industry was particularly undesirable at a time when women were increasingly being encouraged to replace men who had joined the armed forces.[31]

Another area of particular importance in wartime was nursing. Before 1933, sick nursing had been largely conducted by charitable organisations run by the Churches, with nuns playing a central role; there was also the women's section of the Red Cross, which played an important part in nursing during the Great War, and was therefore disliked by pacifist radicals who saw the Red Cross as an instrument of warmongers.[32] In 1934, the nursing corps of the Red Cross came under the leadership of Gertrud Scholtz-Klink, and was closely involved in the work of the NSV. But the decline in the number of nursing nuns, as part of the general decline in recruitment to convents due to 'the change in ideology', led to a serious shortage of nurses in the mid-1930s.[33] The Nazis aimed to create a corps of nurses committed to National Socialism and not to a rival ideological interest group like the Roman Catholic Church, which had challenged official policy by forbidding its nurses to take part in 'certain operations', notably sterilisation. The *NS-Schwesternschaft*, commonly known as the 'Brown Sisters', was therefore founded in 1936.[34] Its leader was the NSV chief, Erich Hilgenfeldt, who appointed two women, Hildegard Rancke and Margarete Liesegang, to assist him in the running of the corps.[35] But a secular organisation had a problem that the Catholic nursing orders could not have: Hilgenfeldt estimated at the beginning of 1938 that the 'Brown Sisters' were losing members through marriage and consequent retirement at a rate of 35 per cent per year.[36] Attempts were made to attract girls into nursing by announcing, in July 1937, that a domestic science course could be counted as a part of the training for the profession,[37] and publicity was given to the activities of the *NS-Schwesternschaft*, which took on a martial tone with the personal oath of allegiance to Hitler administered to each recruit.[38] But the membership of the 'Brown Sisters' in January 1938 looked very meagre at 6,000, especially beside an announcement that the estimated shortage of nurses necessitated the recruitment of 30,000 more women.[39] During the Second World War, the position was so serious that girl medical students had to be compulsorily drafted into nursing for spells of three months each.[40]

The profession in which women were least well represented before 1933 was law. Throughout the Weimar years, women were excluded from the judiciary in Roman Catholic Bavaria,[41] and although elsewhere in Germany women were eligible for appointment as judges, no woman judge was given a place in the Supreme Court of Justice before the 1950s.[42] Still in 1930 there was no female public prosecutor in relatively liberal Prussia.[43] The 1933 census showed women's representation in the legal profession to be very meagre indeed: out of 10,441 judges and public prosecutors thirty-six were women, and only 282 of the 18,766 solicitors were women.[44] The presence of over 1,000 girl law students in the universities at the same time,[45] however, suggested that there would soon be a marked increase in the number of women practising law, if no obstacles were put in their way.

After the Nazi takeover there were, however, to be changes which affected women lawyers. Hitler's deep antagonism towards the judiciary, coupled with his desire to make it politically docile, led to its being purged and also to a restriction of its sphere of competence.[46] The desirability of having women judges, counsel or lawyers was the subject of lengthy discussions; and in August 1936 Hess decided to ask Hitler's opinion, since 'the Party also has a special interest in this matter'. This settled the question, with Hitler pronouncing that women should be neither judges nor counsel, and that women law graduates would in future find State employment only in administrative positions, although the possibility of women continuing as lawyers in private practice was not ruled out.[47]

Hitler's decision was accepted as final although it raised many problems for his Ministers. At least women already employed as lawyers and judges were not to be affected by the ruling, but there remained a considerable number of junior barristers and trainee solicitors who were now obliged to alter their career aspirations. Bormann urged that they all be found administrative posts, and left this to the Ministry of Justice.[48] Freisler, acting for Gürtner, expressed great concern about the prospects for these women, many of whom, he pointed out, had had an expensive training, had pursued their studies diligently, and who often had dependent relatives to support. Freisler wrote to the various Reich and Prussian Ministers saying that his Ministry had found places for several of the women, as had Frau Scholtz-Klink's office, but there remained a number for whom, he hoped, his colleagues would be able to find permanent employment commensurate with their qualifications and ability.[49] While Freisler's concern does him credit, it is remarkable that Hitler could cause so much difficulty for his Government by an arbitrary statement of opinion which his Ministers did not consider opposing. This was, of course, at least partly an ideological question, with Party doctrine opposed to the appearance of women lawyers in courts concerned with criminal cases; the functions of a sentencing judge who represented the authority of the State should clearly be exercised by men alone.[50]

The role of the women's organisations went beyond providing places for some of the women lawyers; it was, in addition, Frau Scholtz-Klink's duty to explain and justify this measure which seemed to discriminate against women who had chosen a legal career. Frau Scholtz-Klink delegated this task to, appropriately, the legal expert in the National Women's Leadership, Dr Ilse Eben-Servaes, who had a lucrative legal practice of her own.[51] Ironically, also in 1936, both she and Frau Scholtz-Klink were accorded the honour of being admitted to membership of the Academy of German Law.[52] Dr Eben-Servaes quickly produced an article describing the remaining opportunities for women with legal training, in the women's organisations, the NSV, in marriage and family law, in the Party's political education courses, and wherever women or children might need legal guidance. Dr Eben-Servaes emphasised that the female lawyer's ability was not in doubt, but that she would serve the community best in areas concerned with women's affairs, leaving fields of less immediate relevance to women to her male colleagues.[53]

Dr Eben-Servaes was particularly anxious that Hitler's ruling should not discourage girls from studying law; neither, she stressed, should the unfortunate fact that some older women lawyers now faced hardship, with a surplus of male lawyers in the older age group, act as a disincentive. On the contrary, she said, 'it is estimated that in two or three years' time there will be a severe shortage of male lawyers, which will presumably work to the advantage of the woman lawyer'. It had already been possible to redeploy most of the junior women lawyers and the women's organisations, particularly, would, she predicted, need even more law graduates, as they expanded.[54] Her views were vindicated when, two years later, Dr Donke of the Party's section for academic affairs announced that 'the sharp decline in the number of young women lawyers is particularly undesirable . . .', since the tasks for which women were especially suited, in the welfare services and in women's and youth organisations, had proliferated rapidly. Dr Donke even suggested that if, as was being planned, a special kind of court were created to deal with legal problems arising from family life, it might be desirable to bring women back into court work, since they had a particularly valuable contribution to make in this area.[55]

The restriction placed on women lawyers in 1936 was an exception to the trend of policy towards women in the professions in that year, which paralleled the change in official attitudes to girl students. By 1936 it had become apparent that, with a few exceptions, such as dentistry,[56] the surpluses there had been in all professions in the early 1930s had been eliminated, and that there would very soon be a serious shortage of candidates for some, if not all, of them. The demands of the Four Year Plan for skilled and qualified personnel from all professions quickly made themselves apparent, and, in the ensuing anxiety on the part of the Government to provide staff — on a scale which they had shortsightedly failed to predict — the appeal for more recruits for the professions was directed at women as well as men. 'Today', asserted a writer in the *Völkischer Beobachter*, 'we can no longer do without the woman doctor, lawyer, economist and teacher in our professional life.'[57]

But even as the demands upon human resources being made by the Four Year Plan became apparent, influential members of both Party and Government continued to be exercised by the question of the place of women in professional life. Those who thought that Frick's assertion that there was not to be a general campaign against women in the professions, made in 1933, had settled the matter may have begun to have doubts after Hitler's restriction on entry to the practice of law by women in 1936. The comprehensive civil service law published in January 1937 had little to say about women; it merely reiterated the 1933 provisions for the possibility of dismissing a married woman official either at her own request or if her financial position would be secure without her own salary.[58] Five months later, an amendment was introduced to exempt the large number of employees of the Minister of Posts and Telegraphs from it, and to permit the re-employment of women whose financial position had changed for the worse to a significant extent after leaving work.[59] This tinkering with the law, along with the absence of any clear guidelines for the employment of women in official positions generally, can only have increased the uncertainty that already existed.

Once again, it was Hess's office which brought the matter to Hitler's personal attention. Sommer wrote to Lammers in May 1937 to ask if Hitler thought that women ought still to be appointed to senior positions in the civil service.[60] Clearly, the Party's central office in Munich, under the leadership of Hess, with Bormann as his deputy, was determined to try to hold the National Socialist Government to original Party doctrine now that it was in power, irrespective of the needs of the economy or of the staffing requirements of the professions; the holding of high office in the State was, according to Nazi ideology, a singularly masculine function. In this case as in the one affecting the legal profession, Hitler responded in his role as leader of the Party: as a matter of principle, he wished to see only men appointed to posts in the higher civil service, although he added that exceptions might be made for individual women in positions connected with the administration of the welfare services.[61]

Once again it fell to the Ministry of the Interior to moderate the Party's policy in favour of women, as it had done in 1933. This time, Pfundtner proposed that education and health, as well as social welfare, be designated areas in which women could be appointed to high ranking official positions,[62] and Lammers incorporated them into his statement of the final decision, which he then communicated to Hess's office in July 1937.[63] A month later, Pfundtner informed the other Reich Ministries of the ruling in a confidential circular.[64] Such was the secrecy involved that one of Frick's staff felt it necessary to ask Lammers if there were any objections to the new order's being intimated to Frau Scholtz-Klink,[65] who, as National Women's Leader, should presumably have been considered an interested party. Lammers replied that there was no objection to Frau Scholtz-Klink's being informed[66] but her exclusion from the original list throws light on how little influence she had, even in matters of special concern to women, in spite of her title.

As it happened, representations on behalf of the *Reichsfrauenführerin* were not necessary, since she had known for some time about the order which 'forbids the employment of women in the higher civil service', as she rather wrongly put it to Bormann. Hess apparently had explained the circumstances of the decision to her, at her own request, and so she was well aware that there were cases in which exceptions to the ruling would be allowed. In her letter to Bormann she now asked for an exception to be made in the case of a talented woman astronomer, Dr Margarete Güssow, who had been proposed by her male superior for promotion to a permanent, senior position in the Berlin Observatory. Dr Güssow's nomination had been rejected by Rust, as Minister of Education, because she was a woman and therefore not eligible for promotion to a post of this kind, according to the order of 24 August 1937.

For the most part, Frau Scholtz-Klink was thoroughly docile, accepting Party edicts and faithfully explaining and justifying them to the women of Germany; this had been true even with Hitler's decision against admitting women to legal practice in the courts. Now, however, she made a rare and rebellious outburst against a situation where 'a woman cannot obtain a position because she is a woman, although she is, by reason of her ability and achievements, suited to it'. Frau Scholtz-Klink asserted that the man who had been suggested by Rust as an alternative candidate for the post had been rejected by Dr Guthnick, the head of the Observatory, because 'his accomplishments bore no relation to Dr Güssow's'; in addition, five astronomers besides Dr Guthnick supported Dr Güssow's candidature. The *Reichsfrauenführerin* openly poured scorn on the way that a gifted woman with an international reputation was being denied the opportunity to realise her full potential, but at the same time voiced deep anxiety about what she saw as an alarming precedent. She referred also to the 'growing tendency to deny gifted and able women the chance of advancement', which had

173

convinced her that it was now necessary 'to put this matter, too, to the Führer, from the women's point of view, so that there can be a fundamental clarification of it'. In particular, the question of the position of women on university staffs was one which she would have liked to broach to Hitler; but the *Reichsfrauenführerin* was never given the chance to talk to Hitler — which is amazing, if her title was supposed to mean anything — and so she had to depend on Bormann to represent her views to him.[67]

Given Bormann's position as Hess's deputy, it was unlikely that Frau Scholtz-Klink would find in him her champion to represent the women's cause to Hitler. In fact, Bormann had influenza in January 1938, and passed Frau Scholtz-Klink's letter on to Lammers, asking that he edit it, submit it to Hitler, and find out his decision. There was, apparently, no need to express a point of view; Hitler's opinion was what counted.[68] It was three weeks before Bormann received his answer, which was simply that there was no objection to Dr Güssow's appointment, with no explanation of this decision, and no mention of the more general points Frau Scholtz-Klink had raised;[69] these had, presumably, been eliminated in the process of editing the letter.

Although she succeeded in her campaign on this occasion, Frau Scholtz-Klink had had to take a firm stand, and the broader issues were no nearer to being clarified. If there was such difficulty in achieving promotion for Margarete Güssow, there can have been little chance for those who were less assiduous in showing an acceptable degree of enthusiasm for the regime and its affiliates. She had joined the Party on 1 April 1933, and the *NS-Frauenschaft* in November 1935. She was also a member of the National Physical Education Association, the NSV, and other groups.[70] Thus, she was 'politically reliable'. In spite of the difficulties surrounding her new appointment, she was given pride of place in the DFW's magazine in February 1939, as an example of what talented and reliable women could achieve. All that was said about the actual appointment was that Hitler personally had been responsible for it;[71] it was very clear that German women were not supposed to know how limited their opportunities had become in some areas of the professions, at the whim of Hitler and his small inner circle of senior Ministers and Party bosses.

But the article on Margarete Güssow seems to have been less a device on Frau Scholtz-Klink's part for deluding German women than part of a campaign which she had begun to wage unilaterally, as leader of the nation's women. Frau Scholtz-Klink took at face value official statements that women were now needed in professional life, and in any case had a growing need for talented and qualified women in her own organisations. Well aware of the dangers of giving these women power and influence, she aimed to utilise their abilities, but at the same time to tie them into the women's organisations so that it was clear that they were a valuable part of them, but only one among others equally valuable. She had begun this process of 'underpinning our practical work with a theoretical basis', as she and her advisers liked to say, in 1936 by making contact with groups of professional women and, especially, women in the universities. The next step was to create a section within the DFW – alongside the sections for political education, German culture and training in domestic science and childcare – for 'academic work', in the summer of 1937.[72] In June a circular announced to the Gau NS-*Frauenschaft* leaders that Ilse Eben-Servaes was to lead this new section, and asked that 'a suitable woman graduate' be selected to head a section for 'academic work' in each Gau office.[73]

Dr Eben-Servaes described the main task of her new section as 'the construction of a bridge between learning and practical work'. There would, for example, be study groups in which women from the DFW's section 'domestic economy-national economy' would meet the small number of women economics lecturers; in other groups, doctors and leaders of the DFW's childcare courses could discuss matters of mutual interest. Women in Arts faculties were to make contact with the mass of German women through the section for 'culture and education'. These activities were to take place not only at the national level but also, it was hoped, in Gau and Kreis units.[74] Wide coverage was given in the DFW's magazine to articles on 'Woman as lawyer', 'The tasks of women in the law', 'The woman doctor', 'The tasks of women in economic science', all of which emphasised that the work of the professions was now being conducted in a new spirit which considered the good of the nation above all, with the interests of individuals secondary. In addition, women were assigned special areas within each profession: childcare and all matters of racial health and population growth were women's chief concern in medicine; in law, it was matters connected with the family and youth; and, with housewives the largest consumers in the home market, women economists ought, it was said, to have a special interest in price movements and patterns of consumption.[75]

The climax of this activity was a conference held early in 1938, to which Frau Scholtz-Klink invited twenty-five women lecturers at universities and teacher-training colleges. The programme for the first day consisted of a tour of a new training centre for domestic science and childcare, a talk by Dr Eben-Servaes on the purpose of the section for 'academic work' in the DFW, followed by a discussion whose theme was 'Women in research at the universities'. Frau Scholtz-Klink spoke briefly to the assembled company, and then left matters in the capable hands of Dr Eben-Servaes.[76] Two lecturers from the technical university at Aachen wrote subsequently of the pleasure and value they had derived from this meeting, secure now in the knowledge that 'we are needed!', after the uncertainties which had surrounded the position of women in the academic life. Further, the isolation they had felt, working away in their own university, had now largely been dispelled by meeting colleagues from other institutions, many of them for the first time.[77] Frau Scholtz-Klink, then, had shown that, in her view, there was a special place in the life of the nation for women lecturers, although she still hoped to have some clarification of the Party's view of the position of these women, preferably from Hitler himself.[78]

In fact, women were still being appointed to positions on university staffs, which indicates that no attempt was being made to phase them out altogether. In autumn 1938, Dr Maria Lipp was promoted to the Chair of Chemistry in the technical university at Aachen. This was the first time a woman professor had been appointed in a technical university. Professor Lipp had begin her lecturing career in the 1920s, managing to survive the purges of the post-1933 period, although she was not a Party member.[79] Earlier in 1938, Gertrud Ferchland, a Party member since May 1933, had become a professor at Schneidemühl teacher-training college,[80] and at the beginning of 1939, Dr Maria Kösters became a senior lecturer in dentistry in the medical faculty of Munich University.[81] She was not a Party member at the time, but did join the NSDAP within a year of her appointment.[82] One Party stalwart to be promoted was Charlotte Lorenz, who moved to a senior lecturing position in political science and economics at the University of Berlin from the post of adviser in the National Statistical Records Office[83] in October 1940. She had joined the Party in May 1933, and was also a member of the NSLB, the *Dozentenbund*, the RDB, and NSV, and a number of other groups in addition.[84] The new trend was summed up by the *Frankfurter Zeitung*:

'In the initial uncertainty about the working of National Socialist principles in practice, the widespread conviction prevailed that in the new State women would sooner or later be phased out of the professions, and particularly out of the academic life. So far, this expectation has not been realised. On the contrary . . .'[85]

The growing shortage of male candidates for the professions, eventually foreseen in 1936, was beginning to make itself felt by 1938, well before the outbreak of the war. Already women's prospects had improved considerably in teaching: whereas only nineteen women had been given permanent jobs in Prussian girls' senior schools in the years 1932-5, twenty-five had been appointed in 1936 alone, with thirteen probationary women teachers also found places in that year.[86] In 1937, the position of male teachers had improved to such an extent that, for the first time for over a decade, every applicant was found a place. This at once raised the prospect of a shortage, which, it was estimated would become acute from about 1942, although there would be enough women teachers, given the number of applicants in 1938, to supply the needs of the senior schools for some time.[87] Far from altering the ratio of male to female teachers in girls' senior schools radically in favour of men — as had been intended — the Government was now obliged to turn increasingly to women to fill these positions; the census returns show that even in 1939, long before the shortage of male teachers was expected to be at its worst, 35 per cent of those involved in education of any kind were female, which was an increase of 1 per cent over the 1933 figure.[88]

Teaching, of course, had always been regarded by the Nazis as a suitable activity for women. But now, in 1938, the Government realised that it would have to make good the shortages of male candidates across the professional spectrum from the significant reserve of qualified women, even in areas which the Party had decreed unsuitable for women. In February 1938, the *Frankfurter Zeitung* reported that women doctors, economists, scientists and 'even women lawyers' were now regarded favourably in high places.[89] Dr Margarete Esch, a careers officer at Berlin University, observed that there were widespread opportunities for women doctors; significantly, she mentioned possibilities for them as medical officers of health and as advisers in administrative positions as well as the fields normally assigned to them by the Nazis, in the care of women and children. Prospects were still limited in dentistry, since there was a continuing surplus of candidates, but there were now opportunities for women in veterinary medicine, and in medical research of all kinds. In the technical and scientific professions, 'which had', said Dr Esch, 'been considered a male preserve for a long time', women were increasingly being employed because of a shortage of men; in fact, women chemists, physicists, engineers and biologists were finding positions in industry or research without difficulty. In spite of the limitations on women's activity in the legal profession, there was a constant need for women lawyers in the organisations, in the employment exchanges and in administrative positions; the same was true for women economists.[90] The 1939 census showed that 15.5 per cent of those employed in administration at the national and local level, including the administration of justice, were women, which was an increase of 4 per cent over the 1933 figure.[91] This was hardly consistent with a rigorous application of the restrictions placed on women in the civil service and the legal profession.

The outbreak of war in September 1939, and the withdrawal of men from the professions into the armed forces, increased the country's dependence on women. In recognition of this, a national agency for advising women graduates about vacancies in positions in the administration, the economy and the social services was opened in Berlin on 1 October 1939.[92] But even in October 1939 reports came in from all over Germany of shortages in every area of the professions. There were not nearly enough doctors,[93] and in teaching the overall situation was so bad that retired teachers and married women who had resigned were being asked to return to work; but even so the situation remained extremely serious.[94] There was also a marked and growing shortage of lawyers, particularly of barristers and judges, so that the Ministry of Justice devised a less lengthy training course for junior members of the profession; the period of training for intending lawyers was shortened as well, whether they were being called up or not, in view of the general shortage of personnel in both the legal profession and the administration.[95] Even the Party eventually had to make sacrifices; in August 1940, it was ordered that teachers should be asked to attend Party meetings in school hours only if their absence would prejudice the Party's interests, and that Party events in which large numbers of teachers would be involved should be held in the school holidays.[96]

The seriousness of this situation did not deter the *NS-Rechtswahrerbund* from complaining to Frick at the end of 1939 about the appointment of women lawyers, who had originally hoped to work in the courts, to permanent positions in the senior ranks of the civil service; although this had been precisely what Freisler had hoped to achieve, after Hitler's order of August 1936, the NSRB claimed that only men should be appointed to such positions. Frick discussed the matter with Hess, and then produced a draft circular in which he explained that Hitler's decision that only men should be appointed to senior civil service positions had allowed for exceptions to be made in cases where the post was one to which a woman would be particularly suited. He went on to say that 'In a rational administration, where there are several possibilities, the most suitable must be chosen. This rule must also hold good for appointments to administrative positions.' From this point he argued that if it were felt that a woman would be a better choice for a particular position, even a permanent post in the higher civil service, then she ought to be appointed. Her suitability, he added, might seem the greater in view of the growing shortage of administrators.[97] Once again, Frick appears to have been determined that doctrinaire Party policy should not be followed blindly, regardless of the practical consequences; as head of a large Government department, he had to ensure that the administrative machinery of the nation worked effectively, particularly in wartime. If there were not suitable men available to fill the gaps in the civil service caused by conscription, then women with the necessary training and qualifications would have to be brought in.

The draft circular went first to Hess, who sent it to Lammers for his opinion. Lammers, who still employed women in responsible positions in the Chancellery,[98] replied that the sense of the circular was not, as far as he could see, in conflict with the ruling Hitler had given in July 1937, about the appointment of women to senior posts in the civil service. He appears not to have consulted Hitler on this occasion,[99] which probably prevented objections from being raised. Frick was, after all, allowing a much wider interpretation of the original order than Hitler's ruling would have permitted. With no obstacles raised, the circular went out in final form to all the Reich Ministers and senior officials of the Party in May 1940.[100] Already, in the same month, a law had provided that women in the service of the State who married 'need not be dismissed if their maintenance seemed guaranteed in the long term from the size of their family income', while women who had resigned or been dismissed for this reason could be reinstated.[101] The wording of the law suggests that this was intended as a wartime measure, at least in the first instance, and not as a statement of a fundamental change of principle. It was still possible for a woman to request to leave the civil service on marriage, and to receive severance pay, as a statement by the Minister of Finance confirmed even in February 1941,[102] at a time when it would have been more practical to discourage women from giving up work, given the chronic shortage of personnel.

As early as February 1940, it was reported that in many areas of the Reich local government was nearing a state of collapse because of the shortage of staff. To try to avert chaos, a number of district governors were beginning to appoint women to manage departments in their offices.[103] But such moves were to be regarded as emergency measures, and in areas of less pressing need women were to continue to be restricted by the orders Hitler had given in 1936 and 1937. Frau Scholtz-Klink discovered this in 1942 when she supported the application of Dr Ilse Esdorn, a Party member since 1937,[104] for promotion to the senior civil service post of scientific adviser in the research institute where she worked as a botanist. Her candidature was also supported by the Director of the institute and by the National Forestry Office, but a dispensation was required for the appointment in view of Hitler's ruling of July 1937. Frau Scholtz-Klink therefore approached an official of the Party office, Dr Klopfer, who put the matter to Lammers with the recommendation that Frick's circular of 1940, allowing for the appointment of women 'in suitable cases', did not apply in this instance.[105] Dr Klopfer received a prompt answer from an official in the Chancellery to the effect that Hitler's order of 1937 was still in force as he had since voiced no other opinion on the matter, and that the post for which Dr Esdorn was being recommended hardly came within the scope of the exceptions to which he had agreed. For this reason, the question of the shortage of senior civil servants, mentioned in Frick's circular, had no

It is hard to make a reasonable projection of what would have happened in peacetime to women brought into professional positions as a result of the war, if Germany had won in 1941 or 1942. No doubt their short-term prospects would have been good, with male casualties and the low numbers of male students during the war. But in the long term — as with employment in general — a new generation of qualified men would presumably have been given precedence, for reasons of population policy. And yet, while the war had precipitated the need for professionally qualified women, the demand was already there before it broke out. If there had been no war, there would still have been a considerable demand for such women, given the expansion, and intended further enlargement, of the Party's own organisations. Indeed, women were supposed to be restricted to matters involving women, children, marriage and the family; but to be able to cope with the administration of the women's organisations, and to provide the training, medical treatment and legal advice necessary in them it was essential that girls be admitted to universities in large numbers and given some practical professional training after graduation. The Party's view was that women should be organised by women — even if they were always ultimately subordinate to male authority — and so the most capable women had to be found for this function. Frau Scholtz-Klink came gradually to the conclusion that women with an academic education were eminently suitable here, as long as they allowed themselves to be wholeheartedly drawn into the women's work of the nation, and did not cut themselves off from members of their sex who were in other occupations — particularly the housewife and mother.

Thus, a division was created between men and women in the same profession, after the massing together of all teachers, doctors, lawyers at first, in 1933, regardless of sex. This can, perhaps, be seen as a return to the pre-Nazi system — the one the Nazis so roundly condemned — in which a strong element of feminism led to the creation of separate organisations for women who nevertheless worked alongside men. The appointment of women representatives in the professional organisations as early as 1934 shows acceptance of the *de facto* situation, that women were quite firmly entrenched in the professions, even if positive encouragement was not given to them until autumn 1936; but it is clear that, almost from the start of the Nazi regime, 'politically reliable', or even neutral, women were not to be driven out of the professions. However meagre the gains of the 1920s may have seemed to the feminists, they were the result of long years of campaigning and were not to be eradicated overnight on the whim of a governing elite whose ideology bore little relation to economic or social reality outside the abnormal conditions of a world depression.

No doubt the fundamental conflict between Party doctrine and the needs of the country would have continued, if the Nazis had survived, with men like Frick — who had to get the results — trying to circumvent orders issued by people removed from the reality of day-to-day government, people like Hitler and Bormann. The case of Ilse Esdorn well illustrates the mindlessness of the bureaucrats who unquestioningly accepted edicts from above, however irrational or impractical they might be, while the increasing use of qualified women by some local authorities for jobs normally done by men shows that those remote from the centre were often prepared to act in what seemed to them the most appropriate way, without feeling the need to ask the central Government or the Party whether there were doctrinal objections to their method.

NOTES

1.   *Die Frau*, June 1934, *op. cit.*, p. 571.
2.   BDC, File on Auguste Reber-Gruber, and Hedwig Förster's Party membership card.
3.   BA, *Slg. Sch.*, 230, 'Angeschlossene Berufsverbände', undated, ? 1938.
4.   Auguste Reber-Gruber, *op. cit.*, pp. 10-11.
5.   BDC, Party Census of 1939 and a personal statement by Dora Hein, 28 July 1939.
6.   'Eine Frauenabteilung beim Reichsbund der Deutschen Beamten', *Die Frau*, November 1934, p. 120.
7.   BDC, File on Ilse Eben-Servaes, answers to a questionnaire for the NSDAP *Reichsleitung*, 2 October 1939.
8.   BA, *loc. cit.*
9.   Reports in *DMäd.*, 15 February 1934, p. 48; 15 May 1934, p. 144; 15 August 1934, p. 240. Promotions and dismissals or demotions were reported on the same page in each issue.
10.   ' "Weibliche Beamte in der Wohlfahrtspflege teilweise unentbehrlich" ', *Der Deutsche*, 5 January 1934.
11.   'Keine Ausschaltung der Frauen von der ärztlichen Tätigkeit', *VB*, 7 February 1934.
12.   Kelchner, *op. cit.*, p. 42.
13.   *St. J.*: 1932, p. 404; 1936, p. 510; 1939-40, p. 586.
14.   'Zahl und Familienstand der Ärztinnen', *Die Frau*, January 1936, pp. 238-9.
15.   Report in *Die Frau*, April 1937, p. 402.
16.   'Was Zahlen lehren', *VB*, 4 September 1936.
17.   See above, Chapter 7, pp. 134-5.
18.   *St. J.*: 1932, pp. 424-5; 1937, pp. 574-6; 1939-40, pp. 611-14.
19.   Article by Auguste Reber-Gruber in *Die Deutsche Höhere Schule*, 1935, no. 14, pp. 480-4.
20.   F. J. Heyen, *Nationalsozialismus im Alltag*, Boppard, 1967, 'Beurteilung

einer Lehrerin durch einen Ortsgruppenleiter in Trier vom 7. Januar 1935', no. 130, p. 256.

21.   'Aus dem NSLB', *Die Deutsche Höhere Schule*, 1935, no. 10, p. 10.

22.   Gertrud Bäumer, 'Zur Berufsgeschichte der deutschen Akademikerin', *Die Frau*, June 1939, p. 453.

23.   Figures from *St. J.*: 1932, p. 431; 1933, pp. 524-7; 1935, p. 525; 1936, pp. 548-9.

24.   'Die deutsche Frau in Lehre und Forschung', *FK*, February 1938, pp. 2-3.

25.   'Dozentinnen an den deutschen Hochschulen', *Die Frau*, November 1936, pp. 432-3.

26.   Irmgard Depres, reported in the feature 'Frau und Beruf', *Die Frau*, March 1935, p. 382.

27.   'Warum nicht: "Fräulein Ingenieur"?', *Die Frau*, November 1938, pp. 94-5.

28.   For the Nazi view of the place of women in social work, see Hildegard Villnov, 'Die Frau in der sozialen Arbeit', *NS-Frauenbuch*, Munich, 1934, pp. 70-73.

29.   'Aus der Arbeit des Frauenamtes der Deutschen Arbeitsfront', *Die Frau*, May 1939, p. 442. See also Chapter 5, pp. 95-6.

30.   Hildegard Villnov, *op. cit.*, pp. 71-2.

31.   'Vermittlung von Volkspflegerinnen in soziale Betriebsarbeit', *RAB*, 1940 I, 16 February 1940, p. 101.

32.   'Die Welt wird schöner mit jedem Tag', *FiS*, May 1929, p. 4.

33.   'Die Frau im Roten Kreuz', *FZ*, 12 November 1936; 'Der Nachwuchs an Krankenschwestern', *FZ*, 10 January 1938.

34.   'Vereidigung von NS-Schwestern', *FZ*, 6 October 1936.

35.   HA, Reel 13, folder 254, report in 'Partei-Archiv', November 1936.

36.   *FZ*, 10 January 1938, *op. cit.*

37.   HA, Reel 13, folder 253, *Reichsfrauenführung*, 'Rundschreiben FW Nr. 66/37', 12 July 1937.

38.   ' "Wo wir stehen, steht die Treue!" ', *Fränkische Tageszeitung*, 20 February 1937.

39.   *FZ, loc. cit.*

40.   Ilse McKee, *Tomorrow the World*, London, 1960, p. 99.

41.   Report in *BF*, July/August, 1932, p. 2.

42.   Johannes Feest, 'Die Bundesrichter', W. Zapf (ed.), *Beiträge zur Analyse der deutschen Oberschicht*, Tübingen, 1964, p. 152.

43.   '10 Jahre weibliche Richter', *Die Frau*, January 1933, p. 249.

44.   'Berufszählung von 1933', *St. J.*, 1938, p. 32.

45.   *St. J.*, 1932, pp. 426-7.

46.   Hubert Schorn, *Der Richter im Dritten Reich*, Frankfurt, 1959, pp. 11-14, 83-4.

47.   BA, R43 II/427, letter from Bormann to Gürtner, 24 August 1936.

48.   *Ibid.*

49.   *Ibid.*, letter from Freisler to the Reich and Prussian Ministers, with the exception of the Chancellery and Hess, 16 January 1937.

50.   Elfriede Eggener, 'Die Aufgabe der Rechtswahrerin', *FK*, July 1939, p. 5.

51.   BDC, file on Ilse Eben-Servaes, answers to a questionnaire for the NSDAP *Reichsleitung*. Letters of 7 and 22 January 1942, reveal that she continued her private legal practice in the face of rules banning outside employment for members of the Party Leadership.

52.   HA, Reel 13, folder 254, 'Partei-Archiv', November 1936; BA, R61/168, letter from Ilse Eben-Servaes to Herr Loyal at the *Akademie für Deutsches Recht*, 12 December 1938.

53.   Ilse Eben-Servaes, 'Die Frau als Rechtswahrerin', *Nachrichtendienst der Reichsfrauenführerin*, January 1937, pp. 6-7. This article was also published in *FK*, January 1937, p. 13.
54.   HA, Reel 13, folder 253, 'Rundschreiben Nr. FW 76/37', from Ilse Eben-Servaes to her representatives in the Gaue, 12 August 1937.
55.   IfZ, MA 205, NSDAP/HA-Wissenschaft, Dr W. Donke, *op. cit.*
56.   'Aufhebung der Sperre des Neuzugangs zum zahnärztlichen Studium und zum Dentistenberuf', *DWEuV* 1937, no. 200, 22 March 1937, p. 187.
57.   'Die Akademikerin von heute', *VB*, 4 September 1936.
58.   'Deutsches Beamtengesetz', *RGB*, 1937 I, 26 January 1937, p. 51.
59.   'Verordnung zur Durchführung des Deutschen Beamtengesetzes', *RGB* 1937 I, 29 June 1937, p. 676.
60.   BA, R43 II/427, letter from Sommer to Lammers, 4 May 1937.
61.   *Ibid.*, letter from Lammers to Hess's office, 8 June 1937.
62.   *Ibid.*, letter from Pfundtner, 18 June 1937.
63.   *Ibid.*, letter from Lammers to Hess's office, 25 July 1937.
64.   *Ibid.*, letter from Pfundtner to the Reich Ministries, 24 August 1937.
65.   *Ibid.*, letter from Dr Schütze to Lammers, 17 December 1937.
66.   *Ibid.*, letter from Lammers to the Minister of the Interior, 31 January 1938.
67.   *Ibid.*, letter from Frau Scholtz-Klink to Bormann, 24 January 1938.
68.   *Ibid.*, letter from Bormann to Lammers, 29 January 1938.
69.   *Ibid.*, letter from Lammers to Bormann, 21 February 1938.
70.   BDC, File on Margarete Güssow.
71.   Report in *FK*, February 1939, p. 2.
72.   'Der Aufruf der Reichsfrauenführerin an die Dozentinnen', *FK*, February 1938, p. 4; Ilse Eben-Servaes, 'Wissen ist uns Verpflichtung', *FK, op. cit.*, p. 13.
73.   HA, *op. cit., DFW Reichsstelle*, 'Rundschreiben Nr. FW 51/37', 18 June 1937.
74.   Ilse Eben-Servaes, *loc. cit.*
75.   Ilse Eben-Servaes, 'Die Frau als Rechtswahrerin', *FK*, January 1937, p. 13; Wiltraut von Brünneck, 'Die Aufgaben der Frau im Recht', *FK*, November 1937, pp. 9-10; Ursula Romann, 'Die Ärztin', *FK, op. cit.*, pp. 8-9; Marilese Cremer, 'Mitarbeit der Frau in der Wirtschaftswissenschaft', *FK, op. cit.*, p. 11.
76.   'Die deutsche Frau in Lehre und Forschung', *FK*, February 1938, pp. 4-5.
77.   Gertrud Savelsberg and Doris Korn, 'Rückblick auf die Tagung der Deutschen Dozentinnen in Berlin 3.-6.1.1938', *FK*, February 1938, p. 12.
78.   BA, *op. cit.*, letter from Gertrud Scholtz-Klink to Bormann, 24 January 1938.
79.   'Zur Lage der deutschen Frau', *Die Frau*, November 1938, p. 98; BDC, Maria Lipp's NSLB card, dated 1.10.38.
80.   *Ibid.*, Gertrud Ferchland's NSLB card, dated 1.1.37; 'Personalnachrichten', *DWEuV* 1938, 5 February 1938, p. 57.
81.   'Zur Lage der deutschen Frau', *Die Frau*, February 1939, p. 271.
82.   BDC, Maria Kösters' Party Membership and NSLB cards.
83.   Stockhorst, *op. cit.*, p. 276.
84.   BDC, Partei-Kanzlei Korrespondenz, and Charlotte Lorenz's Party Membership and NSLB cards.
85.   'Dozentinnen', *FZ*, 4 February 1938.
86.   Luise Raulf, 'Frau und Naturwissenschaft', *FK*, November 1937, p. 13.
87.   'Studienräte und Studienrätinnen an höheren Schulen', *Die Frau*, November 1938, p. 94.
88.   Calculated from figures in *St. J.*, 1941-2, p. 38.
89.   *FZ, loc. cit.*

90.   Maragarete Esch, 'Die Aussichten des Frauenstudiums', *FZ*, 19 March 1939.
91.   *St. J., loc. cit.*
92.   Report in *Die Frau*, December 1939, p. 85.
93.   IfZ. MA 441/1, frames 2-750069 and 2-750043, *BziL*, 13 October 1939 and 9 October 1939.
94.   *Ibid.*, frames 2-750042 and 2-750087, *BziL*, 9 October 1939 and 16 October 1939. Anxiety on this matter featured in a number of reports in the following month, on 10, 17 and 24 November 1939.
95.   *Ibid.*, frames 2-750072/4, *BziL*, 13 October 1939 and 10 November 1939.
96.   BA, NSD 3/5, *Verfügungen, Anordnungen, Bekanntgaben*, vol. 1, 'Teilnahme von Lehrern und Lehrerinnen an Veranstaltungen und Schulungstagungen der Partei – B. 60/40 vom 14.8.40.', p. 129.
97.   BA, R43 II/427, draft circular signed by Frick, January 1940 (exact date not given).
98.   Lists of officials to whom classified documents were to be shown include some women, e.g., on 19 July 1935, 18 September 1937, 17 March 1938, 3 January 1940. Three women (all unmarried) figure on the lists for all of these dates, with an additional three for the last one. BA, R43 II/427.
99.   *Ibid.*, letter from Lammers to Hess, 9 April 1940.
100.   *Ibid.*, circular from Frick to the highest authorities of the Reich, May 1940.
101.   '2. VO über Massnahmen auf dem Gebiet des Beamtenrechts', *RGB*, 1940 I, 3 May 1940, p. 732.
102.   BA, *op. cit., Reichshaushalts- und Besoldungsblatt* Nr. 6, 'Abfindung der weiblichen Beamten bei Verheiratung', 27 February 1941, p. 90.
103.   IfZ, *op. cit.*, frame 2-750855, *MadR*, 'Erneute Meldungen zum Personalmangel bei den Landratsämtern', 19 February 1940.
104.   BDC, Ilse Esdorn's Party Membership card.
105.   BA, *op. cit.*, copy of notes about the case of Ilse Esdorn, 5 February 1942, and of a letter from Dr Klopfer to Lammers, 18 February 1942.
106.   *Ibid.*, letter from Lammers's office to Dr Klopfer, 11 March 1942.

10 WOMEN AND GERMAN SOCIETY IN THE 1930s

The study of even the few selected aspects of women's position in German society in the 1930s which have figured in this work permits the making of observations, and the drawing of tentative conclusions, not only about the position of women in Germany in the 1930s but also about German government before and during the Nazi regime, and about the nature of the Nazi Party. In the general German context, six aspects stand out most clearly, and provide an interesting insight into the politics and problems of the later Weimar period and into the operation of the Nazi regime. In the first place, it appears that the inability of the Reich governments from 1930-33 to take effective action in the economic crisis was in part a product of the democratic system, eroded as it was in these years. In this system, precarious coalition governments of often basically imcompatible elements followed one another in rapid succession; decisions were arrived at only slowly – and sometimes never – at a time when speed was essential; and the power of the Reich government was in any case limited as a result of the substantial autonomy still jealously guarded by the Länder. The stagnation, at times to the extent of paralysis, to which these features contributed caused frustration among the supporters of the Republic and provided ready ammunition for the growing body of opposition to it, on both right and left. In a sense, this created a vicious circle, since governments could not act without further antagonising either the right or the left. And while the last governments of the Republic would hardly have favoured action likely to be offensive to the right, they also feared to generate support for the left by deliberately outraging it. Most of the time, then, inaction seemed the least harmful course.

But if governments did not give clear evidence of energetic attempts to solve Germany's problems in the late 1920s, particularly in the depression, they nevertheless were busy discussing possible plans, appointing committees and consulting experts. The direction in which their investigations took them was, it is clear, often very similar to that subsequently followed – generally with vigour, ruthlessness and effectiveness – by Hitler's Government. The attempt to reduce student numbers in the early 1930s and to pursue a positive population policy are two examples of this. If the policies eventually implemented by the Nazis were often a distortion of those provisionally envisaged by the Brüning Government, particularly, there was nevertheless a strong degree of continuity in the policies considered and followed in the years 1930 to 1935-6. This is hardly remarkable, since any government of Germany at this time, even one with a disproportionate number of prejudices and a heavy weight of ideological lumber, was bound to have as its first priority the alleviating of the problems of the economic crisis. Given the Nazis' basic lack of originality, it was even more natural that they should borrow — even if to intensify and distort — skeleton plans already conceived and tentative schemes still at the experimental stage. Thus, they based a comprehensive public works scheme on the piecemeal expedients introduced under the Papen and Schleicher Governments, and extended and redirected the Labour Service, begun on an official basis under Brüning when already a concept that had been current in Germany for over thirty years.

Certainly, the Nazis introduced new measures in their early years of power; but the real change in the direction of their policies came in the mid-1930s, once the unemployment problem was under control, and when they had had time to design their medium-term plans and were able to begin to implement them within the framework of their long-term objectives. The reform of senior schooling is an obvious example here. The Nazis were indeed — as they claimed — planning for the long term, for the 'thousand-year Reich'; this is why apparent departures from basic principles during the 1930s, and particularly from the outbreak of war in 1939, are far less significant than has been assumed. Critics of the Nazis both at the time and since have delighted in pointing out inconsistencies and the apparent ease with which points of principle were jettisoned. They overlook the timescale to which the Nazis were working, and their list of priorities. Better, they felt, to sacrifice an ideal for a short time in the immediate future, if thereby the long-term future of the Reich would be secured: this is why the Nazis not only tolerated, but even energetically encouraged, the bringing of women into work once publicly designated 'unsuitable' for them, when the needs of war seemed to demand it. Once the war was over and Germany's supremacy assured, women would for ever be relieved of the need to work in heavy industry and other potentially 'biologically' damaging occupations.

This, however, immediately raises another point: the regime in fact failed to persuade women to respond adequately to its appeal for their cooperation in the war effort, and, furthermore, failed to compel them to comply. This was not because the Nazis had abandoned their immediate aim of making Germany supreme, but can be attributed to two other factors. In the first place, in the early years of the war, at least up to the point where German forces failed to take Moscow in November 1941, and conceivably even later, it was still generally believed in Germany and by the Government that a German victory was assured and, more, was imminent. There seemed little point in forcing women into work against their will if in the near future their contribution would not in fact be required. More interestingly, perhaps, in the upper échelons of the Party, at its headquarters in Munich, far from the centre of government and remote from military and economic planning, the ideologues around Hess and Bormann failed to realise that their insistence on upholding the traditional Party view that woman's place was in the home with her family, and certainly not in heavy industry, was incompatible with their real priority, that Germany should establish herself in a position of European, even world, hegemony, by force of arms if necessary. This naivety was a source of continuing irritation and frustration to the men who had to make the system work, and who could see that aims of this kind were indeed — if temporarily — in conflict.

Thus, a man like Wilhelm Frick, a prominent member of the NSDAP before 1933, found himself, as Reich Minister of the Interior, in the first place defending the prerogatives of the State against the encroachments of the Party, and then having to counter objections to policy made on grounds of Party ideology with the plea of expediency. On the whole, given the weight of influence against him, he tended to fail, for example in trying to oppose or circumvent the Party's demand that women be restricted to the areas assigned to them by the Party, areas which did not include the higher civil service. Frick's problem was that Hitler never forgot that he was the Party's leader as well as Germany's ruler, and his few arbitrary pronouncements on women's affairs — on the admission of women to legal practice, for example — reflected the primacy of ideological considerations in his mind, even once the war and its demands suggested that these ought to be put into cold storage for a time. In the constant tension — or, as Schoenbaum says, 'the anarchic relations'[1] — between Party and State in the Third Reich, Hitler's authority as leader of both, and his increasing irrationality and sentimental commitment to the NSDAP, its officers and its theories, all ensured that in most disputed areas the Party won the day — disastrously for the 'thousand-year Reich', as it ironically transpired.

Two other points of general interest remain. Firstly, there is the at times almost comic insistence of the Nazis on voluntary effort and the saving of Government money by encouraging private enterprise in the furthering of the Government's aims. In the name of a spurious — but, to many, convincing — 'socialism' the Nazis wrung money out of German citizens for the Winter Aid scheme to help the poor, rather than release Reich funds for this purpose; the encouragement given to students to work voluntarily and without remuneration to afford fellow citizens extra paid holidays was couched in the same terms, and served much the same purpose. If employers benefited to the extent that they did not have to provide the money for extra holidays, the

Government had nevertheless achieved a propaganda victory without itself putting up the money or antagonising employers by asking them to do so. Private industry as well as the individual was, in any case, expected to play its part in this alleged demonstration of national solidarity. Whether or not the Government had previously brought pressure to bear on the Reemstma cigarette company to induce it to supplement the marriage loan for its female employees out of its own funds,[2] this example was widely publicised as a model for other firms to emulate.

The reluctance of the Government to spend money on social projects was largely the result of its desire to devote as much of its resources as possible to rearmament. No doubt there was also genuine enthusiasm within the Party for the ideological aspect of money for community purposes being raised within the community, without overt Government direction. It is also possible, however, that the fiscal orthodoxy of Krosigk and his advisers at the Ministry of Finance played a part. Certainly, Krosigk was alarmed when large-scale projects necessitated substantial Government expenditure, as he demonstrated when the Labour Service was greatly expanded in the later 1930s.[3] On a smaller scale, the Ministry of Finance felt less than enthusiasm for the SS's scheme to give State aid to unmarried mothers.[4] But the overall picture which emerges from the visible penny pinching in social projects and the encouragement given to private initiatives and voluntary efforts seems somewhat paradoxical in the light of the Nazis' passion for imposing uniformity and nationalising as much of the German people's activity as possible.

Finally, the failure to achieve this uniformity, to impose total control, and to involve everyone in the life of the Nazi state, reveals that the Nazis had not created a fully totalitarian regime, whatever Robert Ley, for one, might claim.[5] They could not even stamp out coeducation or contraception, although they had anathematised both. Their failure was partly due to their continuing dependence on the cooperation of the German people, and their consequent reluctance to antagonise those who were 'politically reliable', 'racially desirable', and who were broadly content under Nazi rule as long as it made few demands on them. Women, particularly, had to be treated carefully: not only were they in a unique position of influence over the nation's youth, but, in addition, the Nazis no doubt remembered the threat of a *Gebärstreik* (strike against childbearing) which had been made before the Great War, when working-class women were urged not to provide cannon fodder for a regime which did not provide adequate sustenance for their children. Thus, persuasion rather than coercion, incentives rather than threats, and withdrawal with a good grace when opposition from the ordinary population seemed formidable, were the tactics to which Hitler's Government was restricted. The limitations thus imposed on Government action left a greater degree of freedom in the Third Reich than is apparent at first sight, and than has generally been supposed, and ensured that Nazi control of Germany was rather less than complete.

It is possible, but it would be misleading, to compile a balance sheet of comparisons of women's position in 1930 with that in 1940. One could, for example, point to the contrast between the opposition to the employment of married women in all areas, from industry to the professions, in the depression years at the start of the decade, and the growing urgency with which attempts were made to persuade married as well as single women to enter employment in the later 1930s, particularly once Germany went to war in the autumn of 1939. Indeed the former situation reveals prejudice, but if this was to some extent a legacy of the German past, in which working-class men as well as members of the middle and upper classes had disliked the appearance of women in large numbers in employment outside the home, its extent in the late 1920s and early 1930s was primarily an automatic response to the desperate economic situation in which job opportunities only diminished in the inexorable deflationary spiral. The changed attitude of the later 1930s was not a reflection of enlightenment, of a desire to encourage women to realise their individual potential outside the home, but was rather indicative of the Government's desire to harness the nation's resources to the war machine it was determined to construct. It is to be hoped that this study has shown that the situation in Germany in both 1930 and 1940 was highly abnormal, with an unprecedented shortage of jobs in the earlier years and a shortage of labour in the latter years which had developed quickly and showed signs of becoming only more acute. Thus, the extent of the prejudice in 1930 was abnormal in the Weimar context, just as the attempt ten years later to winkle housebound wives and mothers out of their domestic routine, and into the factory or the field, was an emergency measure as far as the Nazis were concerned, one which was not expected to continue once the national crisis of the war was over.

It can only be surmised what the position of women in a 'thousand-year Reich' would have been. Clearly, the Nazis' chief concern with women was for their capacity as childbearers. Women with a full-time job might be reluctant to start or add to a family, and so women were to be encouraged to give up work to spend their time in the home, and to have many children in order to fill this time. Girls with an academic education might be reluctant to forego the opportunity of an interesting, responsible, and possibly well paid career, even if they were married; accordingly, the emphasis was to be shifted away from the study of academic subjects, and where a preponderance of these remained in a curriculum, girls were also to be reminded of their maternal role at every opportunity, by taking compulsory courses in domestic science and by mixing socially in the organisations and usefully in the Labour Service with girls and women from different backgrounds, who would be more interested in human relationships than in physics or foreign languages. Above all, women were to be kept physically healthy for childbearing, and had therefore to be removed from work that was actually or potentially damaging to their reproductive capacity.

The motive was world domination; one of the means to this was to be a dramatic increase in the population, by means of creating an atmosphere in which procreation was considered natural and was rewarded in both material and psychological terms, and by attempting to make any means of conception control beyond total abstinence from sexual intercourse unavailable. But some of the side effects were desirable. For example, the Nazis were considered puritanical in their condemnation of tobacco and alcohol — no doubt partly influenced by Hitler's abstinence from and aversion to them[6] — but they were medically correct in urging pregnant women not to smoke or to drink alcohol. While the Nazis claimed to advocate temperance rather than abstinence with regard to alcohol, they were uncompromising in their opposition to cigarette smoking,[7] at a time when it was accepted as fashionable among women as well as men, and before the health hazards directly connected with it were widely accepted. Foreigners were mildly amused by the zeal of some of the Party faithful in encouraging cafes to hang notices prominently on their premises bearing the legend 'The German woman does not smoke',[8] but it was the Rector of Erlangen University, whose own field was medicine, who stated unequivocally that 'For a woman, smoking is without doubt a vice.'[9]

Another aspect of social mores which seemed to the Nazis to have implications for the birth rate was women's clothing. They condemned the foreign influences — of Paris and the United States — which, they claimed, had encouraged German women to adopt a style of dressing that was either frivolous or else an imitation of men's clothes, and was in any case decadent and not conducive to a healthy rate of population growth (*fortpflanzungsfeindlich*); the reasoning behind this assertion was not explained.[10] To give guidance about the kind of clothing that was considered desirable in the Nazi State, the German Fashion Bureau was opened in Berlin in the spring of 1933, under the honorary presidency of Magda Goebbels,[11] who claimed that she was 'trying to make the German woman more beautiful'.[12] At first, there was emphasis on the creation of a 'German style' for German women,[13] but the women's magazines continued to carry fashion articles featuring clothes which were considered fashionable in Paris and London, and eventually in 1937 the DFW denied that there had been, or should be, attempts to devise a 'German style'.[14] These ideas, however, were not new in the 1930s; during the Great War there had been criticism of the 'improper' clothes that some women and girls were wearing, and the call went out for the creation of a 'German style'. The objections were against something which was clearly too terrible to be described explicitly, but the implication was that new styles were being adopted which were at once unpatriotic — presumably imported from enemy countries — and morally risky.[15]

The ideal type of woman in Nazi theory was the peasant wife, whose peaceful, wholesome life was devoted to her work on the land and, above all, her family. The picture of this woman at her spinning wheel[16] was offered as the alternative to the city bred chic sophisticates of the decadent 1920s. To encourage the simple perfection embodied — it was quite unrealistically believed — in this rural figure, edicts were issued castigating and ridiculing women who 'shave their eyebrows, use rouge, dye their hair' in an altogether foreign manner.[17] The Party's puritans conducted a vigorous campaign against cosmetics, although Hitler was apparently not averse to women's using them.[18] Himmler, however, maintained a strict attitude, giving instructions that the mothers in the SS's *Lebensborn* homes should not be permitted to use lipstick, to paint their nails, or to shave their eyebrows.[19] It was further made clear that the SS expected the future wives of its members to demonstrate their wholesomeness by achieving the Reich Sport Medal, since the kind of woman who was suitable for the nation's elite to marry was not the one 'who can dance nicely through five-o'clock teas, but who has proved her fitness by sports activity. For good health, the javelin or the pole-vault are of more value than the lipstick.'[20] This motif ran throughout Nazi speeches about women[21] — naturally enough, since it was directly relevant to the function regarded as most important, childbearing, the function to which all Nazi thought about women was ultimately related.

It is this consistent obsession that renders comprehensible some of the apparent inconsistencies in Nazi thought and practice; for example, while some Nazis undoubtedly took a more puritanical view of social and sexual life than others, there was general acceptance that the family was the essential basic unit of society, to be maintained and protected by every possible means. But the very existence of the family was an obstacle to the Nazis' attempt at totalitarian control, and so the Nazi organisations had to try to exert some influence over individual members of the family in the hope that the family unit as a whole would be permeated by National Socialist ideas and would grow in corporate loyalty to the Nazi regime. A strict line of demarcation was, however, to be drawn between business and pleasure: Hess repeatedly reminded Party members that they were not allowed to wear Party uniform when out on social occasions with women, unless the function was an official one to which wives were invited. Hess particularly condemned those who wore Party uniform when taking their wives for a ride in a car, and ordered that on no account was a woman to be driven in an open car with her husband when he was in uniform.[22] This potential source of petty family friction was, however, trivial compared with the apparent threat to the family unit by some Nazi social policies.

The more tolerant attitude towards unmarried motherhood and the introduction of 'irretrievable breakdown' as a ground for divorce in the Third Reich alarmed some of those who had believed Nazi promises of restoring respectability to German life after the permissiveness of the Weimar Republic. They were, in fact, policies which were more similar to those of liberals and even Communists than to the standard Christian morality of conservatives who had supported Hitler in preference to socialists of any colour. No doubt Himmler and the SS and Hess were in a small minority in the NSDAP in positively encouraging unmarried motherhood, but the Party clearly, after some initial hesitation, moved to a position where it accepted that motherhood was desirable, there-fore those women who became mothers out of wedlock should not be discriminated against, even if they should equally not be acclaimed as examples worthy of imitation. The result was more humane treatment of unmarried mothers, of the kind advocated particularly by radical feminists both before and after the Great War and by Communists, in imitation of the Soviet Russian example. On the whole, the Nazis recognised that there was an implicit contradiction in their claim to be upholding the family unit and their attempt to diminish prejudice against the unmarried mother; but their overriding desire for children led them to welcome any 'racially valuable' child, regardless of the marital status of its parents, and therefore to value the parents them-selves.

Population policy, again, underlay the peculiar situation which arose from the Nazis' being more concerned with the health and welfare of women workers than some of the avowed champions of women's rights. While the Communists and the Socialists were, like the Nazis, anxious to develop schemes of labour protection for women, particu-larly for pregnant women and nursing mothers, the radical feminists of the Open Door International, who were the first to claim that the Nazis had no regard for women and aimed to subject them fully to male domination, denied that special provision for women's welfare was anything other than a device for discriminating against women. Thus, the most militant feminists were prepared to countenance a situation where women and girls were free to work during the day or at night for as many hours as they chose, regardless of the damage they might do to their health. Indeed, they, along with the Communists, demanded equal pay for equal work, which might have discouraged employers from using women for heavy work since men were more obviously fitted for it; but it was the Nazis who actually introduced equal pay in some cases for this very purpose.[23] And the radical feminists never suggested that their aim in agitating for equal pay was to discourage employers from using female labour on the same terms as male. In the end — always for the natalist motive — the Nazis showed more concern for the physical well-being of women.

Perhaps this helps to account for the acceptance of the Nazis by women generally, and even by some of those who had been opposed to the Nazis in the pre-1933 period. Three former DVP Reichstag deputies, Doris Hertwig-Bunger,[24] Elsa Matz[25] and Klara Mende,[26] apparently came to terms with the regime to the extent of applying for Party membership and working in Nazi organisations. Doris Hertwig-Bunger was admitted to the NSDAP in 1937, and was also a member of other organisations, including the *NS-Frauenschaft*, in which she was recognised as a particularly active and diligent member, thoroughly 'politically reliable'.[27] Elsa Matz became a Party member as early as May 1933, on the recommendation of the Berlin Gau leadership of the NSDAP.[28] Klara Mende had been too outspoken against the Nazis before 1933 to be admitted to the Party even in 1938, but she had been a member of the NSF since 1934 and was the Berlin Gau's expert on domestic science training in the NSV.[29] If the DVP was in truth a conservative party, these women must nevertheless have had to compromise their former views in order to cooperate with the Nazi regime to the extent that they did; no doubt personal ambition facilitated this, but it seems reasonable to infer that they also found elements in Nazism which positively, and not necessarily wrongly, recommended themselves to them.

There were, of course, those who could not accept the Nazi system, and who would never be fully acceptable to the Nazis. Of those who for these reasons were unable to continue to work in Germany and who were also possibly in personal danger, some, like Marie Juchacz[30] and Anna Siemsen,[31] both of the SPD, returned to Germany after exile abroad during the Third Reich, while others, like Alice Salomon,[32] remained abroad for the rest of their lives. Of those who stayed, often at great risk, Hilde Benjamin, the former lawyer who suffered imprisonment for her part in the Communist underground, was appointed Attorney-General in Berlin under the Soviet Military Administration in 1945.[33] Marie-Elisabeth Lüders, one of Gertrud Bäumer's associates, was also imprisoned because of some of her publications; after the war, she worked with the United States' occupation authorities before returning to politics as a Free Democrat. As the oldest member of the Bundestag in 1953, she was its President, as well as being Honorary President of the Free Democratic Party.[34]

Gertrud Bäumer herself seems to have managed to arrive at a *modus vivendi* with the Nazi regime. Indeed, she continued to criticise it in her private correspondence, but even there she insisted that there were aspects of National Socialism that were acceptable; this attitude drew criticism from her friend Dorothee von Velsen, who objected above all to the fundamental lack of freedom in the Nazi State, as well as to the anti-semitism, brutality and opportunism of the regime. If open opposition was impossible, Dorothee von Velsen argued that that was no reason to cooperate with Gertrud Scholtz-Klink; 'silent opposition' was, she felt, the only honourable course.[35] Gertrud Bäumer, however, still looked for signs of feminism in the Nazi women's organisation, claiming to discern traces of it among the leaders of the Women's Labour Service in 1940,[36] and with the hope of encouraging a sense of female independence and solidarity she insisted that her magazine, *Die Frau*, must abstain from open criticism – even of the SS's encouragement to girls to procreate outside marriage[37] – and political comment of any kind. No doubt she was sensible to be cautious, having been struck off the list of those permitted to edit magazines for almost two years,[38] but her apparent readiness to cooperate with the National Women's Leadership, albeit on minor matters,[39] suggests something more than prudence. Her priority was to try to keep the spirit and activity of the old Women's Movement alive at all costs, in however small a way, and to try to infiltrate some of its ideas into Frau Scholtz-Klink's organisation. She rather deluded herself in imagining that this was possible – or relevant, given the lack of influence of the Nazi women's organisation. And her policy here was little understood and less welcomed by those women who had formerly admired and supported her and who started from the premise that National Socialism was inherently evil, and that any kind of compromise with it was out of the question.[40]

Perhaps the failure to reconstruct a Women's Movement out of the remains of Gertrud Bäumer's organisation after the Second World War was a reflection of its being discredited by at least tacit cooperation with the Nazis. Certainly, Gertrud Bäumer herself did not return to a position of prominence, dying in 1954 at the age of eighty.[41] But her concern with the young generation of women[42] was perhaps belated, since the Women's Movement had suffered from a generation problem before the Nazi takeover of power, and might in any case have died out with its old leadership. There was, in fact, a vacuum in women's organisational life after 1945, until new groupings emerged, since Frau Scholtz-Klink's organisation was, naturally, disbanded and discredited. The National Women's Leader, too, disappeared into obscurity, after successfully evading arrest with her third husband, former SS officer

Heissmeyer, until March 1948, and then serving an eighteen month prison sentence after trial by a French military court.[43]

It is one of the many ironies of National Socialism that its policies and its defeat created a situation in which discrimination against women in many areas, particularly in employment, was not a practical proposition. The need for many women to assume the role of bread-winner after the Second World War, in the absence of men who were dead, incapacitated, or in prison, led to the opening up of new opportunities for women in the Federal Republic.[44] In the Democratic Republic, that which so many of the Nazis' supporters had feared above all, and which the Nazis had been pledged to prevent, the victory of Communism, has meant that there has been a much more decisive change of policy, so that women have — within the limits of a new dictatorship — equal rights and equality of opportunity.[45] The Nazis, then, unwittingly acted as the agents of the kind of changes they had aimed to prevent or reverse, and women became more self-reliant and were accorded a greater degree of legal and social equality. But the Nazis had certainly given the impression of arresting developments in the direction of greater equality for women; it remains to decide how far this was true.

In the first place, progress was made in improving opportunities for women even before 1914, notably in education; 'emancipation' did not suddenly begin in 1918. After the Great War far less progress was made than feminists had hoped for and conservatives had feared. Indeed, certain areas of activity were opened to women for the first time, including full participation in politics and entry to the legal profession. But the progress made in winning real influence for women in politics and significant representation for them in professions other than teaching, where they were already well-established, was slow and gradual, as it was bound to be, while the provisions of the Imperial Civil Code continued to affirm the superiority of the male sex in society, and especially in marriage. In addition, no sooner were modest reforms introduced after the Great War than the forces of reaction asserted themselves, so that German women — insofar as they were interested — were, like the nation as a whole, bitterly divided between those who resented even cautious change, associating it with 'Bolshevism', and those who poured contempt on the small improvements that were effected. Even moderate feminists, who accepted that evolution was the best course, but a slow one, began to be disillusioned by the later 1920s, and to be alarmed in the early 1930s when the effects of the depression seemed to many justification — or excuse — for a retreat from the Weimar Constitution's commitment to equal rights for members of both sexes. The conservatives, the Churches, and even some trade unionists were very ready to see in, for example, the deliberate discrimination against the employed married woman the solution to Germany's problems which were, in the view of the Churches and the conservatives, at least, not merely of an economic nature but political and moral as well.

Thus, the clock was stopped not in 1933 but in 1930. The Nazis, with their weird, backward looking philosophy, benefited from attitudes which had already developed and hardened, and found at least tacit — and often open — support for their promised policy of restoring women to a position of security, decency and domesticity. But it was not their intention, they repeatedly asserted, to restrict women to the traditional 'three K's' — *Kinder, Küche, Kirche* (nursery, kitchen, church)[46] — as conservatives hoped. Once again, German conservatives had mistaken the Nazis for old style, nationalist reactionaries like themselves, failing to comprehend the essentially revolutionary nature of Nazism. Certainly, in the Nazi State women were to concern themselves to a considerable degree with children and with household matters; but a regime which aspired to totalitarian control had to urge all its citizens to look outward from their private lives, to surrender their privacy and allow themselves to be imbued with the Nazi *Weltanschauung*, and to accept the primacy of the needs of the State as interpreted by the Nazi leadership. Thus, German women were to be less 'requisites of German men'[47] than — like German men — agents at the disposal of the Nazi regime. It was crucial to women's position that the needs of the regime became such that women could be discriminated against to only a very limited extent.

In the Third Reich, men were, after all, controlled and confined to the same extent as women, and often, given the relative immunity of the housewife from official surveillance, even more. If men monopolised positions of power in the Nazi State, only a minority of men exercised power, and the great mass of men were excluded in the same way as women. Male and female opponents and victims of Nazi racist policies were discriminated against and persecuted on an equal basis. Certainly the Nazis were determined to persuade as many women as possible, in the early years, at least, that their natural sphere of activity was the home and family; but it is often overlooked that the majority of women choose to marry and have children in the absence of official pressure to do so. The Nazis were starting their campaign with the advantage of women's biological character and natural disposition on their side. Their aim was to reverse the evident trend towards contempt for the *nur-Hausfrau* (the woman who is 'only a housewife'), which was a side effect of the provision of more opportunities for women outside the home. In this, they to some extent succeeded; where they were wrong was in trying to coerce women into complying with their policy, by limiting opportunities outside the home and by trying to remove all

196

means of birth control.

Attempts to limit opportunities for women outside the home were made, at a time when the massive unemployment problem made them doubly attractive. But the change which came in the economic situation in the mid-1930s made even the campaign against employed married women first redundant and then positively harmful. Similarly, the steps taken to reduce the academic content of girls' school curricula — a reaction against the strong emphasis there had been on academic ability after the Great War — proved to be damaging even before the Second World War gave rise to an urgent demand for girl students in all disciplines. In the later 1930s, women were not only to be given the opportunity to work and to study, whether they were married or single, but were to be positively encouraged to do these things. The motive was, as ever, the serving of the needs of the Nazi State at the time, not the improvement of opportunities for women; but such an improvement was in fact a result. The unrealistic and ideologically motivated barriers raised against women's advancement in the highest echelons of the civil service and to the practice of law by women were indeed indicative of what was, in the Nazi view, ideal, and of what would no doubt have been their aim in the 'thousand-year Reich', if other policies had permitted it. But these instances were exceptions, and the result of the abnormal 1930s — abnormal in political and economic terms and culminating in war — was that women's position in employment outside the home, including the professions as a whole, was consolidated, not eroded, while, in addition, the status of the housewife and mother was raised.

NOTES

1.   Schoenbaum, *op. cit.*, p. 294.
2.   See above, Chapter 4, pp. 87-8.
3.   See above, Chapter 5, p. 103.
4   See above, Chapter 3, p 69
5.   Schoenbaum, *op. cit.*, p. 113, quotes Ley as saying: 'There are no more private citizens. The time when anybody could do or not do what he pleased is past.'
6.   Douglas L. Kelley, *Twenty-Two Cells in Nuremberg*, London, 1947, pp. 178, 190-91.
7.   Erich Bruns, 'Die Bekämpfung des Alcohol- und Nikotinmissbrauchs und die deutsche Frau', *NS-Frauenwarte*, 1938, p. 599.
8.   ' "Die deutsche Frau raucht nicht" ', *FZ*, 1 May 1933; Elizabeth Wiskemann, *The Europe I Saw*, London, 1968, p. 34, relates how in Berlin in March 1933, a Storm Trooper 'snatched a cigarette I was smoking from my mouth, informing me that the *Führer* disapproved of women smoking'.
9.   H. Wintz, 'Die Frau und das Rauchen', *Schriften des 'Verein Deutsche Volksheilkunde e. V.'*, Nuremberg, 1938.
10.   Agnes Gerlach, 'Klarheit in Modefragen', *DAZ*, 23 July 1933.

11. 'Ein deutsches Mode-Amt', *Vossische Zeitung*, 11 June 1933.
12. 'Frau Goebbels über die deutsche Frauen', *Vossische Zeitung*, 6 July 1933.
13. 'Ziel und Aufbau des deutschen Modeamtes', *FZ*, 5 July 1933.
14. 'Keine eigene "Deutsche Mode" ', *FZ*, 23 April 1937.
15. 'Planmässiger Kampf gegen würdelosigkeit im weiblichen Geschlecht, von einem Beobachter am Wege', *Frankfurter Zeitgemässe Broschüren*, January 1916, pp. 2-4.
16. Hildegard von Rheden, 'Bauerlicher Hausfleiss aus Blut und Boden', *VB*, 2 February 1936.
17. 'Muckertum und geschminkten Frauen', *DAZ*, 15 November 1933.
18. Heinrich Hoffman, *Hitler was my Friend*, London 1955, pp. 141-2, describes Hitler's taste in women's appearance thus: 'If he had any preference at all, then I should say that it was a leaning towards the elegant, slim figure. Nor did he object to lipstick and painted fingernails, which were so scornfully castigated in Party circles.'
19. IfZ, Fa 202, frame 78, letter from 'Dr E.' to the Council of *Lebensborn*, 6 September 1940.
20. SS Obergruppenführer Jeckeln, 'Ein Wort an die Frauen', *FZ*, 1 June 1937.
21. E.g., Gertrud Scholtz-Klink, 'Die Frau im nationalsozialistischen Staat', *VB*, 9 September 1934; 'Die Körperschulung und deren Wichtigkeit für die Frauen', *NS-Frauenwarte*, 1938, p. 587.
22. IfZ, Db. 15.02 'Anordnung 214/35', 5 November 1935, signed by Hess, with express orders that it was not for publication.
23. See above, Chapter 4, p. 89.
24. Born in 1882, a senior school teacher and leader of women's organisations in the Weimar period. Horkenbach, *op. cit.*, p. 681.
25. Born in 1881, a senior school teacher and president of the DVP's Women's Committee, *Reichstags-Handbuch*, Berlin, 1930, p. 417.
26. Born in 1869, headmistress of a domestic science school and adviser in the Ministry of Economics in 1929-32. Horkenbach, *op. cit.*, p. 714.
27. BDC, Gestapo report on Doris Hertwig-Bunger, 27 December 1940.
28. *Ibid.*, Partei-Kanzlei Korrespondenz, letter to the Gauschatzmeister of Mark Brandenburg, 5 February 1940.
29. *Ibid.*, Gestapo report to the President of the Reich Chamber of Journalists, 26 April 1938.
30. Max Schwarz, *MdR*, Hanover, 1965, p. 684.
31. Kosch, *op. cit.*, p. 1110.
32. *Ibid.*, p. 1060.
33. Stockhorst, *op. cit.*, p. 51.
34. Kosch, *op. cit.*, pp. 792-3.
35. BA, *Kl. Erw.*, no. 296-(1), letter from Dorothee von Velsen to Gertrud Bäumer, 21 November 1936.
36. *Ibid.*, no. 267-(2), letter from Gertrud Bäumer to Emmy Beckmann, 17 October 1940.
37. *Ibid.*, no. 296-(1), letter from Gertrud Bäumer to Dorothee von Velsen, 4 April 1940.
38. Beckmann, *op. cit.*, letter from Gertrud Bäumer to Emmy Beckmann, May 1935 (exact date not given), p. 82; BA, *op. cit.*, no. 267-(1), letter from Gertrud Bäumer to Emmy Beckmann, 19 March 1937.
39. *Ibid.*, letter from Gertrud Bäumer to Emmy Beckmann, 14 September 1938; *ibid.*, no. 267-(2), letter of 17 October 1940.
40. *Ibid.*, no. 296-(1), letter from Dorothee von Velsen to Gertrud Bäumer, 24 May 1939; *ibid.*, letter from Dorothee von Velsen to Gertrud Bäumer, 11

April 1940.
41.   *Das Grosse Brockhaus*, 1967, vol. 2, p. 393.
42.   BA, *op. cit.*, no. 267-(2), Letter from Gertrud Bäumer to Emmy Beckmann, 17 October 1940.
43.   Wiener Library Personality File G15, reports on Gertrud Scholtz-Klink in several newspapers, e.g., *New York Times*, 3 February 1948; *Neue Zeitung*, 18 November 1948; *Die Welt*, 18 November 1949; *New York Herald Tribune*, 18 November 1949.
44.   B. Rich, 'Civil Liberties in Germany', *Political Science Quarterly*, 1950, p. 81.
45.   David Childs, *East Germany*, New York, 1969, p. 219.
46.   The 'three K's' appear in many different places, in a variety of forms. The one given is the most common of these. In Imperial times, mention was sometimes made of 'four K's', the additional one being for 'Kaiser'.
47.   Hans-Jochen Gamm, *Der Flüsterwitz im Dritten Reich*, Munich, 1966, p. 50, gives one of the popular corruptions of the BdM's initials as 'Bedarfsartikel deutscher Männer'.

BIBLIOGRAPHY

1. Primary Sources

Archival material, listed under each archive:

Bundesarchiv, Koblenz
Schumacher Sammlung: nos. 230 – NS Frauen; 262 – Arbeitsdienst;
  279/1 – NSDStB
R2, Reichsfinanzministerium; R18, Reichsministerium des Innern; R22,
  Reichsjustizministerium; R36, Deutscher Gemeindetag; R43, Reichs-
  kanzlei; R45 II, DVP, 1918-33; R45 III, DDP, 1918-33; R45 IV,
  KPD, 1919-45; R58, Sicherheitspolizei und politischer Nachrichten-
  dienst (including the *Meldungen aus dem Reich*); R61, Akademie für
  Deutsches Recht
NSD 3/5, Verfügungen, Anordnungen, Bekanntgaben; NSD 17/RAK,
  Rassenpolitische Auslands-Korrespondenz; NSD 30/1836, Informa-
  tionsdienst für die soziale Arbeit der NSV
Nachlass Katharina von Kardorff
Nachlass Georg Gothein
Kleine Erwerbungen – nos. 258-(1), 258-(2), 267-(1), 267-(2), 296-(1)
  – the correspondence of Gertrud Bäumer with Marianne Weber,
  Emmy Beckmann, and Dorothee von Velsen.

Berlin Document Center
Schumacher Sammlung: no. 212 – Reichsbund der Kinderreichen
Akten des Obersten Parteigerichts, no. 2684/34
Miscellaneous Personnel Files

Institut für Zeitgeschichte, Munich
Db15.02, Fa 202, MA 47, MA 135, MA 205, MA 306, MA 387, MA
  422, MA 441, MA 468, MA 1163
The reports of Himmler's agents, *Berichten zur innenpolitischen Lage*
  and *Meldungen aus dem Reich*, appear under MA 441

Wiener Library, London
NSDAP Hauptarchiv, Reel 13 and Reel 37
Personality File G15

2. Newspapers, magazines and periodicals

Archiv für Bevölkerungspolitik, Sexualethik und Familienkunde
Archiv für Frauenkunde und Eugenetik
Das schwarze Korps
Der Angriff
Der Deutsche, 1934
Der Deutsche Student
Deutsche Hochschulstatistik, 1934/35
Deutsche Mädchenbildung, 1934
Deutsche Schulerziehung, 1940
Deutsche Wissenschaft, Erziehung und Volksbildung
Deutscher Hochschulführer
Deutscher Reichsanzeiger, 1938
Deutsches Frauenschaffen
Die Arbeit
Die Bayerische Frau
Die Deutsche Höhere Schule
Die Frau
Die Frau im Staat
Fränkische Tageszeitung
Frankfurter Zeitung
Frauenkultur im Deutschen Frauenwerk
Gewerkschaftszeitung, 1930
ILO Yearbook, 1937/38
International Labour Review
Internationales Jahrbuch für Geschichtsunterricht, 1961/62
Jahrbuch des Allgemeinen Deutschen Gewerkschaftsbundes
Keesing's Contemporary Archives, vol. X, 1955/56
Nachrichtendienst der Reichsfrauenführerin
N. S. Frauenwarte
Population Studies
Reichsarbeitsblatt
Reichsgesetzblatt
Statistik des Deutschen Reiches
Statistisches Jahrbuch für das Deutsche Reich
Statistisches Jahrbuch für die Bundesrepublik Deutschland, 1959
Völkischer Beobachter
Westdeutscher Beobachter
Wirtschaft und Statistik
Wissen und Dienst, 1935

The Wiener Library's filed collection of newspaper cuttings is an invaluable source; from it, extracts have been cited from newspapers which do not appear on the above list, e.g., *Vossische Zeitung*.

3. Articles

(1) *Signed:*

Barton, J. L., 'Questions on the Divorce Reform Act of 1969', *Law Quarterly Review*, 1970

Benz, Wolfgang, 'Vom freiwilligen Arbeitsdienst zur Arbeitsdienstpflicht', *Vierteljahrshefte für Zeitgeschichte*, 1968

Brandes, O. Jean, 'The Effect of the War on the German Family', *Social Forces*, 1950/51

Bridenthal, Renate, 'Beyond *Kinder, Küche, Kirche*: Weimar Women at Work', *Central European History*, 1973

Brook-Shepherd, Gordon, 'More Noises from the Bunker', *Sunday Telegraph*, 15 July 1973

Cole, Taylor, 'The Evolution of the German Labour Front', *Political Science Quarterly*, 1937

Epstein, Klaus, 'The Zentrum Party in the Weimar Republic', (review article of Rudolf Morsey, 'Die Deutsche Zentrumspartei 1917-1923', Düsseldorf, 1966), *Journal of Modern History*, 1967

Feest, Johannes, 'Die Bundesrichter', W. Zapf (ed.), *Beiträge zur Analyse der deutschen Oberschicht*, Tübingen, 1964

Fiehler, Karl, 'Sozialgesetzgebung', *Nationalsozialistisches Jahrbuch*, 1927

Führ, Christoph, 'Schulpolitik im Spannungsfeld zwischen Reich und Ländern: Das Scheitern der Schulreform in der Weimarer Republik', *Das Parlament*, 17 October 1970

Grunberger, Richard, 'Lebensborn', *Bulletin of the Wiener Library*, July 1962

Grunfeld, Judith, 'Women Workers in Nazi Germany', *Nation*, 13 March 1937

Hamilton, Alice, 'Woman's Place in Germany', *Survey Graphic*, January 1934

Harden, Maximilian, in *Die Zukunft*, 24 August 1918

Hellersberg, Maria, 'Die soziale Not der weiblichen Angestellten', Gewerkschaftsbund der Angestellten (ed.), 'Die soziale Not der weiblichen Angestellten', Berlin, 1928

Hirschfeld, Julius, 'The Law of Divorce in England and Germany', *Law Quarterly Review*, 1897

Kater, Michael, 'Krisis des Frauenstudiums in der Weimarer Republik', *Vierteljahrschrift für Sozial- und Wirtschaftsgeschichte*, 1972

Lode, M., 'Women under Hitler's Yoke', *The Communist International*, November 1938

Lorenz, Charlotte, 'Die gewerbliche Frauenarbeit während des Krieges', Shotwell, James T. (general ed.), *Der Krieg und die Arbeitsverhältnisse*, Stuttgart, 1928

Lüders, Else, 'Weibliche Aufsicht in Fabriken', *Die deutsche Kämpferin*,

August 1935
Michalke, Otto, 'Die Frauenarbeit', *Jahrbücher für Nationalokonomie und Statistik*, 1935
Petzina, Dietmar, 'Die Mobilisierung deutscher Arbeitskräfte vor und während des Zweiten Weltkrieges', *Vierteljahrshefte für Zeitgeschichte*, 1970
Rich, B., 'Civil Liberties in Germany', *Political Science Quarterly*, 1950
Schuster, E., 'The German Civil Code (1)', *Law Quarterly Review*, 1896
Stephenson, Jill, 'Girls' Higher Education in Germany in the 1930s', *Journal of Contemporary History*, January 1975
Wintz, H., 'Die Frau und das Rauchen', *Schriften des 'Verein Deutsche Volksheilkunde e. V.'*, Nuremberg, 1938
Zodrow, Leo, 'Die Doppelbelastung der Frau in Familie und Erwerbsberuf', *Stimmen der Zeit*, vol. 171, 1962-3

(2)   Unsigned:
'Abtreibung: Massenmord oder Privatsache?', *Der Spiegel*, 21 May 1973
'Aufhebung der Gesetze über die Gemeinschaftserziehung an höheren Schulen (usw)', *Sächsisches Gesetzblatt*, 9 October 1933
'Aus der Rede von Marie Juchacz als erste deutsche weibliche Abgeordnete, 11.2.1919', *Vorwärts*, 14 November 1968
'Bekanntmachung von 3.7.35', *Amtsblatt des Bayerischen Staatsministerium für Unterricht und Kultus*, no. IX 27 409
'Internationaler Kongress für Bevölkerungswissenschaft', *Der Öffentliche Gesundheitsdienst*, 5 December 1935
'München: Kämpferin gegen den Krieg', *Süddeutsche Zeitung*, 15 September 1966
'Planmässiger Kampf gegen Würdelosigkeit im weiblichen Geschlecht, von einem Beobachter am Wege', *Frankfurter Zeitgemässe Broschüren*, January 1916
'Rechtsentwicklung', *Jahrbuch des Deutschen Rechts*, 1934

4.   Dissertations

Ahrens, Hermann, 'Untersuchungen zur Soziologie der Familie in systematischer Absicht', Rostock University, 1931
Brunn-Schulte-Wissing, Josef, 'Die Frühgeburten — ihr Lebensschicksal in den ersten zehn Tagen und ihre bevölkerungspolitische Bedeutung', Rostock University, 1937
Eggener, Elfriede, 'Die organische Eingliederung der Frau in den nationalsozialistischen Staat', Leipzig University, 1938
Evans, Richard J., 'The Women's Movement in Germany, 1890-1919', Oxford University, 1972

Farrensteiner, Egon, 'Schwangerenfürsorge und Geburt', Rostock University, 1939
Freising, Hans, 'Enstehung und Aufbau des Arbeitsdienstes im Deutschen Reich', Rostock University, 1937.
Grasshoff, Karl Heinz, 'Das Schicksal der häuslichen Frühgeburten und ihre bevölkerungspolitische Bedeutung', Rostock University, 1937
Mason, T. W., 'National Socialist Policies towards the German Working Classes, 1925-39', Oxford University, 1971
Meister, Angela, 'Die deutsche Industriearbeiterin', Munich University, 1938
Stephenson, A. Jill R., 'Women in German Society, 1930-40', Edinburgh University, 1974

5. Books

Alexander, G. G. L., *Kämpfende Frauen*, n.p., 1924
Alexander, Thomas and Parker, Beryl, *The New Education in the German Republic*, London, 1930
Anthony, Katharine, *Feminism in Germany and Scandinavia*, New York, 1915
Bade, Wilfrid, *Der Weg des Dritten Reiches*, Lübeck, 4 vols., 1933, 1934, 1935, 1936
Baumgart, Gertrud, *Frauenbewegung Gestern und Heute*, Heidelberg, 1933
Beckmann, Emmy (ed.), *Des Lebens wie der Liebe Band*, Tübingen, 1956 (letters of Gertrud Bäumer)
Boberach, Heinz (ed.), *Meldungen aus dem Reich*, Munich, 1968
Bolte, K. M. and Kappe, Dieter, *Struktur und Entwicklung der Bevölkerung*, Opladen, 1964
Bracher, Karl Dietrich, *The German Dictatorship*, London, 1971
Bracher, K. D., Sauer, Wolfgang and Schulz, Gerhard, *Die nationalsozialistische Machtergreifung*, Cologne and Opladen, 1960
Bremme, Gabrielle, *Die politische Rolle der Frau im Deutschland*, Göttingen, 1956
Broszat, Martin, *Der Staat Hitlers*, Munich, 1969
Browning, Hilda, *Women under Fascism and Communism*, London, 1935
Buresch-Riebe, Ilse, *Frauenleistung im Kriege*, Berlin, 1942
Bry, Gerhard, *Wages in Germany 1871-1945*, Princeton, 1960
Bullock, Alan, *Hitler: a Study in Tyranny*, London, 1962
Bundesrepublik Deutschlands, *Germany Reports*, Bonn, 1961
Büttner, Johannes, *Der Weg zum nationalsozialistischen Reich*, Berlin, 1943
Carroll, Berenice A., *Design for Total War*, The Hague, 1968

Childs, David, *East Germany*, New York, 1969
Dahrendorf, Ralf, *Society and Democracy in Germany*, London, 1967
Das Grosse Brockhaus, 1967
Dent, H. C., *The Education Act, 1944*, London, 1964
Deuerlein, Ernst (ed.), *Der Reichstag. Aufsätze, Protokolle und Darstellungen zur Geschichte des Parlamentarischen Vertretung des deutschen Volkes, 1871-1933*, Bonn, 1963
Deutscher Akademischer Austauschdienst, *German Universities – a Manual for Foreign Scholars and Students*, Berlin, 1932
Deutscher Evangelischer Kirchenausschuss, *Verhandlungen des dritten deutschen Evangelischen Kirchentages 1930*, Berlin, 1930
Domarus, Max, *Hitler: Reden und Proklamationen, 1932-45* (4 vols.) Würzburg, 1962
Douie, Vera (ed.), *The Professional Position of Women: a World Survey immediately preceding World War II*, London, 1947
Eilers, Rolf, *Die nationalsozialistische Schulpolitik: Eine Studie zur Funktion der Erziehung im totalitären Staat*, Cologne and Opladen, 1963
Eschmann, E. W. (ed.), *Wo findet die deutsche Jugend neuen Lebensraum?*, Berlin and Leipzig, 1932
Fainsod, Merle, *How Russia is Ruled*, London, 1963
Fest, Joachim C., *Das Gesicht des Dritten Reiches. Profile einer totalitären Herrschaft*, Munich, 1964
Gamm, Hans-Jochen, *Der Flüsterwitz im Dritten Reich*, Munich, 1966
Glass, David V., *Population Policies and Movements*, London, 1940
Goldmann, Franz and Grotjahn, Alfred, *The German Sickness Insurance Funds*, ILO Studies and Reports, Series M, no. 8, Geneva, 1928
Gottschewski, Lydia, *Männerbund und Frauenfrage*, Munich, 1934
Greiff, M. (ed.), *Bürgerliches Gesetzbuch*, Berlin and Leipzig, 1930
Grunberger, Richard, *A Social History of the Third Reich*, London, 1971
Halle, Fannina, *Women in Soviet Russia*, London, 1933
Halperin, S. W., *Mussolini and Italian Fascism*, New York, 1964
Hasselblatt, Dora (ed.), *Wir Frauen und die Nationale Bewegung*, Hamburg, 1933
Haupt, Joachim, *Neuordnung im Schulwesen und Hochschulwesen*, Berlin, 1933
Heyen, Franz Josef, *Nationalsozialismus im Alltag. Quellen zur Geschichte des N.-s. vornehmlich im Raum Mainz-Koblenz-Trier*, Boppard am Rhein, 1967
Hiller, Friedrich (ed.), *Deutsche Erziehung im neuen Staat*, Langensalza, 1934
Hitler, Adolf, *Mein Kampf*, Munich, 1936
Hitler, Adolf, *Hitler's Table-Talk*, London, 1953

Hodann, Max, *History of Modern Morals*, London, 1937

Hofer, Walter, *Der nationalsozialismus*, Frankfurt, 1957

Hoffmann, Heinrich, *Hitler was My Friend*, London, 1955

Homeyer, Alfred, *Die Neuordnung des höheren Schulwesens im Dritten Reich*, Berlin, 1943

Horkenbach, Cuno (ed.), *Das Deutsche Reich von 1918 bis heute*, Berlin, 1930

Huber, Engelbert, *Das ist Nationalsozialismus. Organisation und Weltanschauung der NSDAP*, Stuttgart, n.d.

Huber, Hans, *Erziehung und Wissenschaft im Kriege*, Berlin, 1940

Hunt, Richard N., *German Social Democracy, 1918-33*, New Haven, 1964

Jüngst, Hildegard, *Die Jugendliche Fabrikarbeiterin. Ein Beitrag zur Industriepädagogik*, Paderborn, 1929

Kaetzel, Gertrud, *Volksgift und Frauenpflichten*, Munich, n.d.

Kandel, I. L. and Alexander, Thomas, *The Reorganisation of Education in Prussia: Based on Official Documents and Publications*, New York, 1927

Karbe, Agnes, *Die Frauenlohnfrage und ihre Entwicklung in der Kriegs- und Nachkriegszeit mit besonderer Berücksichtigung der Industriarbeiterschaft*, Rostock, 1928

Kaufmann, Walter H., *Monarchism in the Weimar Republik*, New York, 1953

Kelchner, Mathilde, *Die Frau und der weibliche Arzt*, Leipzig, 1934

Kelley, Douglas L., *Twenty-Two Cells in Nuremberg*, London, 1947

Kersten, Felix, *The Kersten Memoirs 1940-1945*, London, 1956

Kirchhoff, Arthur (ed.), *Die Akademische Frau*, Berlin, 1897

Kirkpatrick, Clifford, *Women in Nazi Germany*, London, 1939

Kosch, Wilhelm, *Biographisches Staatshandbuch*, 1963

Kracauer, Siegfried, *Die Angestellten*, Frankfurt, 1930

Kriner-Fischer, Eva, *Die Frau als Richterin über Leben und Tod ihres Volkes*, Berlin, 1937

Larenz, Karl (ed.), *Bürgerliches Gesetzbuch*, Munich, 1970

Larkin, Maurice, *Gathering Pace*, London, 1969

Lowie, Robert H., *Towards Understanding Germany*, Illinois, 1954

Lutzhöft, Hans-Jürgen, *Der nordische Gedanke in Deutschland 1920-1940*, Stuttgart, 1971

McKee, Ilse, *To-morrow the World*, London, 1960

Manvell, Roger and Fraenkel, Heinrich, *Heinrich Himmler*, London, 1965

Mannhardt, J. W., *Hochschulrevolution*, Hamburg, 1933

Mayer, August, *Deutsche Mutter und deutscher Aufstieg*, Munich, 1938

Meyers Lexikon, Leipzig, vol. 8, 1940

Milward, Alan S., *The German Economy at War*, London, 1965

Moers, Martha, *Der Fraueneinsatz in der Industrie*, Berlin, 1943

Mosse, George L., *Nazi Culture*, London, 1966

Myrdal, Alva and Klein, Viola, *Women's Two Roles*, London, 1968

NS-Frauenschaft (ed.), *N. S. Frauenbuch*, Munich, 1934

Neef, Hermann, *Das Beamtenorganisationswesen im nationalsozialistischen Staat*, Berlin, 1935

Nicholls, A. J. and Matthias, E. (eds.), *German Democracy and the Triumph of Hitler*, London, 1971

Nieuwenhuysen, P. W. van den, *De Nationaalsocialistische Arbeidsdienst*, Louvain, 1939

Open Door International, Reports of conferences held in 1933, 1935, 1938

Opitz, Reinhard, *Der deutsche Sozialliberalismus 1917-1933*, Cologne, 1973

Organisationsbuch der NSDAP, Munich, 1938

Paulsen, Friedrich, *Geschichte des Gelehrten Unterrichts*, Berlin and Leipzig, 1921

Petzina, Dieter, *Autarkiepolitik im Dritten Reich*, Stuttgart, 1968

Preller, Ludwig, *Sozialpolitik in der Weimarer Republik*, Stuttgart, 1949

Puckett, Hugh Wiley, *Germany's Women Go Forward*, New York, 1930

Rebei-Giubei, Auguste (ed.), *Weibliche Erziehung im NSLB*, Leipzig and Berlin, 1934

Reichenau, Irmgard (ed.), *Deutsche Frauen an Adolf Hitler*, Leipzig, 1934

Reichstags-Handbuch, Berlin, 1930

Roegele, Otto B. (ed.), *Die Deutsche Universität im Dritten Reich*, Munich, 1966

Rühle-Gerstel, Alice, *Das Frauenproblem der Gegenwart. Eine Psychologische Bilanz*, Leipzig, 1932

Russell, James E., *German Higher Schools*, New York, 1907

Samuel, R. H. and Thomas, R. H., *Education and Society in Modern Germany*, London, 1949

Saring, Toni, *Der Deutsche Frauenarbeitsdienst*, Berlin, 1934

Schäfer, Wolfgang, *NSDAP. Entwicklung und Struktur der Staatspartei des Dritten Reiches*, Hanover and Frankfurt am Main, 1956

Scheel, Gustav Adolf, *Die Reichsstudentenführung*, Berlin, 1938

Schlesinger, Rudolf, *The Family in the USSR*, London, 1949

Schoenbaum, David, *Hitler's Social Revolution*, London, 1967

Schorn, Hubert, *Der Richter im Dritten Reich. Geschichte und Dokumente*, Frankfurt a.M., 1959

Schumann, Hans-Joachim von, *Die nationalsozialistische Erziehung im Rahmen amtlicher Bestimmungen*, Langensalza, n.d. (? 1934)

Schwabach, E. E., *Revolutionierung der Frau*, Leipzig, 1928
Schwarz, Max (ed.), *MdR*, Hanover, 1965
Siber, Paula, *Die Frauenfrage und ihre Lösung durch den National-sozialismus*, Berlin, 1933
Siegel, Erich, *Die Deutsche Frau im Rasseerwachen: Ihre Stellung im Recht und ihre Aufgaben im Staat*, Munich, 1934
Social Democratic Party, *Proceedings of the 1927 Party Congress*, Berlin, 1927
Stockhorst, Erich, *Fünftausend Köpfe: Wer war was im Dritten Reich*, Bruchsal, 1967
Stothfang, Walter, *Der Arbeitseinsatz im Kriege*, Berlin, 1940
The Law and Women's Work, ILO Studies and Reports, Series I, no. 4
The Women's Who's Who, London, 1933
Thönnessen, Werner, *Frauenemanzipation*, Frankfurt am Main, 1969
Trevor-Roper, H. R., *The Last Days of Hitler*, London, 1972
Vogel, G., *Die Deutsche Frau, III: im Weltkrieg und im Dritten Reich*, Breslau, 1936
Weber, Hermann (ed.), *Völker hört die Signale: Der deutsche Kommunismus 1916-1966*, Munich, 1967
Wer ist's?, 1928
Wiskemann, Elizabeth, *The Europe I Saw*, London, 1968
Zentral Institut für Erziehung und Unterricht, *Die Reichsschulkonferenz in ihren Ergebnissen*, Leipzig, 1921
Zweig, Stefan, *The World of Yesterday*, London, 1943

GLOSSARY AND LIST OF ABBREVIATIONS USED IN
THE TEXT AND THE NOTES

ADGB	Allgemeiner Deutscher Gewerkschaftsbund (General German Trade Union Association), trade union combine associated with the SPD
ADLV	Allgemeiner Deutscher Lehrerinnenverein (General Union of German Women Teachers)
AfB	Archiv für Bevölkerungspolitik, Sexualethik und Familienkunde (periodical)
AfFr	Archiv für Frauenkunde und Eugenetik (periodical)
AMSO	Arbeitsgemeinschaft marxistischer Sozialarbeiter (Association of Marxist Social Workers), affiliate of the KPD
ANSt	Arbeitsgemeinschaft nationalsozialistischer Studentinnen (Association of National Socialist Girl Students)
AOPG	Akten des Obersten Parteigerichts (Proceedings of the NSDAP's High Court), found in the Berlin Document Center
ARSO	Arbeitsgemeinschaft sozialpolitischer Organisationen (Association of Social Policy Organisations), affiliate of the KPD
BA	Bundesarchiv, Koblenz
BDC	Berlin Document Center
BDF	Bund Deutscher Frauenvereine (Federation of German Women's Associations)
BdM (BDM)	Bund deutscher Mädel (League of German Girls) branch of the Hitler Youth for girls aged from 14 to 18 or 21
BF	Die Bayerische Frau (women's magazine)
BziL	Berichte zur innenpolitischen Lage (early name for the reports of Himmler's security agents)
DAF	Deutsche Arbeitsfront (German Labour Front)
DDP	Deutsche Demokratische Partei (German Democratic Party — from 1930, German State Party, as Deutsche Staatspartei)
DFW	Deutsches Frauenwerk (German Women's Work), the Nazi-led national organisation for women in the Third Reich

DMäd	Deutsche Mädchenbildung (periodical)
DNVP	Deutschnationale Volkspartei (German Nationalist People's Party)
Doppelverdiener	The second earner in a family, generally used to describe a working married woman
DVP	Deutsche Volkspartei (German People's Party)
DWEuV	Deutsche Wissenschaft, Erziehung und Volksbildung (periodical), the Reich Ministry of Education's gazette
FiS	Die Frau im Staat, radical feminist magazine
FK	Frauenkultur im Deutschen Frauenwerk, official magazine of the DFW
FZ	Frankfurter Zeitung (newspaper)
Gau	Administrative unit, most often applied to a province of the NSDAP's organisation. There were 32 Gaue of the NSDAP in 1933, and 40 in the Greater German Reich of 1939
HA	NSDAP Hauptarchiv
IfZ	Institut für Zeitgeschichte Archiv
ILO	International Labour Organisation
ILR	International Labour Review (periodical)
Informations-dienst . . .	Informationsdienst für die soziale Arbeit der NSV (found in BA, NSD 30/1836)
JADG	Jahrbuch des Allgemeinen Deutschen Gewerkschaftsbundes (periodical)
Kl. Erw.	Kleine Erwerbungen (small collections), catalogue description in BA, under which Gertrud Bäumer's letters are found
KPD	Kommunistische Partei Deutschlands (German Communist Party)
Kreis	District — administrative unit of the NSDAP into which the Gaue were divided
Machtübernahme	The 'takeover of power' by the Nazis, generally referring to Hitler's appointment as Chancellor on 30 January, 1933, and on the whole preferred by the Nazis to the term 'Machtergreifung', the 'seizure of power'
MadR	Meldungen aus dem Reich (reports of Himmler's security agents throughout Germany, from late 1939)
n.d.	date of publication not given
n.p.	place of publication not given
NSDAP	Nationalsozialistische Deutsche Arbeiterpartei (National Socialist German Workers' Party — the

	Nazi Party)
NSDStB	Nationalsozialistischer Deutscher Studentenbund (National Socialist Students' Association)
NSF	Nationalsozialistische Frauenschaft (National Socialist Women's Organisation)
NSLB	Nationalsozialistischer Lehrerbund (National Socialist Teachers' League)
NSRB	Nationalsozialistischer Rechtswahrerbund (National Socialist Lawyers' League), formerly the Bund Nationalsozialistischer Deutscher Juristen — name changed in 1936
NSV	Nationalsozialistische Volkswohlfahrt (National Socialist People's Welfare), the national welfare organisation in the Third Reich
ODI	Open Door International for the Emancipation of the Woman Worker (radical feminist organisation)
Ortsgruppe	Local branch of the NSDAP, the subdivision of the Kreis
RAB	Reichsarbeitsblatt (periodical), the Reich Ministry of Labour's gazette
RDB	Reichsbund der Deutschen Beamten (National Association of German Civil Servants), the only civil servants' union in the Third Reich
RdK	Reichsbund der Kinderreichen Deutschlands zum Schutz der Familie (pro-natalist national organisation of large families, founded in 1923 and taken over by the Nazis)
Reichsfrauen-führerin	National Women's Leader, the title conferred on Gertrud Scholtz-Klink in November 1934
RGB	Reichsgesetzblatt (periodical), official publication of German federal statutes and decrees
RGO	Revolutionäre Gewerkschafts-Opposition (Revolutionary Trade Union Opposition), Communist trade union group, founded in 1929
RMdI/NsdL	Nachrichtensammelstelle im Reichsministerium des Innern an die Nachrichtenstellen der Länder, the confidential reports made by the Reich Ministry of the Interior to the Land information offices about KPD activities, 1931-3, found in the BA, R58 files
Slg. Sch.	Schumacher Sammlung (collection of documents about Nazi organisations and projects, found in BA and BDC)

SPD	Sozialdemokratische Partei Deutschlands (German Social Democratic Party)
SS	Schutzstaffeln (Nazi elite bodyguard formations, under the leadership of Heinrich Himmler)
St. D. R.	Statistik des Deutschen Reiches (periodical)
St. J.	Statistisches Jahrbuch für das Deutsche Reich (periodical)
VB	Völkischer Beobachter (official Nazi Party newspaper)
VDEL	Verein Deutscher Evangelischer Lehrerinnen (Union of German Evangelical Women Teachers)
VjfZ	Vierteljahrshefte für Zeitgeschichte (periodical)
VkdL	Verein katholischer deutscher Lehrerinnen (Union of Catholic German Women Teachers)
WILPF	Women's International League for Peace and Freedom (founded at The Hague, 1915)
WuS	Wirtschaft und Statistik (periodical)

INDEX

Police Ordinance of, 69-70, 74n.86
Hindenburg, Paul von, 18
Hindenburg Programme, 15
Hitler, Adolf, 1, 5-6, 12n.17, 27-9,
    49, 61, 84-5, 89, 98, 105, 109-
    10, 115n.92, 116, 127, 132, 138,
    142, 155, 157, 167, 169-74, 176,
    178-9, 181, 185, 187, 189-92,
    198n.18
Hitler Youth, 3, 50
home, 'women's place in', 3, 6, 9,
    11, 14, 31, 81, 85, 87, 110-11,
    131, 152, 168, 187, 189, 196
    attitudes to women working
    outside, 2-3, 9, 18, 81-3, 89, 101,
    110, 134, 189, 196-7
homosexuality, 63
Huch, Ricarda, 3
hygiene, 40, 95, 97

illegitimate, births, 58, 71n.12, 71n.
    13
    child, 20-1, 38, 51, 57-8, 63-5,
    67-9
indoctrination, 95, 141-2
    See also 'political education'
industry, women in, 15, 75-115, 169,
    177, 186-9
    figures, 89-90, 92n.42, 100-1
    women's preserves in, 76-7, 79-
    80, 83, 85, 90, 102, 104, 106, 150
infant mortality, 40, 45, 52n.23, 77
'inferior peoples', 7-8
inflation (of 1923), 11, 75, 79
insurance funds, 45, 58-9, 76
international context, 3-5
internationalism, 22-3, 27, 142, 156

Jena, University of, 156, 168
Jews, 7, 8, 41, 62, 156
    'Jewish-intellectual', 9, 116
    'Jewish women's rights advo-
    cates', 143
    anti-semitism, 194
Juchacz, Marie, 15, 16, 19, 193
judges, 138, 169, 170, 178

K, '3 Ks', 121, 196, 199n.46
Kaiser, 15, 199n.46
Kälin, 132
Kardorff, Katharina von, 16, 38
Karlsruhe, 66
Keitel, Wilhelm, 68
Kersten, Felix, 50, 69, 73n.61

Kiel, 107, 167
Kirchner, Joanna, 28
Klopfer, Dr Gerhard, 179
Koblenz, teacher-training college at,
    135
Kollwitz, Käthe, 3
Kösters, Dr Maria, 176
Kracauer, Siegfried, 75
Krosigk, Lutz Schwerin von, 103,
    188

labour conscription, 15, 98, 106-7,
    109-10, 114n.91
    plans for women's, 103, 106,
    109-11
Labour Front, 63, 96, 100, 111, 209
    women's section of, 95-7, 102,
    140, 168
labour market, 2, 9, 44, 77-9, 82-3,
    85, 104, 153
labour protection for women, 9, 20,
    25, 76-8, 89, 96-8, 112n.14, 192
labour service, 84, 95, 99, 103, 106,
    124, 130, 134, 140, 186, 188
    students', 134, 140-1
    women's, 3, 103-6, 122, 134,
    166-8, 190, 194
labour shortage, 98-101, 103-5, 110,
    124, 189
labour, women as cheaper, 75-6, 79,
    82, 85, 89, 107-8
Lammers, Heinrich, 28, 172-4, 178-9
Länder, 14, 70, 119, 133, 148, 158,
    185
    governments of, 4, 24, 65,
    117-18, 122, 124, 132-3, 149-50,
    152, 154, 170
    See also individual Länder
Lange, Helene, 14, 17, 143, 149
law/legal profession, 138-9, 147, 149,
    160, 164, 169-73, 177, 187, 195,
    197
lawyers, 29, 49, 138-9, 149, 156,
    160, 170-72, 175, 177-8, 180,
    193
League of Nations, 23
League for the Protection of Mothers
    (KPD auxiliary), 58, 61
Lebensborn, 64-5, 68, 73n.61, 191
lecturers, 29, 147, 149, 160, 167-8,
    173, 175-6
Lenz, Elise, 164
Lenz, Friedrich, 68
Ley, Robert, 188

217

222

Wrangell, Margarete von, 168
Württemberg, 150
Würzburg, University of, 140

year of service, compulsory, 103-5,
   121, 124

youth welfare, 23, 155, 158, 169,
   175

Zahn-Harnack, Agnes von, 78
Zeisler, Frau, 24
Zetkin, Clara, 19